I0886384

The Complete Poems

John Crowe Ransom, after he founded the *Kenyon Review*
(*Greenslade Special Collections and Archives of Kenyon College*)

The Complete Poems

JOHN CROWE RANSOM

Edited by

ASHBY BLAND CROWDER

Foreword by

ROBB FORMAN DEW

Louisiana State University Press
Baton Rouge

Published by Louisiana State University Press

Manufactured in the United States of America
LSU Press Paperback Original
First printing

Designer: Laura Roubique Gleason
Typeface: MillerText
Printer and binder: Sheridan Books

ISBN 978-0-8071-7174-5 (pbk.: alk. paper)
Cataloging-in-Publication Data are available from the Library of Congress.

The paper in this book meets the guidelines for permanence and durability of the Committee on Production Guidelines for Book Longevity of the Council on Library Resources. ♾

Toti familiae meae, viventibus manibusque

Lynn O'Malley Crowder
Ashby B. Crowder III
Ashby B. Crowder (1915–1979)
Margaret Hughes Crowder (1918–2000)
Mary Bishop Hughes (1893–1987)

Contents

Foreword
John Crowe Ransom at Home

It takes me aback these days to realize that when I moved to Gambier, Ohio, in 1963 to live with my grandparents while finishing my senior year of high school, my grandfather was only six years older than I am at this very moment. Thinking about my oblivious teen-aged intrusion into my grandparents' well-earned and peacefully established routine makes me shudder, knowing what I know now. There they were, finally able to enjoy the freedom of being unencumbered by the anxiety of *any* child's presence within their household, when suddenly I arrived trailing behind me all the usual havoc that follows in the wake of a seventeen-year-old girl, not to mention other troubling and far-reaching concerns. I was deserting an unhappy situation in Baton Rouge, but I missed my family very much and worried about them incessantly. I don't know how I would have fared if my grandparents hadn't agreed to let me live with them, but I wish I had thought later in my life to thank them wholeheartedly and explain that odd year, although I didn't realize I hadn't done so, of course, until long after they were gone.

My grandparents had never owned a house during their long marriage, and in 1956, when my grandfather retired, they bought land from Kenyon College abutting the yard of the comfortable, rambling twelve-room farmhouse they had inhabited contentedly for twenty years.

Sometimes I am simply blindsided by nostalgia for the satisfactory lives they fashioned for themselves, for their entrenched and unwitting lack of pretension, and for the delight they took in owning that small, modest house with its few eccentric features which they considered great luxuries.

When I arrived, for instance, my grandfather delightedly pointed out the system he had come up with in order to save my grandmother—and in this case, me as well—from the nuisance of making her way down the bare-bones open staircase to the basement in order to summon him to a phone call. The only phone in the house sat accommodatingly in the center hall of the first level of what was essentially a one-story ranch house, accessible to anyone to answer—or to overhear, of course, although I don't imagine that thought had troubled him for a moment.

In the event that someone was trying to reach him by phone, however, all that my grandmother or I needed to do was to press a large brass bell-button which would sound a corresponding buzzer in the basement location of his library and study. "And I can come right up and speak on the telephone, you see," he explained to me with obvious pleasure. I was puzzled initially by the fact that he hadn't simply installed an extension phone in his own office, but I'm still relieved that I didn't ask. It would have spoiled his satisfaction in that carefully thought out solution.

The desires and ambitions that motivated Robb Reavill and John Crowe Ransom seem to me in retrospect substantial and quietly personal, although overall I suppose their wants only *seem* to be modest. The presentation of themselves to the opinion of society was a matter of absolute indifference to each of them. How they appeared to be had absolutely nothing to do with who they were. It never crossed their minds to consider every aspect of their life as a sort of contest, and it may be that the era itself was a less competitive time altogether.

My grandfather, for instance, regularly burned the trash—famously including all his correspondence—which indicates to me that he simply didn't give much thought to whatever his intellectual legacy might be. But burning all paper and safely combustible trash was the only way to get rid of it in the village of Gambier, and I was witness to only one argument between my grandparents during all the years I knew them.

My grandmother was an excellent but offhand sort of cook, and she was often hurried, particularly on the evenings she played bridge. She wasn't terribly concerned about garbage disposal, and, in fact, I doubt that she gave it any thought at all since my grandfather had assumed that responsibility. But one morning my grandfather appeared in the kitchen brandishing several blackened tin cans. "Robb!" he said to my grandmother, "If you keep putting the cans in the same pile as the trash to be burned . . ." and he waved those cans in the air in frustration at not having completely thought his outrage through. "Well! If you keep doing it . . . Robb, if you do that again . . . I'm going to put them under your pillow!"

"Why, John!" she said. "Don't you *dare!*" But I could tell she was hugely amused, and the first thing she said when her bridge partner came by to pick her up was, "Lillian! You'll never guess what John said this morning . . ."

The luxury that pleased her most in the new house, with an enthusiasm equal to my grandfather's delight in having come up with the bell-button for the phone, was the single cupboard built into her new kitchen devoted entirely to neatly holding trays, broiler pans, and baking sheets in vertical rows as opposed having to stack them one atop another in a fragile tower under the sink. The notion of her worrying about choosing among the variations of the requisite granite countertops of today's everyday kitchen amuses me, although I've contemplated them myself.

Naturally they didn't covet items that didn't even exist during their lives, but the nature of the life they most enjoyed had nothing to do with any attempt to satisfy a societal ideal. I look around these days and realize that we have largely lost the capacity to desire so seemingly uneventful an existence, and perhaps we've also lost the devotion to work that is unconcerned with some degree of fame. That's perfectly reasonable; we live in an entirely different age, we are assailed with information, and we do what we can to accommodate an endless flow of ideas, entertainment, astonishing and immediate bulletins about any disaster or celebration in the world, often while it's still occurring. Comparisons to the past are pointless, but now and then I would like to go back and revisit that state of mind. It seems to me that it afforded a greater degree of contemplation and serenity, but perhaps that notion is embedded in my own nostalgia. I miss my grandparents a great deal, and always.

Here I am, however, sitting in my own house in my study that looks out gloriously over a swath of meadow and the rising, modest mountains of the Berkshires, while feeling sentimentally drawn to my grandfather's underground office with its four ceiling-level rectangular windows from which one could gaze at growing grass and occasional feet passing by. At the moment I'm lost in an attempt to fashion a small portrait of my grandfather's character that might accurately introduce readers of his poems to the nature of the man who engendered them. I'm a writer myself, but I have no gift for writing poetry—or even for reading it—which, in any case, I've come to believe is primarily a heritable trait (in my case as singular as being left-handed).

Bland Crowder has done a remarkable job assembling in this volume all of the extant versions of my grandfather's poetry, which include the many and various revisions he made late in his life to what have always seemed to me his unassailable earlier versions. I'm grateful to Professor Crowder in ways that are hard to express, because I feel certain that attached to this effort and its result is the slight concern that my grandfather's endless fiddling with his own poems entailed a variation of tragedy, or at least of regret. I can only speak from my own instinct about this possibility, but I don't think his tinkering was the result of any sort of despair. I believe he was in pursuit of the astonishing ebullience that accompanies the feat of fashioning a work of art, which always begins as little more than a fledgling notion.

I've become intrigued over the years as I remember the awe that accompanied my first acquaintance with my grandfather's brilliant and talented colleagues and students. In fact, I'm still surprised by the general degree of high regard in which the creation of a work of art is held. Certainly the work ethic of a particular artist may be admirable, but it also may be chaotic and seemingly indifferent. The truth is, however, that the character of the artist has very little to do with his or her ability to affect the quality of his or her creation.

Artists come into the world just as everyone else does, of course, naïve and focused on survival. In fact, I see them as particularly innocent bystanders who somewhere along the way are seized with a mercilessly insistent impulse that won't release them until they bring it to its seemingly inevitable conclusion. Whether the result is a mathematical equation, a painting, an arrangement of musical notes, a method of narration, or the shape of a poem, it's a heady business altogether. Once an artist reaches that goal, the temporary euphoria becomes an addiction. Of *course* the rest of us admire the result, but I've realized over the years that the artist's effort is not particularly noble, because it's so rarely his or her choice. I've honestly come to believe through my own experience that the need to work toward so abstract an ideal is simply a biological imperative.

Our shadowy instinct to expect inevitable despair in the life of an artist isn't mistaken, nor is it a mistake to expect the same thing in any human life. I suppose, though, that in my grandfather's case once he had come to a conclusion that led to a finished poem, he had satisfied that particular creative impulse. I've always thought that my grandfather's art tended to be a resolution of an interior question. I can't know if every human mind is continually in a state of needing to have a question to answer, but, if that's your fate, it certainly might be demoralizing to discover that finally your curiosity is sated.

And, too, I don't believe that my grandfather's curiosity was piqued by any examination of his own nature. He wasn't an autobiographical or confessional poet, and therefore the circumstances of his own life remained quite private. He was by nature more of a philosopher, in fact, concerned with universal as opposed to particular ideas and questions. I believe he had exhausted the urgency of discovery of the enormous questions of existence and mortality by the time he was forty years old, and to discuss the daily life he savored wouldn't have occurred to him as being of interest to any audience he could imagine.

My grandfather was a passionately domestic man. By that, I mean that he was unusually delighted by the ordinary richness of his day-to-day life, although it has taken me many years to understand the contours of his contentedness. I want to be careful not to get this wrong, because the nature of his engagement with run-of-the-mill, everyday experience was not sentimental in the least; it was precise and deliberate and, I believe, always acknowledged in his own thoughts with quiet satisfaction. He seems to me to have had a gift for appreciating the pleasure of his own life, and that's fairly rare for anyone who spends whatever effort he or she can afford on a separate and pressing creative endeavor.

I've always thought, as well, that all of those people who have tried to understand my grandfather's seemingly abrupt abandonment of his poetry are looking at his life while giving short shrift to his domestic existence. Clearly John Ransom regretted the loss of his ability to experience the rush of euphoria that he was bound to have felt after satisfactorily completing a poem, but as long as I knew him he seemed to me to be a man largely consumed with contentment.

Anyone thinking of him with melancholy is failing to take into account the remarkable personality of my grandmother, as well. And how could that be otherwise given the era? After all, Jean Stafford never failed to put aside her own work in order to type up Robert Lowell's poems, which sends me into a fruitless rage, because I liked Robert Lowell, and I never met Jean Stafford. But the thought of my grandmother sitting down to type my grandfather's poems is impossible to conjure up. I doubt if she even knew how to type. But my grandfather quite competently pecked away two-fingered at his typewriter, and he had no end of people with whom he could discuss his strong, amorphous ideas in an attempt to realize their shape, which my grandmother certainly wouldn't have ignored, but those were existential questions about which she was incurious or which she had fully answered by the time she met my grandfather.

What very few people can know—or perhaps it never occurred to them to wonder—was that my grandmother was easily my grandfather's intellectual match, and they had a wonderful time together. I can't remember a single moment when either of them ever seemed to avoid the other's company or find the other boring. Well, with the occasional exception of my mother and my grandmother when they were playing their own version of one-on-one croquet. My grandfather was a ruthlessly competitive croquet player, and he made a habit of coming home from his office for lunch in order to make a meal of one of his own sliced, home-grown tomatoes, along with some bread or cheese. If my mother and grandmother were playing croquet, he would take his lunch outdoors and stand beside the croquet court while mildly voicing his disapproval of the rules of their haphazardly invented game. My grandmother was a superb athlete, and she wasn't keen to invite him to play just then, because she and my mother had devised a two-person variation of the game with unorthodox strategies. She knew he would be discontent abiding by those slap-dash rules, and she generally resorted simply to tuning him out by turning off her hearing aid.

I do know that Robb Ransom was not particularly impressed one way or another by the fact of either the extant or the eventual fame and high regard accorded many of my grandfather's acquaintances and close friends. In fact, she wasn't much impressed with anyone, really, simply because of his or her renown or social standing. She summarily resigned from Nashville's Belle Meade Country Club shortly after arriving in Nashville to live with her husband, because when she invited her visiting friend from Wellesley, Trudy Clarfield, to join her there for a game of golf, the club refused Trudy admission because she was Jewish. My grandmother never pretended to any religious belief, and she had no time for prejudices and behavior that she deemed ridiculous.

And as for my grandfather's colleagues, she had known many of them as students and was extremely fond of many of them, but certainly she was never overawed. I can remember being in the house as a teenager for some occasion or another for which she was not only the organizer and the cook but also the hostess, during which one of those celebrated men of letters was clearly vexed at her seeming lack of reverence or even some minor acknowledgment of his importance.

When my grandfather left Vanderbilt for Kenyon College in 1937, I have no idea how my grandmother felt about relocating, but she was always game for just about anything. In Gambier, however, she found herself acting as something of a housemother for her own young son, Jack Ransom, born in 1936, as well as my grandfather's students, Peter Taylor and Robert Lowell, who followed my grandfather to Ohio and because there was a housing shortage ended up living in one of the four bedrooms upstairs in the big house the college had provided for my grandparents.

I think that over the years Peter Taylor and especially Red Warren were her two favorites of my grandfather's friends and students, but Robert Lowell, oddly enough, brought out a rarely tapped maternal impulse not often evident in my grandmother's brisk personality. "It was a little like having a lost bear living over our heads," she told me. Robert Lowell was clearly troubled in some way, and his behavior baffled her, ranging as it did from sullenness to buoyancy, and she insisted he see a doctor in nearby Mount Vernon, who prescribed vigorous exercise as a cure. Cal took up that advice with occasional and extraordinary bouts of enthusiasm, but he required looking after to a degree.

One morning he offered to shovel the long driveway of the house after a heavy overnight snowfall. My grandmother was delighted; she had errands to do in the village later in the day, and she pointed him to the shed where he would find the shovel, and she went off to give Jack his breakfast and to dress them both for their trek to various shops in Gambier. When she and Jack emerged from the house the driveway was thoroughly cleared of snow, but she had come outside just in time to prevent Cal Lowell from his self-appointed task of shoveling all of that snow back onto the driveway in an attempt to follow his doctor's orders.

I'm not certain, either, that my grandfather's friends or colleagues or students had any idea of my grandfather's deep—and largely harmless—eccentricities. His absent-mindedness was part of his character, not a symptom of old age. For instance, when they first relocated from Tennessee to Ohio, my grandparents became quite good friends with Philip Blair Rice, who co-edited the *Kenyon Review* with my grandfather, and his wife Kitty. The two couples spent a good deal of time together. Kitty Rice and my grandmother always chose to sit together in the backseat of the car if the two couples went for a drive in the countryside, as they were one afternoon when they set off for a picnic, and also in search of a roadside apple stand in the splendid fall weather of central Ohio. My grandfather and Philip Rice were discussing various matters having to do with the upcoming issue of the *Review* when Kitty Rice spotted the apple stand and pointed it out to my grandfather, who was driving.

The two women got out, leaving their husbands to their conversation, and discovered that there were apple pies and Amish baskets for sale as well, inside the sheltered storage space beyond the baskets of apples lining the entrance. They became interested in the jars of jams and jellies, the pickled peaches and various relishes displayed on the shelves. But when they came around to the front once more, intending to pay for their goods, they spotted their husbands driving off down the road.

My grandmother grabbed Kitty Rice's hand and the two of them jumped into a car that had just arrived, ordering the startled driver to "Follow that car!" My grandmother was not particularly intimidating, but she was single-minded, and her hearing was very bad. She depended upon a hearing aid which often did not catch a phrase here and there, and whatever the driver of the car may have said had no effect on my grandmother, who pointed determinedly to the car that was rapidly proceeding away. It always surprised me how quickly a person would do exactly what my grandmother said simply because she appeared to brook no argument, when, in fact, she simply *heard* no opposition, and off they went, speeding to catch up with my grandfather and Philip Rice, who were still deeply engaged in conversation.

My grandmother was telling me this story one afternoon when we were sitting together chatting for a little while as we often did when I got home from Mount Vernon High School in the afternoon, and she took a sip of coffee and looked at me dolefully over the rim of her cup. Eventually, she said, they caught up to the two men, and their driver honked insistently until my grandfather pulled over. "And do you know what your grandfather said?" she asked me. "When we got into the car, your grandfather turned around and said, 'Well, I wondered why neither one of you laughed at Philip's fine joke. He'll have to tell it again.'" But once more it was abundantly clear to me that she savored the memory, and the second time she was left behind at a filling station she simply waited until my grandfather returned. "He was bound to realize I wasn't in the car, because there was no one else to talk to." From then on, however, whenever they were stopped somewhere in the car and my grandmother got out, she took the car keys with her in order not to be stranded once more.

Only rarely did I see my grandfather annoyed; he was generally quite accommodating and always pleasant, which often concealed the fact that his mind was engaged otherwise and that he only appeared to have registered whatever might be going on around him. My mother happened to be home from college when unexpectedly two photographers arrived from *Life* magazine; my grandfather had forgotten about the appointment and hurriedly went to change from his gardening clothes to more suitable attire. My grandmother wasn't at home, and my mother stepped in to lend a hand, but my grandfather promptly introduced her absentmindedly as his wife, and she interjected mildly that, in fact, she was his *daughter*, at which he seemed momentarily startled and turned to look at her. "Oh, Helen! Yes, yes! She *is* my daughter!" he assured the two men. My mother took that opportunity to replace the toothbrush he had put in the breast pocket of his suit with the fountain pen he habitually carried.

My grandmother was often referred to by the poets and writers she entertained as being "great fun," and "a good sport," mainly, I think, because she puzzled them mightily, since she was largely indifferent to them except as friends, and a few seemed to feel uncertain about whether or not she understood their distinction in the world of letters. But what no one seemed to understand was how much she, too, savored the absurdities of her fairly rarified circumstances. There were many things she took seriously, of course. Bridge was a serious matter, and she was extraordinarily good at it, playing now and then in tournaments with Charles Goren. In the aftermath of a bridge game I would often be present as she reported to my grandfather a hand her partner had wrongly played, and I resolved never to learn how to play that game in case she was "looking for a fourth" someday when only I was available.

The Cleveland Indians were passionately followed by both of my grandparents, and in my grandmother's case baseball was serious—as was football and the Cleveland Browns, whereas the ins and outs of the debates and political jostling of poets was merely inevitable, but not of much interest to her one way or another. My grandfather was often caught up and distressed by those various intrigues to a point, but as long as he was not disturbed on his own or a close friend's behalf, her relative indifference was a counterbalance to the internecine intrigues afoot in the lives of the poets and writers he knew. My grandfather was a wonderful, reliable, and earnestly loyal friend to the writers he cared deeply about, but he was in love with my grandmother and deeply involved with his children. His domestic situation always trumped any other aspect of his life, although it was an era when that was rarely the case, and was certainly not the norm.

The major literary lights of that generation were generally male, and they took themselves pretty seriously, just as they should, perhaps; most were both ambitious and serious about their life's work. Very few of those men, however, had the capacity to recognize their occasional pomposity, and my grandmother was one of the few wives who simply paid their condescension no heed at all. Their approval or disapproval of her one way or another never seemed to cross her mind, and her approval of them depended upon their personalities—or sometimes on their skill at bridge; she wasn't particularly interested in what they wrote.

I suppose it's natural enough that over the years, whenever I happen to think of my grandfather working diligently in his study each morning as his other faculties began to fail, I am swept through with melancholy. And of course I would like to have more of his careful poetry at hand, but that's for my sake, really. He did become anxious now and then when he grasped the fact that his mind was failing him, as would any human being, but I don't think he left anything unsaid. The assumption that he was somehow frozen in the inability to write more poems is, I think, a skewed perception of my grandfather himself. He was a man who had no choice in the matter of needing to methodically work through the various enthusiasms and investigations of the subjects that required his passionate consideration. Once he resolved his curiosity, however, he continued to consider those ideas as well as various amendments to them, but he moved on to the next pressing and puzzling matter that suddenly occupied his thinking.

His interests and enthusiasms came in waves throughout his life, and he addressed them with zeal, but his immediate family, particularly his wife, absorbed his primary interest in the world. He was very lucky and quite remarkable in his good fortune. Certainly he experienced human loss and tragedy in his life, but I don't think that he was ever heartbroken by his failure to compose more poetry than he had already written, although no doubt he longed to have an idea break open that required nothing less than needing to be resolved in a poem. And I also believe that when his mind began to slip into a less dependable state he turned instinctively to reworking his early poems in an attempt to impose discipline on his fugitive suppositions and wanderings, and although he dismayed his readers in making peculiar changes now and then, I think for his own purposes those efforts sufficed.

—Robb Forman Dew

Preface

When I was a thoroughly innocent-to-poetry first-semester freshman at Randolph-Macon College in 1959, I found myself sitting among an assortment of other scruffy students listening to a white-haired man, not very tall, wearing a plaid shirt and broad suspenders, standing behind a blond podium. I remember thinking he reminded me of a farmer. I enjoyed listening to his voice, though I have no idea which of his poems he read. I had not got around to reading John Crowe Ransom or any other poet that one might encounter in college reading. I cannot help but feel that my early pleasant listening to Ransom had something to do with my putting aside inchoate plans to major in history or political science and casting my lot with belletristic literature. Way led on to way, and over the years I have met many poets, but I have never lost my interest in that first poet that I saw in person. Being addicted to well-made poems, the kind Cleanth Brooks taught me to appreciate and enter into, I would almost always include Ransom on my poetry syllabi at Centre College and Hendrix College.

Yet I had never published anything on Ransom's poetry, as I had done on the poetry of some of those other poets—until I retired from a long teaching career. When a search for a proper edition in order to cite passages I had quoted in an essay for *Mississippi Quarterly* led to a dead end, I discovered that the nearest thing to a collected edition of Ransom's poetry was his *Selected Poems* (1969). This volume contains unfamiliar versions of poems I had come to know. I began to think about rectifying the absence of a proper scholarly edition. I envisioned an edition that reasoned out the best copy-texts, that provided the history of the printed poems through textual notes recording every published version that Ransom was involved in from the earliest newspaper or magazine publication through to the final, albeit unfortunate, revisions that the poet conducted in his senescence. (Seeing how Ransom could in his old age take in hand a perfectly good poem and unwrite it in retrograde fashion can actually enhance one's appreciation for the original excellent poem.) I wished to annotate the poems full of allusions and a vocabulary often drawn from the deep recesses of past ages, and that included poems never published but relegated to archives, as well as those that were published in newspapers or obscure journals decades ago but never collected and effectively lost. I have been as thorough as possible in tracking down all of these poems; I can only hope that I have failed to find all of the poems that Ransom published way back when—when he was just beginning the poetry part of his long life; for any additions that others might find can only enrich the trove. Though I have found several unpublished poems, there are three mentioned in letters that I have been unable to locate—"Religio Medici Kentuckiensis," "Concerning Prohibition," and "Snow Flurries."[1] The letters of Ransom to Robb Reavill before he married her might very well have poems folded into them, poems which he regularly wrote to her—but they are lost somewhere in the family house in Gambier, Ohio, and, for now, searching for them would be an unwelcome intrusion. This edition means to answer, in every way possible, Thomas Daniel Young's urgent call for a variorum edition of Ransom's poetry, a call that he sounded almost forty years ago.

It is not for me here to enter into a critical discussion of Ransom's poetry,[2] but I would like to remind readers that they will find in the poems that follow many voices. Sometimes he sounds like Wallace Stevens (the titles "Adventure This Side of Pluralism," "Parting, Without a Sequel," and "Man Without Sense of Direction" remind one of Stevens's titles); sometimes the voice belongs to an elegant eighteenth-century tradition ("If the young miss with gold hair might not disdain, / We would esteem her company over the pain" ["The Tall Girl"]); sometimes the voice seems rural southern ("She stuffed her ears for fright" and "went to weeping" ["Miriam Tazewell"]); sometimes the voice is King James Version English ("He marshalleth kingdoms like ant-packs, holloweth ships, / He seeketh the bear in the ice and cometh to grips" ["The Handmaidens" (*F*)]); sometimes the voice is conversational ("Go and ask Robin to bring the girls over / To Sweetwater, said my Aunt" ["Vision by Sweetwater"]); and so on the voices sound. This is to sug-

1. In a letter to Allen Tate, 6 May [1924], Ransom says, "You have confirmed my judgment but not my secret wish about Religio Medici Kentuckiensis. I have consigned it to oblivion" (*SL*, 134). In a letter to Morley, 28 April 1919, JCR included "Snow Flurries" and asked if it is "any good." In a letter to Morley, 4 June [1917], JCR says that he had submitted a poem titled "Concerning Prohibition" to *Seven Arts*, which accepted the poem, but the journal ceased to exist before the poem appeared, and it was not published anywhere else (HRC).

2. The best short introduction to Ransom's poetry is still John L. Stewart's *John Crowe Ransom* (Minneapolis: University of Minnesota Press, 1962).

gest that there is a dramatic quality to the poetry, and through the many voices of his poems, from farm boys to scholars and monks, Ransom creates a variety of perspectives, producing a host of characters vivid to readers. Often he presents characters in a moment of crisis, following Robert Browning in this.

That many voices speak in Ransom's poems is no bar to the appearance of frequent themes—the frailty of beauty, for example. One eternal theme in particular occupied Ransom throughout his short career as a poet—the transitory nature of life and everything attached to it, which he over and over re-embodies with fresh perspective. Another is the discrepancy between the way one wishes life were and the way life really is. These themes frequently call for irony, his most common tone, which he never prematurely lays aside. His unusual diction, consisting of Latinisms and archaic terms, helps to introduce the necessary distance; and his deft handling of slant rhyme disquietingly supports the disparities portrayed ("blossom" / "bosom" in "Spectral Lovers"; "said" / "dead" in "Fall of a Leaf" are examples). The sounds of Ransom's poetry support his nuances and ambiguities and his sideways approaches to his subjects.

In commenting on Shakespeare, Ransom spoke of a feature of Shakespeare's poetry that applies also to his own: the style often "consists in smooth classical coherence only up to a certain point, where he lets out a tremendously unexpected crude misfit phrase, which miraculously gives all the vitality to the passage."[3] We see this, for example, in the last stanza of Ransom's "Winter Remembered":

> Dear love, these fingers that had known your touch,
> And tied our separate forces first together,
> Were ten poor idiot fingers not worth much,
> Ten frozen parsnips hanging in the weather.

Ransom's poetry is full of surprising delights and troubling insights; his poems are objects made by a careful craftsman that require close examination so that one can appreciate their intricacy. Randall Jarrell once said of Ransom: "his poetry will always be cared for, since he has written poems that are perfectly realized and occasionally almost perfect—poems that the hypothetical generations of the future will be reading page by page with Wyatt, Campion, Marvell, and Mother Goose."[4] That was said about seventy years ago. It remains true today.

3. Ransom to Robert Graves, 2 December [1925], *SL* 148.
4. Randall Jarrell, "John Ransom's Poetry," *SR* 56:3 (July–September 1948), 388.

Ransom follows the pattern of Matthew Arnold, who, devoting himself to poetry early on, turned to prose and criticism and the workaday world for the remainder of his life; and of S. T. Coleridge, whose poetic output was mainly early and slim, and who gave his energy to philosophical and critical prose and, like Ransom in this too, the editing of a literary journal. Ransom published three slim volumes from 1918 to 1927 (and additional poems in journals and newspapers). After 1927 he wrote only six new poems, the last in 1963. Allen Tate asked often for poems for one of the journals that he was editing, but Ransom responded in some way similar to his letter of 31 January 1932: "I have nothing so far; have never finished that poem of which I showed you a part; have not succeeded . . . in writing the kind of poem I wanted to and have not tried it yet very extensively. . . . The best I can do is say I'll give the muse a chance and will send you anything I can do that seems up to the mark; but doubt whether that undertaking is good for performance. Don't count on me."[5] In 1939, called upon to write a poem for the meeting of the Harvard chapter of the Phi Beta Kappa Society, he squeezed out a seventy-line poem for "the youngling bachelors of Harvard." "Address to the Scholars of New England" was his first poem in five years. Perhaps having a definite audience helped him to overcome the impediment that had blocked him.

Over the years Ransom often spoke of returning to poetry, but he did not. One can only speculate on the reasons. He had written a number of near-perfect poems. What would be the point in continuing to write the kind of poem he had done already? He surely knew, if he were to resume, he would have to produce poems that showed his development from *Two Gentlemen in Bonds*, as *Chills and Fever* had been an obvious advance from *Poems About God*. Yet Ransom might not have seen the stepping stone that he needed to proceed. His editing, critical writing, teaching, reading, and other prose commitments piled up, and he was never able to find the path back to poetry. Had his development of the critical mind found fault with every poem that formed in his mind? We know only that he fiddled, starting in 1963 and carrying on into 1969, with poems he had already written, thinking that he was improving them. He even wrote essays explaining how his revisions had improved the originals. That he was terribly wrong in his judgment and his arguments suggests that even in his criticism Ransom was failing.

5. Young, 333.

Yet he had in his heyday written brilliant poems and brilliant criticism. This edition will enable readers, in the words of Coleridge, to observe "the progress" and "even the decay of genius."

The first object of this edition, then, is to establish the proper texts of Ransom's poems. The second is to be as complete as possible, adding a good number of poems to those included in the first attempt at a *Collected Poems of John Crowe Ransom*, edited by Ben Mazer (Boston: Un-Gyve, 2015). The third is to provide a complete set, for the first time, of all versions of Ransom's often-revised poems (omitting only those to which he relinquished control). And the last aim is to provide for the first time helpful annotations. If ever a poet called for annotation, it is Ransom—whose poems are rife with peculiar and archaic terms and allusions.

A good many generous people and institutions helped me prepare this edition. I must first mention Ray Bonis, Special Collections, James Branch Cabell Library, Virginia Commonwealth University, for his untiring assistance in tracking down Ransom's poems published in magazines and newspapers. And Amber R. Paranick, newspaper and periodical librarian, Library of Congress, offered extraordinary assistance in finding obscure journals containing long-lost poems. There are many others upon whom I depended: Suzanne Huffman, Special Collections, Simpson Library, University of Mary Washington; Teresa Gray and Whitney Mashburn, Special Collections, Jean and Alexander Heard Library, Vanderbilt University; Michael Bright; Rebecca Resinski, Hendrix College; Ellen Wolf and Lynn Vandenesse, Richmond Public Library, Richmond, Virginia; Nanette Hardison, Joyner Library, East Carolina University; the staff of the Library of Virginia, Richmond, especially William C. Luebke, Research Division; W. Donald Kay, University of South Carolina; Michael Berry, curator of published materials, South Caroliniana Library; Michael Zeliff, McKeldin Library, University of Maryland at College Park; Anne P. Benham, Alderman Library, University of Virginia; Ann W. Upton, Special Collections, Haverford College Library; Ann Blackely and Amanda Ferguson, McFarlin Library, University of Tulsa; the staff of the newspaper section of the Free Library of Philadelphia; Sandra Kroupa, book arts and rare book curator, Special Collections, University of Washington, Seattle; Richard B. Watson, head of reference services, and especially Hannah Rainey, graduate research associate, Harry Ransom Center, University of Texas at Austin; Ashby Crowder III, National Archives; Otis

Bland Crowder III; and most of all my wife, Lynn O'Malley Crowder, who has been my constant consultant and who has always given advice that I had utter confidence in.

I owe gratitude to the staff of Louisiana State University Press, especially Margaret Lovecraft, James Long, and Catherine Kadair. My copyeditor, Stan Ivester, has been indispensable.

Finally, I am indebted to Robb Forman Dew, granddaughter of John Crowe Ransom, not only for granting me permission to publish his poems but for providing materials for this project. I am grateful for her encouragement and enthusiasm for this edition.

Abbreviations and Short Titles

AM	*Atlantic Monthly.*
AP	Additional Published Poems.
APM	*American Poetry 1925: A Miscellany.* 1925; rpt. Granger Books, 1977.
AR	*American Review.*
Arma	John Crowe Random, *Armageddon.* Charleston: Poetry Society of South Carolina, 1923.
Buffington	Robert Buffington, *The Equilibrist: A Study of John Crowe Ransom's Poems, 1916–1963.* Nashville: Vanderbilt University Press, 1967.
CA	Oskar Seyffert, *A Dictionary of Classical Antiquities, Mythology, Religion, Literature and Art,* ed. Henry Nettleship and J. E. Sandys. London: Swan, Sonnenschein, 1899.
CB	Cleanth Brooks, "The Doric Delicacy." *Sewanee Review* 56:3 (July–September 1948), 402–15.
CF	John Crowe Ransom, *Chills and Fever.* New York: Alfred A. Knopf, 1924.
Cowan	Louise Cowan, *The Fugitive Group: A Literary History.* Baton Rouge: Louisiana State University Press, 1959.
CV	*Contemporary Verse.*
DD	*Double Dealer.*
EP	*Evening Post* (New York).
F	*The Fugitive: A Journal of Poetry.* Vols. 1–4 (1922–25).
FA	*Fugitives: An Anthology of Verse.* New York: Harcourt, Brace, 1928.
G	*The Guardian: A Literary Monthly*
GAM	John Crowe Ransom, *Grace After Meat.* London: Hogarth Press, 1924.
Haverford	Special Collections, Haverford College Library.
HM	*Harper's Magazine.*
HRC	Christopher Morley Collection. Harry Ransom Humanities Research Center, University of Texas, Austin.

Inde — *Independent.*

JCR — John Crowe Ransom.

Knight — Karl F. Knight, *The Poetry of John Crowe Ransom: A Study of Diction, Metaphor, and Symbol.* The Hague: Mouton, 1964.

KQ — Kieran Quinlan, *John Crowe Ransom's Secular Faith.* Baton Rouge: Louisiana State University Press, 1989.

KR — *Kenyon Review.*

LD — *Literary Digest.*

LR — *Literary Review* (published by *New York Evening Post*).

MQR — *Michigan Quarterly Review*

MS*FA* — Manuscripts prepared for *Fugitives: An Anthology of Verse.* Special Collections, Jean and Alexander Heard Library, Vanderbilt University.

MSFM — Manuscripts read and discussed at meetings of the Fugitives. Special Collections, Jean and Alexander Heard Library, Vanderbilt University.

MS*SP*45 — Manuscript (typescript) prepared for *Selected Poems,* 1945. Stuart Wright Collection, John Crowe Ransom Papers, Joyner Library, East Carolina University.

MW — Miller Williams, *The Poetry of John Crowe Ransom.* New Brunswick, NJ: Rutgers University Press, 1972.

New Int. — *Webster's Third New International Dictionary,* 1986.

NR — *New Republic.*

NV — *New Verse.*

NYR — *New York Review.*

OED — *Oxford English Dictionary.*

PAG — John Crowe Ransom, *Poems About God.* New York: Henry Holt, 1919.

Parsons — Thornton H. Parsons, *John Crowe Ransom.* New York: Twayne, 1969.

PE — John Crowe Ransom, *Poems and Essays.* New York: Vintage, 1955.

PP — Pomegranate Press, Cambridge, MA.

P*SP*63 — Corrected page proofs for *SP*63. Stuart Wright Collection, John Crowe Ransom Papers, Joyner Library, East Carolina University.

RPW Notes — Robert Penn Warren, "Notes on the Poetry of John Crowe Ransom at His Eightieth Birthday." *Kenyon Review* 30:3 (1968), 319–49.

SatR	*Saturday Review of Literature.*
SL	*Selected Letters of John Crowe Ransom,* ed. Thomas Daniel Young and George Core. Baton Rouge: Louisiana State University Press, 1985.
SoR	*Southern Review.*
SP45	John Crowe Ransom, *Selected Poems.* New York: Alfred A. Knopf, 1945.
SP63	John Crowe Ransom, *Selected Poems.* New York: Alfred A. Knopf, 1963.
SP69	John Crowe Ransom, *Selected Poems.* New York: Alfred A. Knopf, 1969.
SR	*Sewanee Review.*
SwR	*Southwest Review.*
TGB	John Crowe Ransom, *Two Gentlemen in Bonds.* New York: Alfred A. Knopf, 1927.
TM	*The Measure: A Journal of Poetry.*
VMS	Manuscripts of Ransom poems prepared for publication as well as those unpublished. Special Collections and University Archives, Jean and Alexander Heard Library, Vanderbilt University.
Young	Thomas Daniel Young, *Gentleman in a Dustcoat: A Biography of John Crowe Ransom.* Baton Rouge: Louisiana State University Press, 1976.

All biblical references are to the King James Version, and all references to Shakespeare are to the *Riverside Shakespeare,* ed. G. B. Evans et al. (Boston: Houghton Mifflin, 1974).

The Complete Poems

Copy-Text

In some cases, it might seem a reasonable course, if a poet has exercised control over the printing of his poems including the final revision, to select for copy-text the last revised version of his complete poems. Such a decision would capture the poet's final intention for his poems and assure consistency, in that all poems would be products of the same process.

Although John Crowe Ransom revised much of his poetry over the years, he never prepared or oversaw a volume of his collected poetry. Instead, he prepared three editions of his *Selected Poems,* the first in 1945 (containing forty-two poems), followed by another in 1963 (fifty-three poems), and a final one in 1969 (seventy-six poems).[1] Determining a copy-text for Ransom is a challenge. In fact, necessity will mean that this collected edition will have different copy-texts for different poems.

The final—and the most extensive—version of *Selected Poems,* with seventy-six poems, many of them revised but all in a state that he was satisfied with, nevertheless contains only a little over half of Ransom's published poems—the first reason for rejecting it as copy-text. Since a large percentage of his published poems would not have been a part of his final revising process, to accept the 1969 edition's text of its seventy-six poems would mean that an edition of Ransom's complete poems would have to combine two main copy-texts from vastly different periods in the poet's life. Mixing in poems of Ransom's youth with revisions made in old age is undesirable on the face of it. Such a scheme would give a confusing view of Ransom's development as a poet.

The other reason—and an even more telling one—for rejecting the final version of some of Ransom's poems as copy-text is that he was essentially a poet for only eleven years, from 1916 till 1927. During these years he published *Poems About God* (1919), *Chills and Fever* (1924),

1. Since Ransom considered the revision of the eight poems presented at the end of the 1969 volume as replacing the "inferior" previous versions, his view would be that there are seventy-two poems in his final selection. I am treating four of the revised poems as entirely new poems.

and *Two Gentlemen in Bonds* (1927).[2] Then his mind turned critical, and he published mainly prose: *The World's Body* (1938) along with many essays in critical journals before he began work on *The New Criticism* in 1938. During the years after *Two Gentlemen,* his stream of poetry dried up. From 1929 on he wrote only six additional poems (though he revised some others so extensively that they can be classified as new poems), the final ones being in 1969. When Ransom turned his critical eye to his own poems, especially when many years had elapsed since the original inspired writing, he did his poems a disservice. Ransom once remarked that he had grown out of several selves "during the years of no poetry," and he acknowledged the "awkwardness when one tries" again to engage in the difficult act of writing a poem.[3] The difficulty pertains as well to the revising of poems, especially in light of the different selves that emerged over the years. To be more specific, in later years, Ransom began to doubt "the advisability of attempting to carry 'two opposing ideas' in the mind 'at the same time' in 'cosmic irresolution,'" a prominent feature of his early poetry; he began to try to synthesize the polarities, to ease the tensions that he had once sought to present, so as to avoid portraying the "torture of equilibrium."[4] The ironic young man who faced in his poetry the hard realities of life became a mellow old man who was more kindly disposed to the world. He even revised "Tom, Tom, the Piper's Son" to give it a happy ending. For the 1969 edition of *Selected Poems,* he revised four of his poems so extensively that they became new poems. These new poems are not as good as the originals that inspired them, and many of the other revisions carried out for the 1969 edition are regrettable. For example, he eliminated the entire third stanza of "Old Mansion," the one containing the most memorable lines of the poem: "it expired as sweetly as Nature / With her tinge of oxidation on autumn leaf," first in the 1963 edition (p. 44) and repeated in the 1969 one (p. 70). The wonderful conclusion to "Judith of Bethulia"—"Inflamed by the thought of her naked beauty with desire? / Yes, and chilled with fear and despair"—was preserved through seven publications of the poem, only to have had its perfection undermined by a flick of the revising pen when the poet stripped her "naked beauty" to mere "nakedness."

2. *Grace After Meat* (London: Hogarth Press, 1924) does not have the same standing as Ransom's other volumes. See "Note on *Grace After Meat,*" below.

3. Young, 134.

4. Young, 371, 471.

Indeed, most critics have frowned on the final two editions of Ransom's poems. Writing in *Sewanee Review,* Roger Hecht said, "It is almost as if John Ransom, Critic, had set out to scold and correct the work of John Ransom, Poet, for a rashness or boldness of past poetic conduct."[5] Ransom's friend Allen Tate spoke of the revisions of some of Ransom's best poetry as "John's mania," the "last infirmity of a truly noble mind."[6] It seems advisable, in the case of Ransom, to steer away from basing copy-text, even partially, on a revised text executed many years after the original writing.

The final revised versions of poems in *Selected Poems* being unacceptable as a basis for a copy-text, we are left, it would seem, with two options (since manuscripts, or typescripts meant as printer's copy are almost nonexistent, they are not in contention): the first option is the original appearance of each poem in print, whether it be in a periodical, a newspaper, or in one of Ransom's first-edition volumes of poems; the second option is the three first-edition texts. Either of these options would fulfill the expectation of consistency in the choice of copy-text.

In deciding between these two options, the issue of whether or not the poet had control over a text when it was published must be considered. In the case of the poems' first appearance in print, almost any poet's access to proofs will vary from publication to publication; we only know for sure that Ransom oversaw the thirty-six poems that appeared in the *Fugitive.* In addition, these very earliest publications might have led the poet to profitable revision (we shall see). At any rate, this possibility for copy-text seems to present some worrisome limitations.

The only other possibility is Ransom's first editions. Ordinarily the first editions of a twentieth-century poet would meet the expectation of authorial oversight. Yet this is not altogether true in the case of Ransom. He had no opportunity to read proofs for his first volume, *Poems About God,* because he was in France from August 1917 until August of 1919, most of the time assigned to the Fifth Field Artillery during World War I. He was still writing poems for this volume while he was in Europe and sending them to his friend Christopher Morley, who was working to secure a publisher for him. In 1919 the volume was published, and Ransom first saw it when he received two copies of the book in the mail.[7] (See the introduction to *Poems About God* in the Anno-

5. Roger Hecht, "John Ransom's Poems," *SR* 71:4 (October–December 1963), 643.
6. Allen Tate, "Reflection on the Death of Ransom," *SR* 82 (Fall 1974), 549.
7. Young, 103, 104, 105.

tations section.) In future years, Ransom took no interest in correcting or revising these poems or including them in any subsequent publication—the four exceptions being "Overtures," in the 1969 edition of *Selected Poems* as a pairing with "Two Gentlemen Scholars," which is a complete re-conception of "Overtures"; "The Lover" and "Under the Locusts," which were the only two poems from *Poems About God* that Ransom selected for *The Fugitives: An Anthology of Verse*; and "The Cloak Model," which was published, significantly altered, in a broadside in 1973.

Resorting for copy-text to the original publication of the three poems in *Poems About God* that appeared in the *Independent* and the one in *Contemporary Verse* is of course not a possibility, for Ransom was in France during that time, having forwarded the poems to his friend Christopher Morley who had found outlets for them. The early newspaper and journal versions of the poems, while not suitable for copy-texts, are essential in the recording of variants, which provide a record of the poems' early forms, allowing one to note the revisions made for the first edition. All forms of all of the poems in *Poems About God*—except for "Overtures," "The Lover," and "Under the Locusts"—are equally lacking in authorial oversight, although there is reason to believe that Morley, who did read the proofs, followed Ransom's wishes. Still, there is no totally suitable copy-text for most of the poems in Ransom's first volume. The only guide that can be followed regarding these earliest poems is the principle of consistency, which would designate the first edition as copy-text. The three poems mentioned above, however, will actually have a proper copy-text. Because Ransom oversaw the re-publication of "Overtures" in the 1969 *Selected Poems,* that version of the poem will be its copy-text; and "The Lover" and "Under the Locusts" have as copy-text *Fugitives: An Anthology of Verse* (1928), a technical distinction, for the most part, because the text of "The Lover" remained unchanged from the first edition, and "Locusts" underwent a single punctuation change, which was in fact an improvement. The anthology reproduced the manuscripts Ransom submitted exactly. Though Donald Davidson was the anthology's compiler and organizer, Ransom worked with him daily at Vanderbilt and without doubt was involved in attending to the proofs, which were ready in early September 1927.[8] That in these three instances Ransom preserved the first edition's texts reflects well on the standing of the rest of the texts in *Poems About God.*[9]

8. Cowan, 222, 252.

9. Originally Ransom had meant to include other poems from *Poems About God*

The other two first editions, *Chills and Fever* and *Two Gentlemen in Bonds,* were published with the ordinarily expected authorial involvement: Ransom finished reading the proofs for *Chills and Fever* on 4 July 1924 and for *Two Gentlemen in Bonds* in mid-December of 1926.[10] These vetted texts, then, are ideal copy-texts and can be put together with *Poems About God* to account for the texts of most of Ransom's published poetry. There is always interest in poems as they appeared together when they made their initial impression on the literary world, and sometimes the original arrangement is significant: for example, "Somewhere Is Such a Kingdom" and the previous poem, "Two in August," speak to each other; in *Selected Poems* 1963 that relationship is not emphasized. Furthermore, many of the poems in the second and third first editions had benefited from Ransom's careful revision before they appeared in *Chills and Fever* and *Two Gentlemen.* He made these revisions as an act of continuing creation, near to the time when they were originally published in various journals, not years later as a critical exercise. Many of these early revisions improved markedly his original poems. The revision of "Blue Girls" originally published in the *Fugitive* for June 1924 is an apt example (see "Additional Published Poems" [pp. 234–35] for the original version, and the revision of it in *Two Gentlemen in Bonds* is on pp. 142–43). The *Fugitive* version of "Blue Girls" is a discursive poem that is all along more about the speaker than the girls observed, even though the speaker links the two somewhat casually at first, and then the speaker turns bitter and seems to jeer at the beautiful girls. This twenty-four-line poem is turned into a more concentrated seventeen-line poem that focuses on the fate of the beautiful girls, and the wisdom of the observer is, in very poignant manner and only at the poem's end, skillfully slipped in, giving the poem a dramatic power: the speaker's sorrow over her own faded beauty extends to the girls unmindful of the frailty of their own loveliness. One knows that the process by which Ransom created an effective poem was still going on when he revised "Blue Girls" for inclusion in *Two Gentlemen in Bonds.*

The superiority of the version Ransom revised for his third volume of poetry is obvious, and what is true for "Blue Girls" is true for many

---

in *Fugitives: An Anthology,* but when he learned that Knopf would not charge a fee to include poems from *Chills and Fever,* he added eight from that volume, removing a number from the first volume.

10. Young, 131, 179.

other poems. Using the first editions as copy-text for this collected edition will capture many of the poet's felicitous revisions; at least this is true for all but the first first edition, yet there is hardly another choice for these early poems. It would seem reasonable to conclude that the first editions, then, ought to serve as copy-text for all except the few poems that Ransom wrote in later life (as well as for those not published in any volume).

This argument would hold but for the real circumstances of Ransom's published texts, which must eclipse somewhat the logic thus far put forth. Though he revised many of his poems optimally before the publication of *Chills and Fever* and *Two Gentlemen in Bonds,* he in fact made some commendable revisions on seventeen of the forty-two poems in the 1945 *Selected Poems.*[11] These alterations of the first-edition texts in *Chills and Fever* and *Two Gentlemen in Bonds* (none of the poems from *Poems About God* appears in the 1945 volume) that clearly make a poem more effective cannot be ignored. The versions of these revised poems in this first book of *Selected Poems* are those that have since been repeatedly published in anthologies and are the forms of the poems that have over the years become so fixed in the minds of readers that they are unchangeable and ought to be left "as they are known and remembered and cherished."[12] It would be a shame to exclude the 1945 revisions from this edition. To illustrate the kind of revision Ransom made for the 1945 *Selected Poems,* let us first consider the small but significant change he made at the end of the first stanza of "Dead Boy." In the first edition of *Two Gentlemen in Bonds,* the first stanza concluded as follows: "And neither the county kin love the transaction / Nor some of the world of outer dark, like me." Ransom changed "love" to "like." As Thornton H. Parsons rightly points out, "'love the transaction' too obviously underscores the irony,"[13] and the word "like" is a better fit with

11. The significantly revised poems from *Chills and Fever* are "Spectral Lovers," "Vaunting Oak," "Miriam Tazewell," "Good Ships," "Necrological," "Armageddon," and "Old Mansion." (There was only one substantive revision for "Bells for John Whiteside's Daughter," but the poem is so well known in its 1945 version that that text will prevail.) The poems from *Two Gentlemen in Bonds* are "Eclogue," "Janet Waking," "Our Two Worthies," "Dead Boy," "Puncture," "Two in August," "Dog," "Antique Harvesters," "Man Without Sense of Direction," and "Survey of Literature."

12. Hecht, 643. *The Literature of the South,* ed. Richmond Croom Beatty, Floyd C. Watkins, Thomas Daniel Young, and Randall Stewart (New York: Scott, Foresman, 1952), set the standard, and others followed the practice. See pp. 751–55.

13. Parsons, 131. Parsons provides an analysis of many of the revisions Ransom made for the 1945 *Selected Poems*; see pp. 130–35.

the cold business language of "subtraction" and "transaction." Next, the wordy and somewhat cumbersome "He was not a beautiful boy, nor good, nor clever" became "A boy not beautiful, nor good, nor clever" (l. 4). In the final line, the emotionally more resonant "Grieving" replaced "Aggrieving," which carries the sense of merely "annoying" (*OED*) and thus reduces the devastating loss to the family that the speaker, in the end, realizes that the boy's death represents. "Spectral Lovers," from *Chills and Fever*, was also the object of some felicitous revisions in Ransom's 1945 volume. The original line 3—"Else two immaculate angels fallen on earth"—contains two problems that required elimination: these angels are not immaculate if they are fallen, and that they are "on earth" had been established in the two preceding lines. Ransom's revision is apposite: "Else angels lost in each other and fallen." The ineffective tenth line was also given life. "But for all the red heart beating in the pale bosom" became "The heart was bold that clanged within her bosom." In addition to eliminating the unnecessary anatomical allusion and the tired reference to the fact of the heart's beating, Ransom gives force to feeling with "bold," and the word "clanged" emphasizes the woman's powerful heartbeat as well as her alarm at those feelings that made it beat so.

One can be too scrupulous, then, in blindly following a common principle of editing, the principle of consistency, for it can force an editor to present a deficient version of a poem. Surely an editor's first principle should be to offer not only an accurate text but the best version of a text. Therefore, I shall substitute the texts from the 1945 *Selected Poems* for those seventeen poems that Ransom revised successfully and substantially.[14] It would not be prudent to accept all of the minor changes made for all of the poems in *Selected Poems* 1945, for Ransom was not immune to introducing errors—for example, in "Tom, Tom, the Piper's Son," he turned "councils" into "council" in the following line: "And against me the council of spirits were not then darkened" (l. 21), thereby creating a subject-verb disagreement, which would then need to be emended.

The order of poems according to *Chills and Fever* and *Two Gentlemen in Bonds* will be preserved, and the copy-texts imported from the 1945 *Selected Poems* will be designated with a parenthetical "(*SP*45)."

14. On a number of the other poems in the 1945 *Selected Poems,* Ransom made only minor revisions in punctuation, capitalization, single-word deletion or revision, and, in one case, number. There is no reason that these slightly revised poems should supersede the first-edition copy-text.

It remains to settle on copy-text for the poems that Ransom wrote after 1927, and it will become inevitable that this 1945 volume will be copy-text for at least some of the poems in this collected edition. He wrote six more poems between 1929 and 1969, and he revised nine other poems to such an extent that they must be judged new poems. Determining a copy-text for these fifteen poems that is consistent with the practice regarding the majority of Ransom's poems is in some cases impossible. It would be helpful if we could find something within the principle of consistency to guide the decision on most of these remaining poems. Five post–*Two Gentlemen in Bonds* poems—"What Ducks Require," "Prelude to an Evening," "Of Margaret," "Painted Head," and "Address to the Scholars of New England"—appear at the end of the 1945 *Selected Poems,* and this is the first publication of these poems after their initial appearance in periodicals. A copy-text for these poems based on the versions in the 1945 *Selected Poems* is thus consistent with the treatment of those earlier poems substantially revised for the 1945 volume, the principle being that the poet had the same opportunity to improve upon the poem following soon after its earlier publication.

For different reasons a few poems must depend on the *Selected Poems* of 1963 for copy-text. This edition offers the only volume publication of "Old Man Pondered," which had previously appeared only in the *Saturday Review* in 1929. In his preface to the 1963 volume, Ransom says that he had changed the title of "Tom, Tom, the Piper's Son" to "The Vanity of the Bright Young Men"—but Ransom had actually written an entirely new poem to go with that new title; and since this is this new poem's only publication, the poem being radically revised in the 1969 *Selected Poems* and thus creating yet another new poem with a new title, "The Vanity of the Bright Boys," the 1963 text must be designated copy-text for "The Vanity of the Bright Young Men." Also a new version of "Prelude to an Evening" was included, in addition to the original one, in the 1963 volume. In his 1963 preface, Ransom acknowledged that "Masters in the Garden Again," which appears for the first time in 1963, "is a completely new version of the old and rather ignominious 'Conrad in Twilight,' . . . which did not try to resemble that of the original." These last two poems were periodically published before being put in the 1963 volume, and so these 1963 versions will be copy-text for those versions, following the principle referred to above of first revision after the original publication.

Several remaining poems require the 1969 *Selected Poems* as copy-text, because it is the only volume in which they appear; these are the total rewrites of earlier poems—"Nocturne" and "April Treason"—as well as the totally new versions in the section titled "Sixteen Poems in Eight Pairings" at the end of the volume: "Two Gentlemen Scholars (a pastoral)," "*Agitato ma non troppo*," "Birthday of an Aging Seer," and "The Vanity of the Bright Boys," which is a complete overhaul of "The Vanity of the Bright Young Men."[15] Although "Birthday of an Aging Seer" is essentially the same poem as "Semi-Centennial," the word and line revisions are so extensive that it will nonetheless be included in the section of "Additional Published Poems" (otherwise the textual notes required for reconstruction of the revisions would discourage that process).[16]

Finally, there are a good number of poems that were published only once in newspapers or journals, the earliest one that I have found being "What the Old Leaf Said," published in the *Independent* on 27 October 1917. The copy-text for these can be nothing other than their one-time publication. Most of the alternate versions of poems, whether they were made before or after the standard version, were published only once.

It is clear, then, that the circumstances of Ransom's texts determine that an eclectic copy-text for this collected edition cannot be avoided. Too many of his poems have no common textual history, and the decision about copy-text for many poems must be done on an ad hoc basis. Briefly, then, the following plan has been followed: Ransom's three first editions—*Poems About God*, *Chills and Fever*, and *Two Gentlemen in Bonds*—will be copy-text for most of the poems herein, the exceptions being the seventeen poems effectively revised for the 1945 *Selected Poems*, which will be copy-text for them. The six poems introduced in *Selected Poems* 1945 and 1963 will have those editions as copy-text, and all of the uncollected poems as well as those revised into new poems will be represented as they appear either in a newspaper or periodical or in a subsequent volume. The poems that exist only in manuscript (typescript) will appear at the end of the volume, and this volume will mark their first publication. The manuscripts will of course be copy-text for unpublished poems.[17]

15. The revised versions in the "Sixteen Poems in Eight Pairings" at the end of the 1969 volume that are not sufficiently revised to be considered new poems are "Masters in the Garden Again," "Here Lies a Lady," "Of Margaret," and "Prelude to an Evening."

16. There are five other alternate versions of poems, published periodically between 1920 and 1925, that are also included in the AP section.

17. There are six unsigned poems among Ransom's papers at Vanderbilt—"Daily," "This Lady," "Question and Answer," "My Dog," "Mother and Child," and "I Would Do Violence"—that were published under Ransom's name in the *Michigan Quarterly*

A remaining issue is how to arrange the early poems included in the "Sixteen Poems in Eight Pairings" feature of *Selected Poems* (1969), some of which were completely rewritten. Though it might be tempting to replicate the pairing arrangement, to do so would destroy the chronology and the record of Ransom's development as a poet. Therefore, the early versions will appear in the order of their original publication, and the same will be done for the new poems based on those earlier ones (notes will direct the reader to the corresponding early or late version of a poem).

A Note on *Grace After Meat*

Grace After Meat, with an introduction by Robert Graves, was published by Leonard and Virginia Woolf at the Hogarth Press in 1924, a few months before *Chills and Fever* appeared in America. The volume contains twenty-one poems (counting "The Southern Mansion," which appears in a shortened version in the introduction), nine from *Poems About God* and twelve from *Chills and Fever.*

When Ransom sent the manuscript that was the basis for *Grace After Meat* to Graves in the hope that Graves would find a publisher for it, he stated unequivocally that Graves was to change any title he wanted to as well as "edit" the manuscript "as you please," for he believed that Graves was "much further along than I in technique." Ransom reiterated this permission on 1 February 1923: "make any revisions, excisions, changes you want to." What is more, in November he asked Graves to "handle my proof," reiterating this in the next month: "You are considerate in offering to try to get proofs for me. I don't care a hang about them, *provided* you can stand the strain of correcting them for me."[18]

There is evidence that Graves took Ransom at his word, wanting to keep to the agreement even when Ransom on specific issues wanted to have his own way. Graves went so far as to add a poem that Ransom had not included. That poem is "Grace," from *Poems About God.*

Review 35:3 (Summer 2006). Subsequently, Charles Stephen Dew pointed out to the editor of that review that those poems had actually been written by his grandmother, Helen Ransom Forman. One other poem in the folder, "Hallowe'en Poem," is actually by Ransom and is published for the first time in this volume.

18. Ransom to Graves, 22 October 1922, *SL,* 113; 1 February 1923, *SL,* 118; 19 November 1923, *SL,* 124; and 30 December 1923, *SL,* 126.

Graves liked the poem so much that he not only insisted upon including it in the volume against Ransom's wishes but alluded to it in the title that he gave to the entire volume, over-riding the title that Ransom had originally given the collection—"Philomela." In his introduction to *Grace After Meat,* Graves says that in the end "Ransom has conceded me 'Grace,'" which Ransom did in fact do in a 19 November 1923 letter: "Personally, I'd say 'Grace' is an artistic offense, and I'd rather pose for an artist than exhibit my history. But if you'd like to have written it, my judgment is wrong."[19] Ransom remained opposed, however, to Graves's desire to name the book "Grace After Meat": on 20 November 1923 Ransom proposed eight titles in addition to his original preference. Graves was adamant, even though Ransom had told him that he was so opposed to the title that he put down one of the alternative titles he had suggested—"Vaunting Oak"—when filling out a questionnaire for *Who's Who in America* ("I'd just as soon be in error in that tome. But it came a little hard to write "Grace After Meat"—it emphasizes a poem I don't like").[20]

Another indication that Graves was really in charge of this publishing adventure shows in his disregard of Ransom's appeal that Graves correct two errors that Ransom had detected in looking over his retained copy of the manuscript of "Adventure This Side of Pluralism." In "the last quatrain, third line, the word *respective* should be *invective,*" Ransom wrote.[21] The word *respective* remains in *Grace After Meat.* In regard to "Vaunting Oak," Graves changed the title to "Ilex Pricus." To this Ransom objected, for this Latin name "can mean only a holm-oak, which is evergreen, and useless for my peculiarly devastating intentions." Then he suggests the title "Old Oak." Ransom was so concerned about the title that Graves had chosen that he wrote again the next day: "I feel that *Ilex* must go; it's a glaring inaccuracy which an Englishman like yourself . . . ought not to have smiled upon!"[22] Graves kept the title he had chosen.

Although it was a real feather in Ransom's cap to have a collection of his poems published by the Hogarth Press, this volume does not qualify, for the reasons outlined above, to be included in the variants

19. Robert Graves, "Introduction," *Grace After Meat* (Hogarth Press, 1923), 8; Ransom to Graves, 19 November 1923, *SL,* 124.

20. Ransom to Graves, 4 January 1923, *SL,* 117.

21. Ransom to Graves, 22 October 1922, *SL,* 113.

22. Ransom to Graves, 19 November 1923, *SL,* 124; 20 November 1923, *SL,* 125.

to Ransom's poems. That would be to give standing to differences in texts that they do not deserve. Although Ransom had given Christopher Morley similar leave to revise *Poems About God,* Morley refrained from doing so, and when Ransom sent revisions from Europe to Morley, he inserted those changes diligently. Significant differences between *Grace After Meat* and *Poems About God* and *Chills and Fever,* however, will be indicated in the annotations.

Variants

Though Ransom's habit was to revise his poems upon each publication following their initial publication—sometimes to a great extent—the result of his revisions varies: early in his life, his revisions were often felicitous; as the years progressed, the revisions often proved unfortunate. The textual notes record any variants from the various copy-texts, those preceding in chronology the established text and the changes in text that occurred afterwards. The copy-text reading will not appear in the textual notes, as is sometimes done when a final revised version is copy-text.

Primary Materials

The primary materials, which will serve as copy-texts or as variants recorded in the textual notes, are as follows:

1. *Manuscripts.*

The manuscript (typescript) of a poem obtains when the poem was unpublished (including those sent in letters to Christopher Morley, those in the Heard Library at Vanderbilt University, and those poems in the 1922 typescript "Chills and Fevers" that were later not included in the *Chills and Fever* volume (this manuscript is at the Harry Ransom Center, University of Texas at Austin). When a manuscript was clearly prepared for a poem's publication, it is a primary item. Almost all of the manuscripts of published poems at the Heard Library are not connected directly with any published versions of the poems. Though it is interesting to know that Ransom at some point thought of titling "These Winters" as "These Winters and Those," there is no way to know if the manuscript containing that option precedes or follows the title as it appears in *Chills and Fever*; and though the poem was published only in this first edition, the poet might well have revised it in contemplation of a subsequent publication. The same can be said of the manuscript line "And a wild weather empties upon our pride" and its relationship to the corresponding line in *Chills and Fever*," "And a great weather was emptied on our pride." Any such differences in texts that cannot clearly be shown to have a connection with a published version of a poem will not be recorded in the textual variant notes.

The manuscripts that were clearly prepared for publication are the typescripts for those poems published in *Fugitive: An Anthology of Verse* (1928) and the typescript for the 1945 *Selected Poems* (this manuscript contains printer's marks indicating galley-proof numbers and other directive notes, notes that new stanzas begin as the text goes from one page to another, for example). There are a very few relevant manuscripts of individual poems.

2. *Newspapers and Journal Publications.*

Some of the poems published in newspapers or periodicals appeared only in one of these forums, and it is possible that even Ransom himself might have forgotten about some of them. Examples are "What the Old Leaf Said," which appeared in the *Independent,* 27 October 1917, and "Halted at the Altar," which was in the *Evening Public Ledger* (Philadelphia) on 26 May 1919. There are a good number of long-lost poems included, and their once-only publication provides their copy-text.

Those poems published in newspapers and journals and later revised for either additional journal publication or for inclusion in a volume will furnish variants that shall be recorded in the notes. *The Fugitive,* the journal created in 1922 by the group of nine poets at Vanderbilt known as the Fugitives, contains the majority of Ransom's early poems. For the first two issues, the poets used pen names, Ransom's being Roger Prim.

Although in the acknowledgment for *Poems About God* Ransom says that one or more of the poems in that volume had been published in the *Liberator,* a left-wing journal published in New York City and edited by Max Eastman and contributed to by Carl Sandberg and E. E. Cummings, it appears that he was mistaken (though he was correct in his other acknowledgments): Theodore F. Watts's *The Liberator Index, 1918–1924* (Easthampton, MA: Periodyssey Press, 2001) lists no poems by Ransom.

3. *The First Editions.*

Poems About God. New York: Henry Holt, 1919.
Chills and Fever. New York: Alfred A. Knopf, 1924.
Two Gentlemen in Bonds. New York: Alfred A. Knopf, 1927.

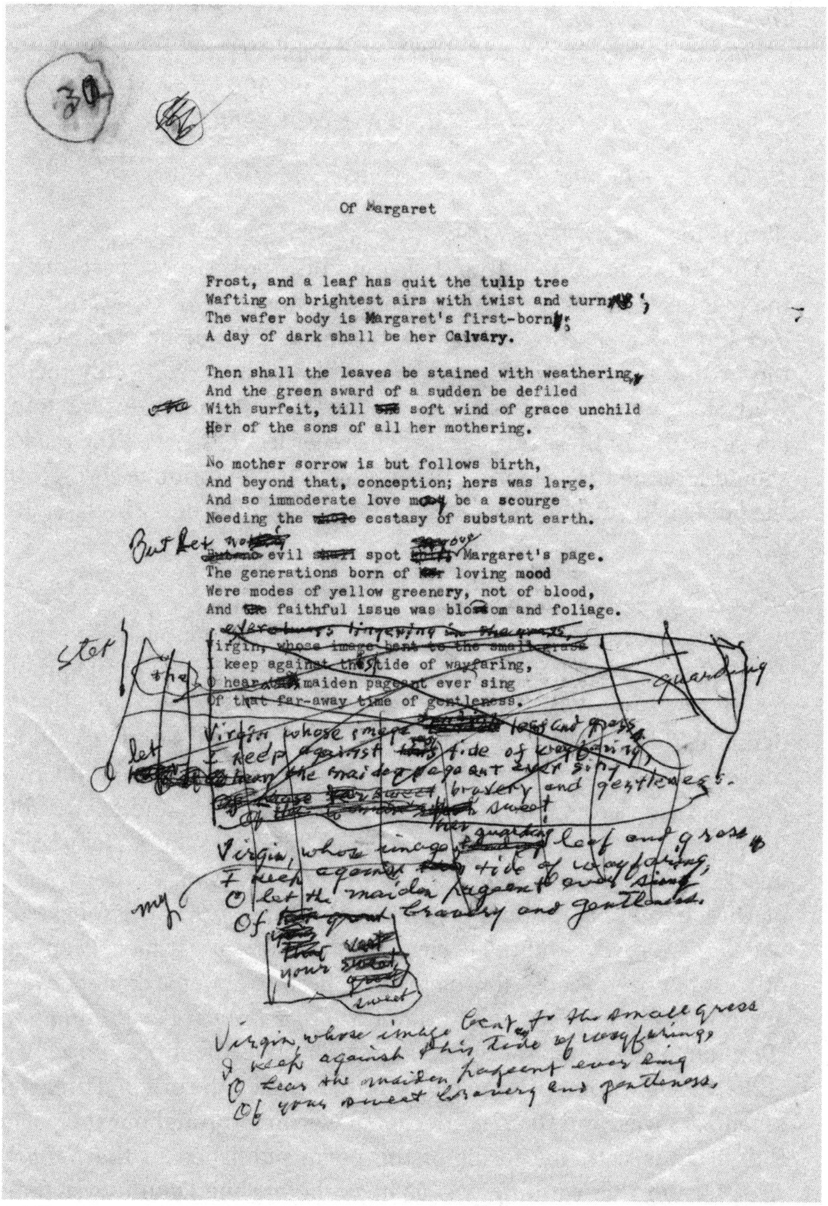
Of Margaret

Frost, and a leaf has quit the tulip tree
Wafting on brightest airs with twist and turn;
The wafer body is Margaret's first-born;
A day of dark shall be her Calvary.

Then shall the leaves be stained with weathering,
And the green sward of a sudden be defiled
With surfeit, till the soft wind of grace unchild
Her of the sons of all her mothering.

No mother sorrow is but follows birth,
And beyond that, conception; hers was large,
And so immoderate love may be a scourge
Needing the whole ecstasy of substant earth.

But no evil shall spot this Margaret's page.
The generations born of her loving mood
Were modes of yellow greenery, not of blood,
And the faithful issue was blossom and foliage.

Virgin, whose image bent to the small grass
I keep against this tide of wayfaring,
O hear the maiden pageant ever sing
Of that far-away time of gentleness.

Virgin, whose image bent to the small grass
I keep against this tide of wayfaring,
O hear the maiden pageant ever sing
Of your sweet bravery and gentleness.

This manuscript page of "Of Margaret" illustrates Ransom's penchant for revision. This revision is not directly related to any published version of the poem. (*Vanderbilt University Special Collections and University Archives*)

4. *The Selected Editions.*

Selected Poems. New York: Alfred A. Knopf, 1945.
Selected Poems. New York: Alfred A. Knopf, 1963.
Selected Poems. New York: Alfred A. Knopf, 1969.

5. *Author's Page Proofs.*

5a. Proofs for *Selected Poems* 1945.

The author's marks on these page proofs, for the most part, direct the printer to fix broken fonts, eliminate stray bits of type, and correct improper spacing. These "corrections" will not be recorded in the textual notes. Only five poems—"Miriam Tazewell," "Philomela," "Old Mansion," "Lady Lost," and "What Ducks Require"—were actually revised, and these revisions will be recorded. Otherwise the reader should assume that the page proof for the 1945 edition accords with the published edition and that therefore a duplicate entry in the notes will not occur.

5b. Proofs for *Selected Poems* 1963.

In most cases these page proofs accord with the published form of *Selected Poems* 1963, and therefore an additional record of the proofreading will not ordinarily be recorded in the textual notes. In the main, at this stage Ransom cleaned up the text by signaling marks made by stray bits of type. Variants in the these page proofs will, however, be recorded for the heavily revised introduction and for the following poems: "*Agitato ma non troppo*," "In Process of a Noble Alliance," "The Vanity of Bright Young Men," "Dog," "Man Without Sense of Direction," and "Prelude to an Evening: Revised and Explicated," which were revised on these page proofs. There must have been another set of page proofs, for the texts of these few poems do not always agree with the final 1963 edition of *Selected Poems.* For example, in "Prelude to an Evening: Revised and Explicated," an entire stanza was added at some point prior to publication between the original first and second stanzas, and there is additional wording throughout the poem that accords with the forms of the poem published in the *Kenyon Review,* and this wording was changed before the volume was published. Further, there is a word crossed out and replaced on the "Prelude" page proof that was countermanded before the volume's publication. In addition, the poem "Old Man Pondered" was added to *Selected Poems* 1963 after the correction of these page proofs.

6. Louis Untermeyer, ed. *American Poetry 1925: A Miscellany.* 1925. Rpt. Granger Books, 1977.

   This publication began in 1920, and the original twelve contributors in subsequent years invited the new contributors, who were given twenty pages in which to place unpublished poems representing their latest work. Ransom published his sonnet sequence from *Two Gentlemen in Bonds* in the 1925 issue.

7. *Fugitives: An Anthology of Verse.* New York: Harcourt, Brace, 1928.

   Although Donald Davidson was the organizer, collecting manuscripts and "fitting them into the limitations of space," each of the eleven Fugitive poets was responsible for selecting his own poems (vi).

8. *Poems and Essays, Selected, Edited, and Arranged by the Author.* New York: Vintage Books, 1955.

9. The broadside "Cloak Model." Cambridge, MA: Pomegranate Press, 1973.

Secondary Materials

Secondary materials are either not directly connected to the poems' publication or were published without Ransom's involvement in or control over the text. Secondary materials are sometimes discussed in the notes and occasionally can play a role when emendation is required.

1. The typescripts prepared for *Fugitives: An Anthology of Verse* but not included in that volume.

2. *Grace After Meat.* London: Hogarth Press, 1924.

   This volume lacks authorial authority (see "A Note on *Grace After Meat,*" above).

3. Typescript of Ransom's poems read and discussed at Fugitive meetings.

   Several of these poems (VMS, box 2, folder 12, contains carbon-paper copies) vary significantly from any of the published versions; they appear in Appendix C.

4. The typescript of the original version of "Chills and Fevers" produced in 1922.

   It was the basis of what became *Chills and Fever* in 1924, but it does not qualify as part of the poems' publishing history. The four poems eliminated from this manuscript and never published are Primary Materials (item 1).

5. Assorted manuscripts not prepared for publication.

Principles Pertaining to Textual Notations

The textual notes will represent a thorough history of Ransom's texts in the line of publication; that is, the notes will record all word and punctuation variants. It would be pointless to record differences in spelling—for example, the shifts back and forth between "grey" and "gray," which were probably owing to the inclinations of printers and of no interest to readers. Older forms like "to-night" and "to-morrow" will be modernized. Ransom's compulsion to employ British spelling was a literary pretense to gentility that he shared with other early twentieth-century American writers—Ellen Glasgow, Edith Wharton, William Dean Howells, and others. Ransom had begun to employ American spelling in 1927, and in 1945, he indicated in various instances his desire to shift from English spelling in earlier poems, for example in a marginal note on the proofs for *Selected Poems* 1945, when beside stanza seven of "Armageddon" he marked the deletion of "u" in "honourable" and added that this deletion was to be carried out in "all copy." Again, on the typescript of "Eclogue" for *Selected Poems* 1945, he marked out the British double "l" in "travellers." Therefore, for those copy-texts that retain British spelling I have silently altered "defence," "sombre," "spectre," "practise," "centres," "flavoured," and so on to American spelling, except when a poem makes special use of archaic British forms, as in "Boris in Britain," in which "chymist" and "gaol" play a role. Another exception is "Adventure This Side of Pluralism," in which "centred" and "accoutred" make a sight rhyme (ll. 90, 92).

Shifts in capitalization will generally be ignored, unless the move from upper case to lower case, or the other way, is particularly significant. Most of the time the change in capitalization is simply in line with standard practice. Occasionally, if the change is very deliberate, as when in *The Fugitive* he capitalized the words "South" and "North" in "Judith of Bethulia" and then reintroduced capitals for the words in 1969, the variants will be noted. He saw significance in the difference.

Finally, I have silently corrected obvious errors in the copy-texts and ignored obvious errors in other texts, as, for example, when *Poems and Essays* misprints "I till" instead of "I tell" or when the *Fugitive* version of

"The Miller's Daughter" has "dalight" instead of "daylight"; also I have silently eliminated the holdover from the nineteenth-century practice of using a comma with a dash (as in "In their easy practiced throats, — / Smooth as orators are the thrushes"), a habit that Ransom had in fact abandoned by 1927. In at least two instances I have recorded as variants Ransom's unusual combination of a dash with semicolon and full stop, being unable to determine which mark was meant to dominate.

Mechanics of Presenting Variants

In recording a variant from the copy-text, the variant will ordinarily be preceded by a pickup word and followed by a drop word. For example, from "On the Road to Wockensutter":

Copy-text, line 4: The pulver of her brimstone scratched my throat.
Variant note: 4| *DD*: brimstone itched my

The list of abbreviations indicates that *DD* = *Double Dealer;* the annotations for the poem give the particulars of this first publication of the poem.

When there is more than one variant in a line, the mark < > means that the word or words and punctuation between the two variants agree with the copy-text. For example, in "Vaunting Oak":

Copy-text, line 6: Only his temporal twigs are unsure of seat.
Variant note: 6| *F, CF*: Only the temporal < > are abashed on their seat.

The abbreviations *F* and *CF* refer to *The Fugitive* and *Chills and Fever.*

Next, no textual note ends with a punctuation mark unless the punctuation mark appears at the end of the line. If the point of a note is to record a variant in punctuation, the word preceding and following the punctuation mark will be included, though if the variant in punctuation occurs at the end of a line, obviously no drop word will be necessary. The examples below are from "Vaunting Oak" and "Somewhere Is Such a Kingdom":

Copy-text, line 38: And if they stayed would perish miserably
Variant note: 38| *F, CF*: stayed, would

Copy-text, line 26: This I know, that if they wrangle
Variant note 26| MS*SP*45, *SP*45, *PE, SP*63, *SP*69: wrangle,

If the would-be pickup word is capitalized, and is not the first word of the line in the copy-text, then the next-previous uncapitalized word is included. For example, from "Noonday Grace":

Copy-text, line 40: But God was behind it, it seems to me.
Variant note: 40| *Inde*: But God is in it

No pickup word is used when the first word of a line is a variant from the copy-text.

Most of the variant notes apply to only one line, but when additional lines appear—or when lines have been deleted—the entry will cover all of the lines involved, with a pickup word from the preceding line and a drop word from the line that follows. The copy-text for "Plea in Mitigation" ends the penultimate stanza with the line "Pursue your gods faster than most of creatures!" and the last stanza begins with "And if an alien, hideously at feud[.]" The earlier *Fugitive* version of the poem has a stanza inserted between these two lines, and so the variant note will appear as follows, incorporating any variants that appear in the lines before or after the additional lines.

Variant note: 32–33| *F*: creatures; // So I take not the vomit where they do, / Comporting downwards to the general breed; / I have run further, matching your heat and speed, / And tracked the Wary Fugitive with you; // And

(Double virgules [//] indicate a stanza break.)

When lines in a variant text are absent from what is given in the copy-text, a pickup word from the line preceding the variant and a drop word following the same are also required. Any additional differences in the lines involved will be folded into the note. For example, the version of "Dead Boy" in *Sewanee Review* does not contain the second stanza that we find in the copy-text, and there are other differences in the preceding and following lines; therefore, the note reads as follows:

Variant note: 4–9| *SR*: And some < > me. // A pig < > face, I had

When there is a small difference between two versions of a long variant, the discrepancy will be noted at the end of the entry in lieu of repeating the entire entry. The example is from "Prometheus in Straits":

Variant note: 6| *SP63*, *SP69*: Lest I seem to identify your wits with your nation's #*your* in italics in *SP63*#

Changes that Ransom made on a typescript or on page proofs are described between these marks: # #; drop words do not follow the change remarked upon, as long as the change is clear from the editorial description. For example, from "Vaunting Oak":

Variant note: 23| MS*SP45*: of grim #last word crossed out and replaced above by one word# much

No pickup or drop words are called for when a variant is internal—for example, in a tense change or in a change in number (singular/plural).

POEMS ABOUT GOD

The Swimmer

In dog-days plowmen quit their toil,
And frog-ponds in the meadow boil,
And grasses on the upland broil,
And all the coiling things uncoil,
And eggs and meats and Christians spoil.

A mile away the valley breaks
(So all good valleys do) and makes
A cool green water for hot heads' sakes,
And sundry sullen dog-days' aches.

The swimmer's body is white and clean,
It is washed by a water of deepest green
The color of leaves in a starlight scene,
And it is as white as the stars between.

But the swimmer's soul is a thing possessed,
His soul is naked as his breast,
Remembers not its east and west,
And ponders this way, I have guessed:

I have no home in the cruel heat
On alien soil that blisters feet.
This water is my native seat,
And more than ever cool and sweet,
So long by forfeiture escheat.

O my forgiving element!
I gash you to my heart's content
And never need be penitent,
So light you float me when breath is spent
And close again where my rude way went.

And now you close above my head,
And I lie low in a soft green bed
That dog-days never have visited.
"By the sweat of thy face shalt thou eat bread:"
The garden's curse is at last unsaid

What do I need of senses five?
Why eat, or drink, or sweat, or wive?
What do we strive for when we strive?
What do we live for when alive?

And what if I do not rise again,
Never to goad a heated brain
To hotter excesses of joy and pain?
Why should it be against the grain
To lie so cold and still and sane?

Water-bugs play shimmer-shimmer,
Naked body's just a glimmer,
Watch ticks every second grimmer:
Come to the top, O wicked swimmer!

Noonday Grace

My good old father tucked his head,
(His face the color of gingerbread)
Over the table my mother had spread,
And folded his leathery hands and said:

"We thank thee, Lord, for this thy grace,
And all thy bounties to the race;
Turn not away from us thy face
Till we come to our final resting-place."

These were the words of the old elect,
Or others to the same effect.

I love my father's piety,
I know he's grateful as can be,
A man that's nearly seventy
And past his taste for cookery.

1| *Inde*: head
3| *Inde*: spread
4–5| *Inde*: said: / #no stanza break# "We < > grace
8–9| *Inde*: our last resting place." #no stanza break# These

But I am not so old as he,
And when I see in front of me
Things that I like uncommonly,
(Cornfield beans my specialty,
When every pod spills two or three),
Then I forget the thou and thee
And pray with total fervency:

Thank you, good Lord, for dinner-time!
Gladly I come from the sweat and grime
To play in your Christian pantomime.

I wash the black dust from my face,
I sit again in a Christian's place,
I hear the ancient Christian's grace.

My thanks for clean fresh napkin first,
With faint red stain where the fruit-jar burst.

Thanks for a platter with kind blue roses,
For mother's centerpiece and posies,
A touch of art right under our noses.

Mother, I'll thank you for tumbler now
Of morning's milk from our Jersey cow.

And father, thanks for a generous yam,
And a helping of home-cured country ham,
(He knows how fond of it I am.)

For none can cure them as can he,

18| *Inde*: specialty
19| *Inde*: three)
20| *Inde*: forget formality
21| *Inde*: pray along half-consciously.
22| *Inde*: you, God, for
24–25| *Inde*: pantomime #no stanza break# I < > face
26| *Inde*: And set < > place
27| *Inde*: And hear the good old Christian's
28| *Inde*: Thanks for my clean
29–30| *Inde*: With its faint < > burst. #no stanza break# And thanks for plates with such blue roses
31| *Inde*: And mother's
33 *Inde*: Mother is filling my tumbler
34| *Inde*: With sweet milk fresh from
35| *Inde*: Father calls for a golden yam
36| *Inde*: And gives me a < > of country
37–38| *Inde*: He < > am. / #no stanza break# No one can cure it as well as he,

And he won't tell his recipe.
But God was behind it, it seems to me.

Thank God who made the garden grow,
Who took upon himself to know
That we loved vegetables so.
I served his plan with rake and hoe,
And mother, boiling, baking, slow
To her favorite tune of Old Black Joe,
Predestined many an age ago.

Pearly corn still on the cob,
My teeth are aching for that job.

Tomatoes, one would fill a dish,
Potatoes, mealy as one could wish.

Cornfield beans and cucumbers,
And yellow yams for sweeteners.

Pickles between for stepping-stones,
And plenty of cornmeal bread in pones.

Sunday the preacher droned a lot
About a certain whether or not:
Is God the universal friend,
And if men pray can he attend
To each man's individual end?

They pray for individual things,
Give thanks for little happenings,

39| *Inde*: tell the recipe,
40| *Inde*: But God is in it
41| *Inde*: I'm sure God made our garden
42| *Inde*: Because he certainly would know
43| *Inde*: We loved the vegetables
44| *Inde*: I did my part with < > hoe
45| *Inde*: mother boiled and baked them slow
46| *Inde*: of "Old < > Joe,"
47| *Inde*: For so he planned them years ago.
49–50| *Inde*: for their job; / #no stanza break# Tomatoes
51–52| *Inde*: wish; / #no stanza break# Cornfield
53–54| *Inde*: sweeteners; / #no stanza break# Pickles
56| *Inde*: preacher talked a
57| *Inde*: About the question whether < > not
58| *Inde*: God is a universal friend
60–61| *Inde*: And favors individual men. / #no stanza break# We pray

But isn't his sweep of mighty wings
Meant more for businesses of kings
Than pulling small men's petty strings?

He's infinite, and all of that,
The setting sun his habitat,
The heavens they hold by his fiat,
The glorious year that God begat;
And what is creeping man to that,
O preacher, valiant democrat?

"The greatest of all, his sympathy,
His kindness, reaching down to me."

Like mother, he finds it his greatest joy
To have big dinners for his boy.

She understands him like a book,
In fact, he helps my mother cook,
And slips to the dining-room door to look;
And when we are at our noon-day meal,
He laughs to think how fine we feel.

An extra fork is by my plate,
I nearly noticed it too late!

Mother, you're keeping a secret back!
I see the pie-pan through the crack,
Incrusted thick in gold and black.

There's no telling what that secret pair
Have cooked for me in the kitchen there,

64| *Inde*: for the business of kings,
65| *Inde*: And not for pulling little strings?
67–74| *Inde*: habitat, / But the preacher and I, we say out flat: / You can never compute his sympathy, / His time and love reach down to me // Like
76| *Inde*: My mother knows him
78| *Inde*: And steals to < > dining room < > look.
79| *Inde*: noonday meal
81| *Inde*: plate.
82| *Inde*: late.
85–86| *Inde*: And strips of crust in < > black, / #no stanza break# There's
87–88| *Inde*: there. / #no stanza break# There's

There's no telling what that pie can be,
But tell me that it's blackberry!

As long as I keep topside the sod,
I'll love you always, mother and God.

The Ingrate

By night we looked across my field,
The tasseled corn was fine to see,
The moon was yellow on the rows
And seemed so wonderful to me,
That with an old provincial pride
I praised my moonlit Tennessee,
And thought my poor befriended man
Would never dare to disagree.

He was a frosty Russian man
And wore a bushy Russian beard;
He had two furtive faded eyes
That some old horror once had seared;
I wondered if they ever would
Forget the horrors they had feared;
Yet when I praised my pleasant field
This stupid fellow almost jeered.

"Your moon shines very well, my friend,
Your fields are good enough, I know;
At home our fields in the winter-time
Were always white, and shining so!
Our nights went beautiful like day,
And bitter cold our winds would blow;
And I remember how it looked,
Dear God, my country of the snow!"

89–90| *Inde*: blackberry! / #no stanza break# And long < > upside the sod

Sunset

I know you are not cruel,
And you would not willingly hurt anything in the world.
There is kindness in your eyes,
There could not very well be more of it in eyes
Already brimful of the sky.
I thought you would some day begin to love me,
But now I doubt it badly;
It is no man-rival I am afraid of,
It is God.

The meadows are very wide and green,
And the big field of wheat is solid gold,
Or a little darker than gold.
Two people never sat like us by a fence of cedar rails
On a still evening
And looked at such fat fields.
To me it is beautiful enough,
I am stirred,
I say grand and wonderful, and grow adjectival,
But to you
It is God.

Cropping the clover are several spotted cows.
They too are kind and gentle,
And they stop and look round at me now and then
As if they would say:
"How good of you to come to see us!
Please pardon us if we seem indifferent,
But we have not much time to talk with you now,
And really nothing to say."
Then they make their bow,
Still kind and calm,
And go their way again
Towards the sunset.
I suppose they are going to God.

2| *Inde*: world,
3| *Inde*: For there
6| *Inde*: me.
10| *Inde*: green

Your eyes are not regarding me,
Nor the four-leaf clovers I picked for you,
(With a prayer and a gentle squeeze for each of them),
Nor are they fretting over dress, and shoes,
And image in the little glass,
Restlessly,
Like the eyes of other girls.
You are looking away over yonder
To where the crooked rail-fence gets to the top
Of the yellow hill
And drops out of sight
Into space.
Is that infinity that catches it?
And do you catch it too in your thoughts?
I know that look;
I have not seen it on another girl;
And it terrifies me,
For I cannot tell what it means,
But I think
It has something to do with God.

We are a mile from home,
And soon it will be getting dark,
And the big farm-bell will be ringing out for supper.
We had better start for the house.
Rover!
O here he is, waiting.
He has chased the rabbits and run after the birds
A thousand miles or so,
And now he is hungry and tired.
But he is a southern gentleman
And will not whimper once
Though you kept him waiting forever.
He knows his mistress' eyes as well as I,

37| *Inde*: dress, or shoes,
38| *Inde*: Or image
44–45| *Inde*: sight / #no line break# into
49| *Inde*: girl,
54| *Inde*: home
55| *Inde*: dark
60| *Inde*: the birds and < > the rabbits
61| *Inde*: so
65| *Inde*: Tho you

And when to be silent and respectful.
I will try to be as patient as Rover,
And we will be comrades and wait,
Unquestioningly,
Till this lady we love
And her strange eyes
Come hone from God.

One Who Rejected Christ

There's farmers and there's farmers,
There's many a field and field,
But none of the farmers round about
Can haul such harvest-wagons out
As I from an acre's yield.

There's plenty and plenty of farmers
That leave the ground by the fence,
Thinking it's nice if a patch of roses
Should scratch out the hay and tickle their noses
With nice little wild-rose scents.

I'm not like other farmers,
I make my farming pay;
I never go in for sentiment,
And seeing that roses yield no rent
I cut the stuff away.

A very good thing for farmers
If they would learn my way;
For crops are all that a good field grows,
And nothing is worse than a sniff of rose
In the good strong smell of hay.

69–70| *Inde*: comrades #line break# / And wait #no line break# unquestioningly

14| *Inde*: And since the roses

Grace

Who is it beams the merriest
At killing a man, the laughing one?
You are the one I nominate,
God of the rivers of Babylon.

A hundred times I've taken the mules
And started early through the lane,
And come to the broken gate and looked,
And there my partner was again,
Sitting on top of a sorrel horse
And picking the burrs from its matted mane,
Saying he thought he'd help me work
That field of corn before the rain;
And I never spoke of the dollar a day,
It's no use causing hired men pain,
But slipped it into his hand at dark
While he undid the coupling chain;
And whistled a gospel tune, and knew
He'd join in strong on the refrain.
For I would pitch the treble high,
"Down at the cross where my Savior died,"
And then he rolled along the bass,
"There did I bury my sin and pride."

Sinful pride of a hired man!
Out of a hired woman born!
I'm thinking now how he was saved
One day while plowing in the corn.
We plowed that steamy morning through,
I with the mule whose side was torn,
And keeping an eye on the mule I saw
That the sun looked high and the man looked worn;
I would take him home to dinner with me,
And there! my father's dinner horn.

The sun blazed after dinner so
We sat a while by the maple trees,
Thinking of mother's pickles and pies

And smoking a friendly pipe at ease.
I broached a point of piety,
For pious men are quick to tease:
Was it really true John dipped his crowd
Down in the muddy Jordan's lees?
And couldn't the Baptists backslide too
If only they went on Methodist sprees?
And finally back to the field we went,
The corn was well above my knees,
The weeds were more than ankle high,
And dangerous customers were these.
We went to work in the heat again,
I hoped we'd get a bit of breeze
And thought the hired man was used
To God's most blazing cruelties.

Sundays, the hired man would pray
To live in the sunshine of his face;
Now here was answer come complete,
Rather an overdose of grace!

He fell in the furrow, an honest place
And an easy place for a man to fall.
His horse went marching blindly on
In a beautiful dream of a great fat stall.
And God shone on in merry mood,
For it was a foolish kind of sprawl,
And I found a hulk of heaving meat
That wouldn't answer me at all,
And a fresh breeze made the young corn dance
To a bright green, glorious carnival.
And really, is it not a gift
To smile and be divinely gay,
To rise above a circumstance
And smile distressing scenes away?

But this was a thing that I had said,
I was so froward and untamed:
"I will not worship wickedness
Though it be God's—I am ashamed!

For all his mercies God be thanked
But for his tyrannies be blamed!
He shall not have my love alone,
With loathing too his name is named."

I caught him up with all my strength
And with a silly stumbling tread
I dragged him over the soft brown dirt
And dumped him down beside the shed.

I thought of the prayers the fool had prayed
To his God, and I was seeing red,
When all of a sudden he gave a heave
And then with shuddering—vomited!
And God, who had just received full thanks
For all his kindly daily bread,
Now called it back again—perhaps
To see that his birds of the air were fed.
Not mother's dainty dinner now,
A rather horrible mess instead,
Yet all of it God required of him
Before the fool was duly dead.

Even of deaths there is a choice,
I've seen you give a good one, God,
But he in his vomit laid him down,
Denied the decency of blood.

If silence from the dead, I swore,
There shall be cursing from the quick!
But I began to vomit too,
Cursing and vomit ever so thick;
The dead lay down, and I did too,
Two ashy idiots: take your pick!
A little lower than angels he made us,
(Hear his excellent rhetoric),
A credit we were to him, half of us dead,
The other half of us lying sick.

The little clouds came Sunday-dressed
To do a holy reverence,
The young corn smelled its sweetest too,
And made him goodly frankincense,
The thrushes offered music up,
Choired in the wood beyond the fence.

And while his praises filled the earth
A solitary crow sailed by,
And while the whole creation sang
He cawed—not knowing how to sigh.

Moonlight

He feigned a fine indifference
To be so prodigal of light,
Knowing his piteous twisted things
Would lose the crooked marks of spite
When only moonbeams lit the dusk
And made his wicked world seem right.

But we forget so soon the shame,
Conceiving sweetness if we can,
Heaven the citadel itself
Illumined on the lunar plan;
And I the chief of sinners, I
The middlemost Victorian!

Now I shall ride the misty lake
With my own love, and speak so low
That not a fishy thing shall hear
The secrets passing to and fro
Amid the moonlight poetries.
O moonshine, how unman us so?

Street Light

The shine of many city streets
Confuses any countryman;
It flickers here and flashes there,
It goes as soon as it began,
It beckons many ways at once
For him to follow if he can.

Under the lamp a woman stands,
The lamps are shining equal well,
But in her eyes are other lights,
And lights plus other lights will tell:
He loves the brightness of that street
Which is the shining street to hell.

There's light enough, and strong enough,
To lighten every pleasant park;
I'm sorry lights are held so cheap,
I'd rather there were not a spark
Than choose those shining ways for joy
And have them lead me into dark.

Darkness

When hurrying home on a rainy night
And hearing tree-tops rubbed and tossed,
And seeing never a friendly star
And feeling your way when paths are crossed:
Stop fast and turn three times around
And try the logic of the lost.

Where is the heavenly light you dreamed?
Where is your hearth and glowing ash?
Where is your love by the mellow moon?
Here is not even a lightning-flash,
And in a place no worse than this
Lost men shall wail and teeth shall gnash.

Lightning is quick and perilous,
Thc dawn comcs on too slow and palc,
Your love brings only a yellow lamp,
Yet of these lights one shall avail:
The dark shall break for one of these,
I've never known this thing to fail.

Geometry

My window looks upon a wood
That stands as tangled as it stood
When God was centuries too young
To care how right he worked, or wrong,
His patterns in obedient trees,
Unprofited by the centuries
He still plants on as crazily
As in his driveling infancy.

Poor little elms beneath the oak!
They thrash their arms around and poke
At tyrant throats, and try to stand
Straight up, like owners of the land;
For they expect the vainest things,
And even the boniest have their flings.

Hickory shoots unnumbered rise,
Sallow and wasting themselves in sighs,
Children begot at a criminal rate
In the sight of a God that is profligate.
The oak-trees tower over all,
They seem to rise above the brawl,
They seem—but just observe the hoax,
They are obscured by other oaks!
They laugh the weaklings out of mind,
And fight forever with their kind.

For oaks are spindling too, and bent,
And only strong by accident;
And if there is a single tree

Of half the size it ought to be,
It need not give him thanks for that,
He did not plan its habitat.

When tree-tops go to pushing so,
There's every evil thing below;
There's clammy fungus everywhere,
And poison waving on the air,
A plague of insects from the pool
To sting some ever-trusting fool,
Serpents issuing from the foot
Of oak-trees rotten at the root,
Owls and frogs and whippoorwills,
Cackling of all sorts of ills.
Imagine what a pretty thing
The slightest landscape-gardening
Had made of God's neglected wood!
I'm glad man has the hardihood
To tamper with creation's plan
And shape it worthier of man.
Imagine woods and sun-swept spaces,
Shadows and lights in proper places,
Trees just touching friendly-wise,
Bees and flowers and butterflies.

An easy thing to improve on God,
Simply the knowing of even from odd,
Simply to count and then dispose
In patterns everybody knows,
Simply to follow curve and line
In geometrical design.

Gardners only cut their trees
For nobler regularities.
But from my window I have seen
The noblest patch of quivering green
Lashed till it never quivered again.
God had a fit of temper then,
And spat shrill wind and lightning out
At twinges of some godly gout.

But as for me, I keep indoors
Whenever he starts his awful roars.
What can one hope of a crazy God
But lashings from an aimless rod?

The Lover

I sat in a friendly company
And wagged my wicked tongue so well
My friends were listening close to hear
The wickedest tales that I could tell.
For many a fond youth waits, I said,
On many a worthless damozel;
But every trusting fool shall learn
To wish them heartily in hell.

And when your name was spoken too,
I did not change, I did not start,
And when they only praised and loved,
I still could play my secret part,
Cursing and lies upon my tongue,
And songs and shouting in my heart.

But when you came and looked at me,
You tried my poor pretence too much.
O love, do you know the secret now
Of one who would not tell nor touch?
Must I confess before the pack
Of babblers, idiots, and such?

Do they not hear the burst of bells,
Pealing at every step you make?
Are not their eyelids winking too,
Feeling your sudden brightness break?
O too much glory shut with us!
O walls too narrow and opaque!

Copy-text is *FA*.
2| *PAG*, MS*FA*: well,
18 MS*FA*: tell or touch?

O come into the night with me
And let me speak, for Jesus' sake.

Dumb-Bells

Dumb-bells left, dumb-bells right,
Swing them hard, grip them tight!
Thirty fat men of the town
Must sweat their filthy paunches down.
Dripping sweat and pumping blood
They try to make themselves like God.

One and two, three and four,
Cleave the air and smite the floor!
Five and six, seven and eight,
Legs apart, shoulders straight!
Thirty fat men grunt and puff,
Thirty bellies plead, Enough!

Dumb-bells up, dumb-bells down,
Dumb-bells front, dumb-bells ground!
Thirty's God has just the girth
To pull the levers of the earth,
They made him sinewy and lean
And washed him glittering white and clean.

Dumb-bells in, dumb-bells out,
Count by fours and face about!
Put by dumb-bells for today,
Wash the stinking sweat away
And go out clean. But come again;
Worship's every night at ten.

Overtures

My dear and I, we disagreed
When we had been much time together.

For when will lovers learn to sail
From sailing always in good weather?

She said a hateful little word
Between the pages of the book.
I bubbled with a noble rage,
I bruised her with a dreadful look,

And thanked her kindly for the word
Of such a little silly thing;
Indeed I loved my poet then
Beyond my dear, or anything.

And she, the proud girl, swept away,
How swift and scornfully she went!
And I the frightened lover stayed,
And have not had one hour's content

Until today; until I knew
That I was loved again, again;
Then hazard how this thing befel,
Brother of women and of men?

"Perhaps a gallant gentleman
Accomplished it, who saw you bleed;
Perhaps she wrote upon the book
A riddling thing that you could read;

"Perhaps she crept to you, and cried,
And took upon her all the blame."
O no, do proud girls creep and cry?
"Perhaps she whispered you your name."

O no, she walked alone, and I
Was walking in the rainy wood,
And saw her drooping by the tree,
And saw my work of widowhood.

15| *SP69*: stayed
20| *SP69*: men.
25| *SP69*: *you and*
27| *SP69*: girls cry for shame?

Under the Locusts

What do the old men say,
Sitting out of the sun?
Many strange and common things,
And so would any one.

Locust trees are sorry shade,
They are good enough;
Locust trees are sweet in spring
For trees so old and tough.

Dick's a sturdy little lad
Yonder throwing stones;
Agues and rheumatic pains
Will fiddle on his bones.

Grinny Bob is out again
Begging for a dime;
Niggers haven't any souls,
Grinning all the time.

Jenny and Will go arm in arm.
He's a lucky fellow;
Jenny's cheeks are pink as rose,
Her mother's cheeks are yellow.

War is on, the paper says,
Wounds and enemies;
Now young gallivanting bucks
Will know what trouble is.

Parson's coming up the hill,
Meaning mighty well;
Thinks he's preached the doubters down,
And old men never tell.

Copy-text is *FA*.

27| *PAG*, MS*FA*: down.

Worship

I know a quite religious man
Who utters praises when he can.

Now I find God in bard and book,
In school and temple, bird and brook.

But he says God is sweetest of all
Discovered in a drinking-hall.

For God requires no costly wine
But comes on the foam of a crockery stein.

And when that foam is on the lips,
Begin then God's good fellowships.

Cathedrals, synagogues, and kirks
May go to the devil, and all their works.

And as for Christian charity,
It's made out of hilarity.

He gives the beggar all his dimes,
Forgives his brother seven times.

"I love the rain," says thirsty clod;
So this religious man of God.

For God has come, and is it odd
He praises all the works of God?

"For God has come, and there's no sorrow,"
He sings all night—will he sing tomorrow?

The Cloak Model

"My son," the stranger thus began,
And drew me to the window side,
"Now here are beauties better than
You ever have dreamed, or ever can.
But yet beware!" he cried.

A tidy citizen was he
Although a dismal daffy one.
"See this one pose and pout for me
And march around magnificently.
But I'm immune, my son.

"Observe how ripe the lady's lips,
How Titianesque the mop of hair,
And where the great white shoulder dips
Beneath its gauzy half-eclipse,
You well may stare and stare.

"When I was young I said as you
Are saying in your sapphic youth,
That ah! such lips were certain cue,
And look! her bosom's rhythm too,
It signified her truth;

"Her broad brow meant intelligence
And something better than a bone,
Her body's curves were spirit's tents,
Her fresh young skin was innocence
Instead of meat that shone.

Title| PP: *Cloak Model*
1| PP: began
2| PP: side:
3| PP: "Here are smart beauties
4| PP: ever dreamed, and never can,
5| PP: But be beware," he said.
6| PP: citizen looked he
7| PP: Though possibly a daffy
9| PP: magnificently,
14| PP: Beneath the gaudy half-eclipse
15| PP: may stand and
17| PP: your Sapphic youth
18| PP: That ah, such lips are certain
19| PP: And oh, her < > rhythms
20| PP: They signify her truth.
21| PP: "Her wide brow says intelligence
23| PP: curves are spirit's
24| PP: skin is innocence

"I wish the moralists would thresh
(Indeed the thing is very droll)
God's oldest joke, forever fresh:
The fact that in the finest flesh
There isn't any soul."

By the Riverside

A great green spread of meadow land,
(Must rest his weight on an ample base),
A secret water moving on,
A clean blue air for his breathing-space,
A pair of willows bending down
In double witness to his grace,
And on the rock his sinner sprawls
And looks the Strong One face to face.

The sinner's mocking tongue is dry,
Wonder is on that mighty jeerer,
He loves, and he never loved before,
He wants the glowing sky no nearer,
He likes the willows to be two,
He would not have the water clearer,
He thinks that God is perfect once:
Heaven, rejoice! a new God-fearer.

And now each quiet thing awakes
And dances madly, wavers, dips;
These are God's motions on the air,
His pulse for the sinner's finger-tips,
His arrows shot across the blue,
His love-words dropping from his lips,
And who ever heard such whisperings,
Who ever saw such fellowships?

26| PP: "We think the
28| PP: Their oldest
29| PP: They know that
30| PP: There's never much of soul."

The Bachelor

The wind went cold as the day went old,
And I went very sad,
Till I saw something by the road
That brought me round and glad.

The keen wind nipped me northerly
And bent me back almost,
And I was the worst discouraged man
Abroad on any boast,

The road was rocks and wilderness
And never a sign of a town,
It tapered up a wicked hill,
I tried to curse it down,

But like an undefeated man
I mounted, slow and hard:
And round the top was a little house
With a woman in the yard.

She was a housewife in her yard,
Tending her husband's place;
The broom was busy in her hand,
The goodness in her face.

She brushed the yard, she brushed the step,
She made the leaves to spin,
Tidying up her husband's place
Outside as well as in.

I knew no woman and no house
And night was just ahead;
Yet I went cheerful down the hill,
Rested and warmed and fed.

For some man had a woman there
To keep his board and bed;

"I have seen women by these bad roads,
Thank God for that," I said.

Roses

I entered dutiful, God knows,
The room in which I was to sit
With dreary unbelieving books.
It was surprising, I suppose,
To find such happy change in it:
There stood a most celestial rose
And looked the flower that my love looks
Who, where she turns her smiling face
Makes heavy earth a hopeful place.

I blessed the heart that wished me well
When I had been bereft of much,
And brought such word of beauty back.
I went like one escaping hell
To drink its fragrance and to touch,
And stroked, O ludicrous to tell!
A horrid thing of bric-a-brac,
A make-believe, a mockery,
And nothing that a rose should be.

Red real roses keep a thorn,
And save their loveliness a while
And in their perfect date unfold.
But you, beyond all women born,

Title| *SP69*: The Rose
1| *SP69*: entered weary of my woes
3| VMS, *SP69*: books,
4| VMS, *SP69*: Astonished, as you may suppose,
8–9| *CV*: When men are mad for her sweet face. / I waited by the door a space.
VMS, *SP69*: When men are mad to see that face / Whose smile is very Heaven's grace.
12| VMS, *SP69*: back;
14| VMS, *SP69*: drink the fragrance
15| VMS, *SP69*: tell,
17| VMS, *SP69*: make-believe and mockery
19|VMS: But #blotted out and replaced by# Red real
VMS and *SP69*: thorn
20| VMS, *SP69*: To save their sweetness for a
21| *CV*: Till all the fragrance may unfold.
VMS, *SP69*: unfold,
22| *CV*: you, above all
VMS, *SP69*: you beyond < > born

Have spent so easily your smile,
That I am not the less forlorn
Nor these ironic walls less cold,
Because it smiles, the chilly rose,
As you are smiling, I suppose.

November

There's a patch of trees at the edge of the field,
And a brown little house that is kept so warm,
And a woman waiting by the hearth
Who still keeps most of a woman's charm.

She traffics in her woman's goods
And is my woman of affairs.
Yet not so fast, my moral men,
November's most poetic airs
Are heavy with old lovers' tales,
How hearths are holy with their prayers,
How women give their fragrance up
And give their love to the man that dares.
Now who goes heedless hearing that?
At last we trade, we laissez-faires.

O moralizers, it is hard
When I am not a candidate
For holy wedlock's offices,
That mother has picked me out a mate,
And couldn't have made a sorrier choice
Than that same Smiley's daughter Kate,
Who prays for the sinners of the town
And never comes to meeting late,
Who sings soprano in the choir
And swallows Christian doctrine straight.
Of all the girls deliver me
From the girl you haven't the heart to hate!

23| *CV*: spent the radiant ready smile,
VMS and *SP69*: smile
24| *CV*: And I
25| VMS and *SP69*: cold
26| VMS and *SP69*: the heartless rose,

Piety: O what a hideous thing!
And thirty-odd pounds she's underweight.

The winds of late November droop
(Poor little failures) very low,
As up and down the farm they pass,
Pass up and down, and to and fro,
And look for a home they are not to find,
For they were homeless years ago.

But years ago I knew a girl,
Beautiful, fit for a Grand Vizier's,
A girl with laughing on her lips
And in her eyes the quickest tears,
And low of speech, as when one finds
A mother cooing to her dears.
I took the note into my heart,
And so did other cavaliers.
If God had heard my prayer then,
The good folk couldn't point and say
As mother says they're pointing now:
Behold, one stands in the sinners' way!
The stiffest sceptic bends his neck
And stands on no more vain parley
If such as she would have him come,
Worship with her in the Baptist way,
Accept the fables as he can,
A Jewish God, a Passion Play;
And such a lover never comes
To fondling dirty drabs for pay.
But God had another man for her,
He cannot answer all that pray.

November winds are weak and cold,
They lie at last beneath the blue
And sleep in the fields as cold as they.
I know but one good thing to do,
So hearken, all ye mutineers:
Every man to his rendezvous!

My woman waits by the hearth, I say,
And what is a scarlet woman to you?
Her sins are scarlet if you will,
Her lips are hardly of that hue,
And many a time I've seen her sit
Beside the hearth an hour or two,
And set the pot upon the fire
And wait until she's spoken to.
A hateful owl is roosting near
Who mocks my woman, Hoo, Hoo, Hoo,
But the pot sings back just as shrill as it can,
And the angry fire-log crashes through;
And there the woman waits, and I,
I ponder the ways of God—and rue!

A Christmas Colloquy

The country farmer has his joys
Of little city girls and boys
When brother Thomas brings his brood
Of motherless brats in Christmas mood
To try our country air and food.
And O what splendid pies and cakes
Their pleased and pretty grandma makes!
And O what squeals and stomach-aches!

Poor Thomas shepherds him a flock
Of city souls as hard as rock,
And though they will not fill his larder
He only preaches Christ the harder.
But Ann, though seven years my niece,
Is still a pagan little piece,
And as she often hints to me
She hates the sound of piety.
Fair Inez is my ancient setter
Who lies by the fire when we will let her:
Alas, this amiable dog
Heard all the bitter dialogue

That passed between my niece and brother
Misunderstanding one another.

ANN:
Father, what will there be for me
Tomorrow on the Christmas tree?
Have you told Santa what to bring,
My pony, my doll, and everything?

THOMAS:
My daughter, Santa will know best
What to bring you, and what the rest.
But father and his little girl
And everybody in the world
Should dwell tonight on higher things,
For hark! the herald angel sings,
And in a manger poor and lowly
Lies little Jesus, high and holy.

ANN:
Father, don't talk of little Jesus,
You're only doing it to tease us,
It isn't nearly time for bed,
And I want to know what Santa said.

THOMAS:
Jesus is better than any toys
For little sinning girls and boys,
For Jesus saves, but sin destroys.
And O, it gives him sad surprise,
There must be tears in Jesus' eyes,
When little girls with bad behavior
Forget to own their Lord and Savior.

ANN:
I didn't, you know it isn't true!
I say my prayers, I always do,
I know about Jesus very well,
And god the Father, Heaven, and Hell.

O please don't say it any more,
You've said it so many times before,
But tell me all about Santa instead,
And about the horns on his reindeer's head,
And what he will bring me on his sled.

THOMAS:
This night he was born on earth for us,
And can my daughter mock him thus,
And care more for her worldly pleasures
Than Jesus' love and heavenly treasures?
For Jesus didn't like to be
So crowned with thorns and nailed to tree,
But there was a sinful world to free,
And out he went to Gethsemane—

ANN:
And left the twelve and went apart—
O father, I know it off by heart,
Please, father, please don't finish it out,
There's so much else to talk about!
I ask about Santa, and there you go,
And now you're spoiling my Christmas so,
And you are the wickedest man I know!

Disgraceful scenes require the curtain,
But lest the moral be uncertain,
I briefly bring the good report
That valiant Thomas held the fort,
And wicked Ann was quite defeated,
In vain denied, in vain entreated,
In vain she wailed, in vain she wept,
And said a briny prayer, and slept.
While Inez, who had been perplexed
To see good kinsfolk so much vexed,
When peace descended on the twain,
Lay down beside the fire again.

The Power of God

If the power of God were mine, and the ample turn,
I never could dwell in my law, which is 'stablished and stern,

But my pity would plague me still! In the fare of my state
I would summon my ministers often to reprobate:

"Do ye see them walk on the unwaked streets of the town?
Are they not of my handmaidens, burdened and bending down?

"It is not yet day, and my tale of the stars not told,
But already they bear of their burdens, and tremble of cold.

"Do ye heed not her, ye stony and reconciled,
One gathering sticks for a fire, who is heavy with child?

"And one was so heavy with sleep that she watched not, and slept
Till it nearly was dawn, and then she arose and wept.

"Previsal I made, and the burning of quenchless gold,
Yet still they bedevil my kingdom, the dark and the cold.

"There is labor appointed, I know not if it shall cease,
Yet anon cometh night, and my daughters shall lie in peace.

"What avoideth my glory of firmaments keeping the way,
If the poor soft flesh must trouble before the day?

"Or spectacular stars, as they race to encircuit the deep,
If my littlest people is driven, and needeth sleep?

"For my absolute heaven is high, and nothing dependeth,
Yet it twitcheth my heart, when weeping of women ascendeth.

"Then arrange ye again how the people's task be done,
There shall no woman toil till they see my sign of the sun."

Resurrection

Long, long before men die I sometimes read
Their stoic backs as plain as graveyard stones,
An epitaph of poor dead men indeed.
I never pass those old and crooked bones,
Ridden far down with burden and with age,
Stopping the headlong highway till they lean
Aside in honor of my equipage,
But I am sick and shamed that Heaven has been
So clumsy with the inelastic clay!
"What pretty piece of hope then have you spun,
My old defeated traveler," I say,
"That keeps you marching on? For I have none.
I have looked often and I have not found
Old men bowed low who ever rose up sound."

Men

"How many goodly creatures are there here!"
Miranda doted on the sight of seamen,
The very casual adventurers
Who took a flood as quickly as a calm,
And kept their blue eyes blue to any weather.
This was the famous manliness of men;
And when she saw it on the dirty strangers,
She clapped her pretty hands in sudden joy:
"O brave new world!"

The Christian

I heard a story of a sailing man.
He was a surly sort of mariner,
He used to swear at all the seven seas,
And rode them dauntless up and down the earth.

But when he sickened of the windy wash,
He took to wife a proper village woman

And put her in a precious little house;
And there he weathered many winter seasons,
Knocking the ashes neatly from his pipe
Upon the tended hearth.

And only when he went upon the moors,
And felt the sting and censure of the winds,
And tasted of the salt blown in from sea,
Then only would he curse the marriage morning,
And swear he'd not go skulking back again
To sit that hearth like any broken bitch
Whose running time was over.

Morning

The skies were jaded, while the famous sun
Slack of his office to confute the fogs
Lay sick abed; but I, inured to duty,
Sat for my food. Three hours each day we souls,
Who might be angels but are fastened down
With bodies, most infuriating freight,
Sit fattening these frames and skeletons
With filthy food, which they must cast away
Before they feed again.

April

Savor of love is thick on the April air,
The blunted boughs dispose their lacy bloom,
And many sorry steeds dismissed to pasture
Toss their old forelocks, flourish heavy heels.
Where is there any unpersuaded poet
So angry still against the wrongs of winter
Which caused the dainty earth to droop and die,
So vengeant for his vine and summer song,
As to decline the good releasing thaw?
Poets have temperature and follow seasons,
And covenants go out at equinox.

The champions! For Heaven, riding high
Above the icy death, considered truly;
"My agate icy work, I thought it fair;
Yet I have lacked that pretty lift of praise
That mounted once from these emaciate minstrels.
They will not sing, and duty drops away
And I must turn and make a soft amend!"
At once he showered April down, until
The bleak twigs bloom again; and soon, I swear,
He shall receive his praise.

Wrestling

At last came threshing-time, the manly season.
We kept the thresher thundering by daylight,
And rested all the sweeter after dark,
Telling of tales, and washing in the river.
But one there was, some twenty miles a stranger,
Who boasted that he was a mighty wrestler
And had not met that valiant pair of shoulders
That he could not put down.

We had a champion there. He looked and listened,
He measured off his man, he made his mind up,
And thus he brought great honor to his country:
"My friend, I've heard you bragging, heard you braying,
And now I say, for God's sake come and wrestle."
And thus appealed, the other came, for God's sake,
And they did wrestle.

They sprang, they gripped, they strained and rocked and twisted,
They pounded much good sod to dust and powder,
They ripped the garments off each other vainly
And showed us many naked bulging muscles,
And still were even.

But while the tide of battle ran so equal,
I heard a sound, I took it for a voice,
I almost saw it, spitting out a passage

Between the haggard jaws of my poor hero,
The voice as of a man almost despairing,
Hoping again though all his hopes had failed:
"By God, I'll have you down in one more minute!"
And it was as he said; for in a minute
He had him down, by God.

Prayer

She would not keep at home, the foolish woman,
She would not mind her precious girls and boys,
She had to go, for it was Sunday morning,
Down the hot road and to the barren pew
And there abuse her superannuate knees
To make a prayer.

She had a huge petition on her bosom—
A heavy weight for such a lean old thing—
Her youngest boy made merry in the village
And had not entered into the communion;
And having labored with him long for nothing
She meant to ask of God to save him yet.
Thank God she asked that favor!

The manner of it echoes still in Heaven.
Before she dared to utter her desire
The strange old woman made approach to God
With many a low obeisance and abasement,
As having done so many things she ought not,
And left undone so many things she ought,
And being altogether very wicked;
She testified she had not kept his temple,
Which was her heart, all swept and white and ready;
She testified it—O the shameless woman,
The spotless housekeeper!

Now God sat beaming on his burnished throne
And swept creation with appraising eye,
Finding, I fear, not all was free from blemish,

Yet keeping his magnificent composure;
But wearing certain necessary airs,
To suit with such incumbency of court,
He still at heart was quite a gentleman;
For when he saw that aged lady drooping
And wearying her bones with genuflections
For her unworthiness, he fell ashamed
To think how hard it went with holy women
To ease their poor predicaments by prayer:
There on his heaven, and heard of all the hosts,
He groaned, he made a mighty face so wry
That several seraphin forgot their harping
And scolded thus: "O what a wicked woman,
To shrew his splendid features out of shape!"

Friendship

I viewed him well, the visible fat fool,
And yet I took him in; for I contended,
Friends are not sent in order of our choosing,
They come unsuited like the gifts of God.
I would not do a perfidy to friendship,
I let him past the private inner gate
And made him be at home among my treasures
Like my true friend.

Now I am ground with a grim torture daily
That I have been befriended by a fool.
He forages at will upon my garden,
He noses all its pretty secrets out,
And still the fool finds nothing to his liking.
Meeting a modest velveteen affair,
Peevish he hangs his sad and silly head:
"Alas! such unsubstantial gaudy goods!"
Thus he meets pansies; meeting zinnias,
He nearly faints at such a rioting:
"Alas! what fruit will these red wantons bear?"
And not a perfume spills upon the air
But his malicious nose suspects a poison,

As he goes browsing like an ancient ass,
An old distempered ass.

I'd almost rather be a friendless man
And have my house my own. The prying fool
Asks me the queerest idiotic questions:
"O friend, is this the harvest of your hands?
How will you stand before the lord of harvests?
These are the gardens of your idleness;
Where is the vineyard, friend?"

The Four Roses

Four sisters sitting in one house,
I said, these roses on a stem
With bosoms bare. But wayfaring
I went and ravished one of them.

So one was taken. But the three,
They spread their petals just the same,
They turned no decent pale for grief,
They drew no fragrance back for shame.

The canker is on roses too!
I cried, and lifted up the rod
And scourged them bleeding to the ground.
All, all are sinners unto God.

The School

I was not drowsy though the scholars droned.
Hearing the music that they made of Greek,
Whenever Helen's unforgotten face
Sent other young men whisking off to war;
Hearing much mention of the hecatombs,
And Pericles, and fishes that were purple,
Temples in white, and trees that they named olive;
And thinking always of proud Athens shining
Upon her hill, that slanted to her sea:

Equipped with Grecian thoughts, how could I live
Among my father's folk? My father's house
Was narrow and his fields were nauseous.
I kicked his clods for being common dirt,
Worthy a world which never could be Greek;
Cursed the paternity that planted me
One green leaf in a wilderness of autumn;
And wept, as fitting such a fruitful spirit
Sealed in a yellow tomb.

The Lord preserves his saints for Christian uses.
He sent a pair of providential eyes.
They would have sat in any witless head,
Although I deemed them deep as classic seas,
As strange as any woman written smiling,
And much more near; the merest modern eyes,
The first my Athens faced; and yet her lamp,
It flickered rather low.

Then he commanded me to scrutiny
As to a fingered thing of no great matter,
A circumstantial sorry little coin.
A friendly thing, I owned, to lie so warm
Against the side of any friendless man;
And in the hand—O if the happy hand
Accommodate the cunning rounded scepter,
Then is dominion seated in that palm,
And coveting is seated in men's eyes.
Make haste, my hands, about your own inclosures!
And what were dead Greek empires to me then?
Dishonored, by Apollo, and forgot.

Sickness

The toughest carcass in the town
Fell sick at last and took to bed,
And on that bed God waited him
With cool, cool hands for his frantic head,
And while the fever did its dance

They talked, and a good thing was said:
"See, I am not that Scriptural!
A lesser, kinder God instead."

Fever must run its course, and God
Could not do much for the countryman.
At least he saved him certain dreams:
"I die! O save me if you can,
I am a bruised, a beaten slave,
I march in a blistering caravan,
They dash a stone upon my head—
Ah no, but that is God's white hand."

God plucked him back, and plucked him back,
And did his best to smoothe the pain.
The sick man said it was good to know
That God was true, if prayer was vain.
"O God, I weary of this night,
When will you bring the dawn again?"
The night must run its course, but God
Was weary too with watching-strain.

A cluck of tuneless silly birds,
A guilty gray, and it was dawn.
The sick man thumped across the floor
And slid the curtain that was drawn:
"O pale wet dawn! O let it shine
Lustrous and gold on the good green lawn!
The luster, Lord!" Alas, God knows
When sad conclusions are foregone.

The sick man leant upon his Lord,
On that imperfect break of day,
"Now, Lord, I die: is there no word,
No countervail that God can say?"
No word. But tight upon his arm,
Was God, and drew not once away
Until his punctual destiny.
To whom could God repair to pray?

Now God be thanked by dying men
Who comrades them in times like these,
Who dreads to see the doom come down
On these black midnight canopies
And on this poisonous glare of dawns.
The whole world crumples in disease,
But God is pitying to the end,
And gives an office to my knees.

CHILLS AND FEVER

Agitato ma non troppo

I have a grief
(It was not stolen like a thief)
Albeit I have no bittern by the lake
To cry it up and down the brake.

None there hath been like Dante's fury
When Beatrice was given him to bury;
Except, when the young heart was hit, you know
How Percy Shelley's reed sang tremolo.

"If grief be in his mind,
Where is his fair child moaning in the wind?
Where is the white frost snowing on his head?
When did he stalk and weep and not loll in his bed?"

I will be brief,
Assuredly I have a grief,
And I am shaken; but not as a leaf.

Spectral Lovers (*SP*45)

By night they haunted a thicket of April mist,
Out of that black ground suddenly come to birth,
Else angels lost in each other and fallen on earth.

#The poem is printed in italics except for *F*, P*SP63*, and *SP*63. A new and expanded version of the poem appears in the "Additional Published Poems."#

P*SP63*, *SP63* begin with two lines, designated here as *a* and *b*:
a| This is what the man said,
b| P*SP*63: Accused of having the grief in his head. #eight words crossed out and replaced by seven words# Who shook, but stood upon his head# these seven words crossed out and replaced by five words# Insisting, standing on his head.
*SP*63: #retains revision#

1| P*SP63*, *SP63*, *SP*69a: grief,

2| *F*, *SP*69a: thief),
P*SP*63, *SP*63: It < > thief,

5| *F*, *SP*69a: There hath been none like
P*SP*63, *SP*63: there has been

9| P*SP*63, *SP*63: "Yes, there is grief in

10| P*SP*63, *SP*63: But where

11| *F*, *SP*69a: whitefrost

14| P*SP*63: Assuredly I have a grief, #last four words crossed out and replaced by four words# I know my grief,
*SP*63: #retains revision#

1| *F*: They walked, they haunted

2| *F*, *CF*: As out of that rich ground strangely come

3| *F*, *CF*: Else two immaculate angels fallen

Lovers they knew they were, but why unclasped, unkissed?
Why should two lovers go frozen apart in fear?
And yet they were, they were.

Over the shredding of an April blossom
Scarcely her fingers touched him, quick with care,
Yet of evasions even she made a snare.
The heart was bold that clanged within her bosom,
The moment perfect, the time stopped for them,
Still her face turned from him.

Strong were the batteries of the April night
And the stealthy emanations of the field;
Should the walls of her prison undefended yield
And open her treasure to the first clamorous knight?
"This is the mad moon, and shall I surrender all?
If he but ask it I shall."

And gesturing largely to the moon of Easter,
Mincing his steps and swishing the jubilant grass,
Beheading some field-flowers that had come to pass,
He had reduced his tributaries faster
Had not considerations pinched his heart
Unfitly for his art.

5| *F*: lovers be frozen asunder in
CF: lovers go frozen asunder in
SP69: lovers be frozen
8| *F*: Her thrilling fingers < > him, quick < > care;
CF: him quick < > care;
9| *F*: Of many delicate postures she cast her share;
CF: Of many delicate postures she cast a snare;
10| *F*: But for all the red heart beating in her pale bosom,
CF: But for all the red heart beating in the pale bosom,
MS*SP45*: Ungovernable the heart clanged in her bosom,
11–12| *F, CF*: Her face as of cunningly tinctured ivory / Was hard with an agony.
13| *F, CF*: Stormed by the little batteries of an April night,
MS*SP45*: There were the
14| *F, CF*: Passionate being the essences of the field,
15| *F, CF*: the penetrable walls of the crumbling prison yield
17| *F, CF*: and must I
18| *F, CF*: it, I
19| *F, CF*: the very moon
20| *CF*: steps, and
PE: grass.
21| *F, CF*: And beheading
22| *F, CF*: faster,

"Am I reeling with the sap of April like a drunkard?
Blessed is he that taketh this richest of cities;
But it is so stainless the sack were a thousand pities.
This is that marble fortress not to be conquered,
Lest its white peace in the black flame turn to tinder
And an unutterable cinder."

They passed me once in April, in the mist.
No other season is it when one walks and discovers
Two tall and wandering, like spectral lovers,
White in the season's moon-gold and amethyst,
Who touch their quick fingers fluttering like a bird
Whose songs shall never be heard.

Bells for John Whiteside's Daughter (*SP*45)

There was such speed in her little body,
And such lightness in her footfall,
It is no wonder her brown study
Astonishes us all.

Her wars were bruited in our high window.
We looked among orchard trees and beyond,
Where she took arms against her shadow,
Or harried unto the pond

The lazy geese, like a snow cloud
Dripping their snow on the green grass,
Tricking and stopping, sleepy and proud,
Who cried in goose, Alas,

25| *SP*69: Do I reel
26| *F*: is He that < > cities.
27| *F, CF*: stainless, the < > pities;
28| MS*SP*45: that #next word blotted out and replaced by# marble
32| *F, CF*: it, when
33| *F, CF*: Two clad in the shapes of angels, being
MS*SP*45: wandering, #comma inserted# like
34| *F, CF*: Trailing a glory of moon-gold

Title| *F, CF, FA*: Whitesides'
F: #alternate lines are indented#
3| *F, CF, FA*: wonder that her
6| *PE, SP*63, *SP*69: beyond
12| *F*: goose, Alas

For the tireless heart within the little
Lady with rod that made them rise
From their noon apple-dreams and scuttle
Goose-fashion under the skies!

But now go the bells, and we are ready,
In one house we are sternly stopped
To say we are vexed at her brown study,
Lying so primly propped.

Winter Remembered

Two evils, monstrous either one apart,
Possessed me, and were long and loath at going:
A cry of Absence, Absence, in the heart,
And in the wood the furious winter blowing.

Think not, when fire was bright upon my bricks,
And past the tight boards hardly a wind could enter,
I glowed like them, the simple burning sticks,
Far from my cause, my proper heat and center.

Better to walk forth in the murderous air
And wash my wound in the snows; that would be healing;
Because my heart would throb less painful there,
Being caked with cold, and past the smart of feeling.

And where I went, the hugest winter blast
Would have this body bowed, these eyeballs streaming,
And though I think this heart's blood froze not fast,
It ran too small to spare one drop for dreaming.

Dear love, these fingers that had known your touch,
And tied our separate forces first together,

15| *CF*: apple dreams, and
16| *F*: skies.
17| *CF, SP63, SP69*: ready;
20| MS*SP45*: so primply #altered to# primly

8| MS*SP45*: proper heart #crossed out and replaced by# heat
9| *PE, SP63, SP69*: the frozen air
13| *PE, SP63, SP69*: where I walked, the
15| MS*SP45*, *SP45*, *PE*, *SP63*, *SP69*: fast
17| MS*SP45*: fingers which had

Were ten poor idiot fingers not worth much,
Ten frozen parsnips hanging in the weather.

Triumph

Athens, a fragile kingdom by the foam,
Assumed the stranger's yoke; but then behold how meek
Those unbred Caesars grew, who spent their fruits of Rome
For ever after, trying to be Greek.

I too shook out my locks like one born royal;
For she dissolved in tears, and said my barbarous name,
And took my oath, she was so piteous and loyal:
Vote the young Caesar triumph, spread his fame!

But oh, I find my captive was not caught.
It was her empty house that fell before my legions;
Of where her soul inhabits I have conquered naught;
It is so far from these my Roman regions!

Two Sonnets

I. Yea

It was beside the fire that I had lit,
Out of the rain that drummed upon my roof,
She leant against my bosom, fluttering it,
And stared beyond my world, far, far aloof.

And neither spoke, and thus we might have sat
Till angry Gabriel trumpeted for change,

Title| *EP*: On a Superior Woman
2| *EP*: then how
3| *EP*: their Rome
4| *EP*: Forever after trying
6| *EP*: my name,
7| *EP*: oath, so piteous
9| *EP*: captive is not caught,
10| *EP*: her house < > legions,
11| *EP*: inhabits I know naught.
12| *EP*: Save it is far < > regions.
EP: #two lines added, making a sonnet# I mourn for heavens that I cannot reach, / And such poor earth am I, she cannot teach.

But she said, "Heart of stone, look not like that!
O unconcessive husband, you are strange."

For joy I could not answer, being taxed
By such a star, so distant in the sky,
With being cold. But think how the poor heart waxed,
The chidden wonder of women, the huge I!

And I played the god; disdaining her no more
I smiled, and drew her closer than before.

II. Nay

With such strong arms I shut my love about,
She rested there, which was to me a token
This was a house she never could walk without,
Securely bricked, and never to be broken.

But no, the tight imprisonment was vain,
Too physical and wide to catch a heart;
When we had come most near, and scarce were twain,
Some soul was still unmet, and much apart.

Therefore I knew the most unperjured lips
That ever sweetly bargained love's exchange
Must lie; love must be blacked with this eclipse,
That she and I could live, and still be strange!

And as for death, whose stroke dissevers men,
What fool would hope for firm possession then?

Spring Posy

Running to meet us came neighbors' daughters nigh,
Fluting like birds, and calicoed bright and clean;
And beautiful else had been their bosoms poutering by!
"But ye are a cloud," I said, "too much between."

Title| *F*: The Sure Heart
F: #alternate lines indented#
1| *F*: As we two walked in the path, came
2| *F*: birds they passed, and < > clean,
3| *F*: by,

I was waylaid in a depth of woody grot:
Was it a fox in his fern, was it a wing's blue sheen?
In her widow's weed the balsam? But how ye prospered not,
When full of her images I saw not your scene!

Up once I rose in a fury of heard-of things
To travel the splendid sphere that twirleth in its fame;
But the wars and ships and towns, and pestilent roaring kings,
These angered me, and why? They fought unknowing her name!

To a Lady Celebrating Her Birthday

Too quick the annual sun returns,
Mounts to the ledge and scans the pillowed face
Whereon four seasons hardly have writ the trace,
Though even he on his timeless circuit mourns
That faintlier his fire burns.

Bring proper gifts to beauty then:
Bring topaz, emeralds, gold, and minerals rare,
Musk that will ever be sweet on mortal air,
Bright stiff brocades outlasting the short ken
Of usual mortal men.

Bring only tokens fixed and sure:
Bring kind affections, merited deep and strong,
And though poor hearts never have lasted long,
Swear splendidly to how they shall perdure
As true as now, as pure.

5–6| *F*: Beauty waylaid me once, in < > grot, / It was a fox < > sheen,
7| *F*: balsam: but how did ye prosper not!
8| *F*: With an image of her I filled your empty scene.
9| *F*: rose and hasted in < > things,
11| *F*: and the pestilent
12| *F*: me, for they fought < > name.
F: #four additional lines follow# Lovely the moons will rise, loudly the brave will shout. / Now meanly my house is reared, but my dear love keepeth therein: / Ye kingdoms may fight and fail, ye stars as ye please go out, / O world I have honored not, be off and spin!

2| *F*: Mounts on the
5–6| *F*: burns. / Vainly the year's much weather has beat:
The world is aged, aged, and love's own breath
Goes speedily rank with the odor of age and death,
Yet this frail beauty is flushing freshly sweet
Unthinking of a defeat. / Bring

But bring no gift of trembling flowers;
Dear comrade, never on pain of pain suppose
From the blowing of any little wasted rose,
Up clomb the enemy in the airy towers
To number beauty hours.

Ah, but I think you clearly know:
Sure eyes, you have observed on what hard terms
Beauty has respite from voracious worms;
Her moment comes; thereafter fast or slow
Her daily funerals go.

Dear love, rise up and proudly sing:
For even foreboding soldiers deep at night
Make up no prayers against tomorrow's fight;
They fling sweet oaths on high, not honoring
The dismal nearing Thing.

Come to the company and play:
For even that sinful Babylon when surprised
Put not her sackcloth on nor sacrificed;
The revel roared, and few stood off to stay
And greet the mournful day;

Unearthèd liquors were poured out,
The burghers dined, in no constricted rage
At sudden death as fearsomer than age,
The harlots danced, the elders at least with shout
Tossed brittle bones about.

Small, small my heart inclines to boast:
What can a virtuous poor pale lover do
Who's prey to dissolution quick as you?

16| *F*: bring not roses nor delicate flowers:
18| *F*: rose
19–20| *F*: That enemies hide within her chastest bowers / For numbering beauty's hours!
21| *F*: you surely know
22| *F*: Clear eyes
23| *F*: worms.
26| *F*: and clearly sing:
28| *F*: fight,
29| *F*: high not
31| *F*: Come let the waiting company play:
34| *F*: roared and
36| *F*: Unearthed
37| *F*: Fat burghers
38| *F*: sudden doom as
42| *F*: do,

This day smells mortuary more than most
To me upon my post.

Know this, though desperate our cases:
Thus will I hold you out of other harms
Till these be palsied paralytic arms;
Then be we grizzled polls and yellow faces
In these respective places.

Vaunting Oak (*SP*45)

He is a tower unleaning. But how will he not break,
If Heaven assault him with full wind and sleet,
And what uproar tall trees concumbent make!

More than a hundred years, more than a hundred feet
Naked he rears against the cold skies eruptive;
Only his temporal twigs are unsure of seat,

And the frail leaves of a season, which are susceptive
Of the mad humors of wind, and turn and flee
In panic round the stem on which they are captive.

Now a certain heart, too young and mortally
Linked with an unbeliever of bitter blood,
Observed, as an eminent witness of life, the tree,

48| *F*: these are palsied

1| *F, CF*: unleaning. But he may break,
MS*SP*45: unleaning. But will break, O break,
*SP*69: how he'll break
2| *F, CF*: If Heaven in a rage try him too windily;
3| *F*: tall towers concumbent make:
CF: make!
4| *SP*69: years and a
5| *F*: Of time less trunk that is too vast to shake;
CF: Of timeless trunk
*SP*69: against cold < > eruptive,
6| *F, CF*: Only the temporal < > are abashed on their seat,
*SP*69: twigs unsure
8| *F, CF*: turn and beat
9–10| *F, CF*: Ecstatic around the < > captive. // But he casts the feeble generations of leaf, / And naked to the spleen of the cold skies eruptive / That howl on his defiant head in chief, // Bears out their frenzy to its period, / And hears in the spring, a little more rheumy and deaf, / After the tragedy the lyric palinode. . . . // Now < > young, and
11| *F, CF*: Yoked with
*SP*69: Yoked with < > of bantering brood,
12| *F, CF*: tree.
*SP*69: tree;

And exulted, wrapped in a phantasy of good:
"Be the great oak for its long winterings
Our love's symbol, better than the summer's brood."

Then the venerable oak, delivered of his pangs,
Put forth profuse his green banners of peace
And testified to her with innumerable tongues.

And what but she fetch me up to the steep place
Where the oak vaunted? A flat where birdsong flew
Had to be traversed; and a quick populace

Of daisies, and yellow kinds; and here she knew,
Who had been instructed of much mortality,
Better than brag in this distraught purlieu.

Above the little and their dusty tombs was he
Standing, sheer on his hill, not much soiled over
By the knobs and broken boughs of an old tree,

And she murmured, "Established, you see him there! forever."
But, that her pitiful error be undone,

13| *F, CF*: And she exulted—being given to crying,
MS*SP45*: exulted, in a fond #last three words crossed out and replaced above by three words# wrapped in her phantasy
SP69: She exaulted

14| *F, CF*: "Heart, heart: love is so firm an entity,

15| *F, CF*: It must not go the way of the hot rose dying"—
MS*SP45*: symbol, and #last word inserted above, then crossed out# nothing of #last two words crossed out, replaced above by three words# better than the summer's
SP69: Our symbol of love, better < > brood!"

16| *F, CF*: For the
SP69: the patient oak

17| *F, CF*: forth his flames of green with profuse joying

20| *F, CF*: vaunted? A meadow of many songs

21| *F*: a thick populace
SP69: traversed, and

22| *SP69*: kinds, and

23| *F, CF*: had sorely been < > much decease,
MS*SP45*: of grim #last word crossed out and replaced above by one word# much mortality,
SP69: Instructed well by much

25| *F, CF*: But above
SP69: Above their pied and dusty clumps was

26| *F, CF*: hill, soiled by few

27| *F, CF*: Of the
SP69: tree.

28| *F*: murmured, "He is established you see forever."
CF: murmured, "He is established, you see, for ever."
SP69: She looked and murmured, "Established there, forever!"

29| *F, CF*: But thinking that she had lied too piteously,

I knocked on his house loudly, a sorrowing lover,

And drew forth like a funeral a hollow tone.
"The old gentleman," I grieved, "holds gallantly,
But before our joy shall have lapsed, even, will be gone."

I knocked more sternly, and his dolorous cry
Boomed till its loud reverberance outsounded
The singing of bees; or the coward birds that fly

Otherwhere with their songs when summer is sped,
And if they stayed would perish miserably;
Or the tears of a girl remembering her dread.

In Process of a Noble Alliance

Reduce this lady unto marble quickly,
Ray her beauty on a glassy plate,
Rhyme her youth as fast as the granite,
Take her where she trembles, and do not wait,
For now in funeral white they lead her
And crown her queen of the House of No Love:
A dirge, then, for her beauty, Musicians!
Ye harping the springe that catches the dove.

30| *SP69*: knocked upon his house, a
31| *SP69*: And like a funeral came the hollow
32| *F*: "Largely, the old gentleman is—" I grieved—"cadaver.
CF: "Largely, the old gentleman is," I grieved, "cadaver.
MS*SP45*: grieved, "is holding gallantly,
SP69: "The grand old fellow," I
33| *F, CF*: Before < > even, he is gone."
SP69: joy has lapsed
34| *SP69*: I beat more < > and the dolorous
35| *F, CF*: its round reverberance had outdone
MS*SP45*: reverberance had #last word crossed out# outsounded
38| *F, CF*: stayed, would
39| *F*: girl discovering her
SP69: the weeping girl

Title| *MQR:* Grim Wedlock
F: #lines are alternately indented#
1| *MQR:* Liken this lady to a marble statue,
2| *MQR:* Record her < > painter's plate,
3| *F:* granite:
SP63: #typographical error, *youth at fast,* instead of youth as fast#
MQR: Rime her virtue as
4| *SP63*: trembles and
MQR: Know her as victim and
6| *F:* of No love.
MQR: Crowning her Queen
7| *F:* dirge then for
P*SP63*: dirge then for < > Musicians, #comma replaced by exclamation mark#
SP63: musicians!
MQR: Dirge is the right thing, you musicians!
8| *PSP63*: Not harping
MQR: Harp not the Gay Lord producing his dove.

Parting at Dawn

If there was a broken whispering by night,
It was an image of the coward heart,
But the white dawn assures them how to part—
Stoics are born on the cold glitter of light,
And with the morning star lovers take flight.
Say, then, your partings; and most dry should you drain
Your lips of their wine, your eyes of the frantic rain,
Till these be as the barren Cenobite.

And then? O dear Sir, stumbling down the street,
Continue, till you come to wars and wounds;
Beat the air, Madam, till your house-clock sounds;
And if no Lethe flows beneath your casement,
And when ten years have brought no full effacement,
Philosophy was wrong, and you may meet.

Miriam Tazewell (*SP45*)

When Miriam Tazewell heard the tempest bursting
And his wrathy whips across the sky drawn crackling
She stuffed her ears for fright like a young thing
And with heart full of the flowers took to weeping.

But the earth shook dry his old back in good season,
He had weathered storms that drenched him deep as this one,
And the sun, Miriam, ascended to his dominion,
The storm was withered against his empyrean.

1| MS*SP45*: was an image #last two words crossed out# < > night, #comma blotted out#
SP45, *PE*: night
4| *SP69*: light
6| *F*, MS*SP45*, P*SP45*, *SP45*, *PE*: Say then your < > parting
7| *SP69*: of the wine,
8| *SP69*: barren anchorite.
11| *SP45*: air, Madame
13| MS*SP45*, P*SP45*, *SP45*: have not brought full

1| *LR*, *CF*: bursting,
MS*SP45*: bursting, #comma blotted out#
2| *LR*, *CF*: crackling,
MS*SP45*: crackling, # comma blotted out#
3| *LR*, *CF*: thing,
MS*SP45*: thing, #comma blotted out#
4| *LR*: And, with < > flowers, went to
CF: flowers, went to
6| P*SP45*: one. #full stop replaced first by dash, which is marked out and then replaced by comma#

After the storm she went forth with skirts kilted
To see in the strong sun her lawn deflowered,
Her tulip, iris, peony strung and pelted,
Pots of geranium spilled and the stalks naked.

The spring transpired in that year with no flowers
But the regular stars went busily on their courses,
Suppers and cards were calendared, and some bridals,
And the birds demurely sang in the bitten poplars.

To Miriam Tazewell the whole world was villain
To prosper when the fragile babes were fallen,
And not to unstop her own storm and be maudlin
For weeks she went untidy, she went sullen.

Here Lies a Lady

Here lies a lady of beauty and high degree.
Of chills and fever she died, of fever and chills,
The delight of her husband, her aunts, and infant of three,
And of medicos marveling sweetly on her ills.

For either she burned, and her confident eyes would blaze,
And her fingers fly in a manner to puzzle their heads—
What was she making? Why, nothing; she sat in a maze
Of old scraps of laces, snipped into curious shreds—

10| *SP69*: the hot sun
13| *LR, CF*: flowers,
MS*SP45*: flowers, #comma removed#
14| *LR*: courses;
17| *LR, CF, SP69*: villain,
MS*SP45*: villain, #comma removed#
18| *LR, CF*: prosper, when < > fallen; #*CF* has no comma after "prosper"#
SP69: The principle of the beast was low and masculine, #line is taken from its place in *LR* and *CF*, line 19#
19| *LR, CF*: The principle of the beast was low and masculine!
MS*SP45*: And, #comma marked out# < > maudlin, #comma marked out#
PE, SP63, SP69: maudlin,

1| *LR, SP69b*: degree,
2| *LR*: she perished, of
3| *SP45, PE, SP63, SP69a,b*: aunt
LR: aunts, her infant
SP69b: three
4–5| *SP69b*: ills. / First she was hot, and her brightest eyes
5| *LR*: blaze
MS*SP45*: For #followed by word illegibly blotted out#
6| *LR*: a way to
SP69b: And the speed of her flying fingers shook their heads.
7–8| *SP69b*: making? God knows, she sat in those days / With her newest gowns all torn, or snipt into shreds.

Or this would pass, and the light of her fire decline
Till she lay discouraged and cold as a thin stalk white and blown,
And would not open her eyes, to kisses, to wine;
The sixth of these states was her last; the cold settled down.

Sweet ladies, long may ye bloom, and toughly I hope ye may thole,
But was she not lucky? In flowers and lace and mourning,
In love and great honor we bade God rest her soul
After six little spaces of chill, and six of burning.

The Tall Girl

The Queens of Hell had lissome necks to crane
At the tall girl approaching with long tread
And, when she was caught up even with them, nodded:
"If the young miss with gold hair might not disdain,
We would esteem her company over the plain,
To profit us all where the dogs will be out barking;
And we'll walk by the windows where the young men are working
And tomorrow we will all come home again."

But the Queen of Heaven on the other side of the road
In the likeness, I hear, of a fine motherly woman
Made a wry face, despite it was so common
To be worsted by the smooth ladies of hell,
And crisped her sweet tongue: "This never will come to good!
Just an old woman, my pet, that wishes you well."

9| *LR*: decline,
SP69: But that would < > the fire of her cheeks decline
10| MS*SP45*, *SP45*, *PE*, *SP63*: cold, like a stalk
SP69a: cold, like
SP69b: lay dishonored and wan like a rose overblown,
11| *LR*: wine:
12| *LR*: last, the
SP69: her final. The cold came down.
13–15| *SP69b*: Fair ladies, long < > and sweetly may thole! / She was part lucky. With flowers < > / With love and bravado, we
16| MS*SP45*: of mourning #last word crossed out and replaced by# burning.
SP69b: six quick turns of quaking, six

Title| *F*: Ada Ruel
6| MS*SP45*, *SP45*, *PE*, *SP63*, *SP69*: barking,
7| MS*SP45*, *SP45*, *PE*, *SP63*, *SP69*: we'll go by
9| *F*: the Queen of Heaven who had advanced and stood
10| MS*SP45*, *SP45*, *PE*, *SP63*, *SP69*: a plain motherly
12| *F*: the shrewd ladies

Fall of Leaf

With a rocking and guffawing,
Winter set his wind to blowing.
Oaken leaves of pale or brown,
Hickory leaves of sere,
Leaves of ash that tumbled down,
Weary, weary were.

Farthest from the living green
The sumac pitched his blood-red scene;
But pale or red the leaves were failing,
His dear hearts and hers;
Dick and Dorothy were quailing,
Summer foresters.

Dick and Dorothy look forth
And every quarter is a north.
Each old comrade is forlornest,
Bush, and trumpet-vine, and tree;
Is it jest? or in good earnest
Goes the somber colloquy?

"Dorothy, the year's played out,
His green young armies all in rout.
Some are pale and some are bleeding,
Green the summer long,
And the rattle-throats are pleading
With a foe too strong."

"Dick, the play is done for them
And every leaf that grows on stem.
And leaves and lovers have in common
That the leaves are dry and blown,
And the husk of man and woman
Withers on the bone."

F: #alternate lines set in and indented after first two lines of each stanza#
8| *F*: Was the sumac's blood-red scene.
13–18| *F*: #stanza not included#
22| *F*: long;
23| *F*: Hear the rattle-throats a-pleading
25| *F*: them,
26| *F*: Such is leaf

"Dorothy, we grow no younger,
Need we play it any longer?
Methinks eastward is a gate
Rusted, and a slim white spire;
Go tell them you come cold and late
To help them tend their fire."

"Dick, those are the Holy Rood
And sweet Saint Margaret's sisterhood.
Fearful are the maids, nor many,
Narrow is their bed;
They must open not to any
Woodwife wrapped in red."

"Dorothy, then westward come
Where the night-bells promise home.
For the arduous dome is black
But the gate is golden;
They will joy to have us back,
Loyal and beholden."

"Dick, they tend Saint Gregory's tomb,
The strictest monks in Christendom.
Tenants of a godly house,
Of cleanly gear and hallowed,
They will think but little use
Of woodman stained and yellowed."

"Dorothy, then will you tell
The way that goes from Lovers' Hell?
All the potent charms are said,
We that clasp are cold and wearied;
Heartless lovers are as dead
That walk the earth unburied."

"Dick, they found the ending good,
The Babes that ventured in the Wood.

35| *F*: Tell them
40| *F*: is the bed;
50| *F*: Strictest

So tell the leaves that die and fall,
As we lie a-shiver,
Stop and stitch us one close pall
To hide us deep for ever."

Rapunzel Has Submitted Herself to Fashion

Rapunzel, and Rapunzel,
All this day will I cry upon you,
Accusing, Was it well
How the old witch has enviously undone you?

Undone of your tangled snare
By which the midnight moon was sifted and stranded;
Forlorn of the rippling stair
Whereon the secret lover had ascended.

For when it came to night,
And the breath-shortening of the most shut hour,
Should he have mounted light
And delivered you with a kiss, and possessed the tower.

But the beldame spat between
The crooked blades of shears,
And put her warty hands to the sheen
Of your hair, and hacked it off, and maybe hacked your ears.

Do you sit at the casement still,
Braving the ruins of your smile but wanly?
Prince there shall come not till
He may climb to his kiss on a rippling ladder, only.

The Vagrant

Now what can he want,
The vagrant, the lout,
Who leers in the parson's face,
Lolls with tongue out?

12| *F*: tower,

F: #alternate lines indented#

Nothing that you have,
Men with a motor car;
God keep you your high hats
And fine things that are!

With a knot in his bosom
And a bee in his brains,
He goes full of pictures
Around the flat lanes.

His breeches are patchy,
His shirt full of thread,
But the hair's plastered neat
On his great hollow head.

Then think you he means
To harm our precious daughters?
Why, gentlemen, he fishes
In deeper waters.

Lou Margaret, Kittie,
Em with the country curls,
Are sweet bites for red lips,
Very fine girls;

But he visits with others,
With the Queen Guinevere,
Troy's women, Eden's,
Towns not near.

So leave him leering,
Loitering in the lanes;
There's no mischief in him
But a bee in his brains.

6–7| *F*: Men in a < > car, / Good folk with starch-fronts
8| *F*: are.
22| *F*: with country
31| *F*: him,

Boris of Britain

If ever your sleep goes bad,
Have in the chymist that Boris had.
When Boris' head was blown with trouble,
This man picked the bubble;
For Boris, loath to take to his bed,
To the cunning chymist took his head;
But Boris' heart knocked louder and louder,
As chymist mixed him the green powder,
And he shook it, and he shook it,
And with misgiving took it.

How did Boris get to court?
By a conveyance of a sort,
Hardly wood, hardly steel,
Beetle's wing, snail's wheel—
Sprawled upon the chymist's bed
Boris lay an hour like dead,
For the chymist went to look
And saw him there at three o'clock,
So he deposeth in a book;
One minute after, in the court,
Was Boris, arguing a tort,
Boris in his periwig,
Looking learned, talking big.
It was the great Boris—none
Could get a sweeter justice done.

What did Boris do there?
Got deliverance of a snare.
Poison brewing at the bone
Exploded against the chymist's one.
Too many prisoners in docks,
Liars in the witness box,

4| *F*: bubble.
7| *F*: louder
15| *F*: Sprawled on apothecary's bed,
16–20| *F*: dead, / When, it is claimed, at three o'clock / Chymist heard a brantgoose squawk, / And Boris had gone when he could look! / One
23| *F*: big,
28| *F*: Poison growing at
29| *F*: one;

Advocates hired to the devil,
Fed his ingrowing evil.

Accused was in a stinking tale
Conceived in terror of the gaol,
When to the whole court's surprise
Old Boris thunders, Lies! Lies!
And for not telling what he knows,
Old Boris smites him on the nose.
Gentlemen are on their feet,
Boris willing to repeat,
And there's your easy barrister
As mad as the March-most hare.
Up with hate, contempt, grudge,
Which in the white bosom lodge!
Order, order! It was not,
Boris too infernal hot,
Drew his fist and let 'em have it,
Got it back as good as gave it,
Went for eye and went for wig
Of coward, tattler, meddler, prig.

Boris darted in and knocked 'em,
Boris laid about and crocked 'em,
Jurors, gentlemen, and clients,
Neo-British bobby giants:
A man by pea-green powder charmed,
For down he dropped unharmed.
Now the barrister is disbarred.
'Twould have hit the old Boris hard;

36| *F*: When now, to < > surprise,
37| *F*: thunders, "Lies! Lies!"
39| *F*: Boris
51| F: Of tattler, coward, meddler
51–52| *F*: prig. // Down from public seats in rear
Tripped his dainty lady Clare,
Cried her shrew's tongue shrilling down
To make no scandal for the town,
Stop, remember, think, behave,
Something there was yet to save!
But he boxed the lady's ears,
Smartly dashed her pearls of tears,
Gave her such an awful shove
She was persuaded to remove;
She departs the Boris scene,
And they are not what they have been.
// Boris
55–58| *F*: Official neo-British giants, / And the green powder made him charmed, / For he dropt down unharmed. // A barrister, and disbarred!

This was not he—the wind in the head
Escaped when Boris dropped like lead.

Boris, a single-minded man,
Has turned an honest publican,
With a preference for quiet
But an aptitude for riot;
Serves the trade without deceit
And shows the merry ones the street;
And as for the lass named Nellie—no man
Has a helpfuller woman.

April Treason

So he put her in his picture.
Of a lady he was painting,
Put her lips, which smiled but faintly,
And her eyes, which leveled quaintly,
While her length of limb and noble Roman bust,
These he copied as he must.

And she was a perfect model,
Never restless with her features,
Never agitating greatly,
More than still and less than stately,
Till he knew that he could limn the dream aright
In his honest Northern light.

He had nearly done his portrait,
But there came a day in April;
There was treachery come winging
On the dust of flowers springing;
It was not a day for artist to play host
Lest the man come uppermost.

68| *F*: Nellie Cobbit helps him—no

3| *F*: lips which < > faintly
4| *F*: eyes which < > quaintly;
12| *F*: In the honest northern
14| *F*: in April.
15| *F*: treachery a-winging
16| *F*: springing—

And he knew that he was changed,
Was changed the wintry lady.
It was but their way of speaking,
It was but their way of looking,
But the cunning all had fled his fingertips;
So he bent and kissed her lips.

Then for all his giddy pulses
He laid grim hands on the picture,
And he trampled it with loathing,
Flung it many miles to nothing,
And it screamed to wake the devils as it fell
Till it thundered into hell.

Then a silence straightway took them
And they paced the woodland homeward.
What a bitter noon in April
(It was April, it was April)
As she touched his fleeting fingers cold as ice
And recited, "It was nice!"

First Travels of Max

As hath been, lo, these many generations,
The best of the Van Vroomans was the youngest;
And even he, in a chevroned sailor's blouse
And tawny curls far from subdued to the cap,
Had slapped old Katie and betaken himself
From games for children; that was because they told
Him never, never to set a wicked foot
Into Fool's Forest, where the devil dwelt.

19| *F*: he saw that
26| *F*: picture
31| *F*: them,
33| *F*: in April—
34| *F*: It < >April, it < >April—

1| *F*: been lo
SP63: In that old house for several generations
SP69: In that old house of many generations
2| *SP63*, *SP69*: youngest.
3| *F*: in chevroned
SP63, *SP69*: But even Max, in a chevroned
5| *F*: and delivered himself
SP63, *SP69*: and removed himself
7| *F*: never, to set his wicked
SP63: never never to
SP69: never never < > a naughty foot

"Become Saint Michael's sword!" said Max to the stick,
And to the stone, "Be a brand-new revolver!"
Then Max was glad that he had armed so wisely,
As darker grew the wood, and shrill with silence.
All good fairies were helpless here; at night
Whipped in an inch of their lives; weeping, forbidden
To play with strange scared truant little boys
Who didn't belong there. Snakes were allowed there
And lizards and adders—people of age and evil
That lay on their bellies and whispered—no bird nor rabbit.
There were more rotten trees than there were sound ones;
In that wood, timber was degenerate
And rotted almost faster than it grew;
There were no flowers nor apples; too much age.
The only innocent thing in there was Max,
And even he had cursed his little sisters.

The black tarn rose up almost in his face—
It was as black and sudden as the pit
The Adversary digs in the bowels of earth;
Bubbles were on it, breath of the black beast
(Formed like a spider, white bag for entrails)
Who took that sort of blackness to inhabit
And dangle after bad men in Fool's Forest.
"Must they be bad?" said casuistical Max.
"Mightn't a good boy who stopped saying his prayers
Be allowed to slip into the spider's fingers?"
Max raised his sword—but what can swords do
Against the Prince of the Dark? Max sheathed his point
And crept around the pool.

In the middle of the wood was a Red Witch.

9| *F*: St.
10| *SP63*, *SP69*: a forty-four revolver!"
11| *F*, *SP63*, *SP69*: wisely
15| *F*: strange, scared, truant, little
19| *F*: than sound
SP63, *SP69*: ones.
20| *F*, *SP63*, *SP69*: wood timber
21| *SP63*, *SP69*: grew.
22| *SP63*, *SP69*: apples. Too
23| *SP69*: thing was really Max,
24| *F*: even Max had
SP69: had beat his
25| *SP63*, *SP69*: face.
27| *F*: the Adversary digged in < > earth.
30| *F*: That took
32| *F*: casuistical Max,
38| *F*: red witch.
SP63: was the Red
SP69: There in < > the Red

Max half expected her. He never expected
To find a witch's house so dirty and foolish,
A witch with a wide bosom yellow as butter,
Or a witch combing so many obscene things
From her black hair into her scarlet lap;
He never believed there would attempt to sing
The one that taught the rats to squeal and Bashan's
Bull to bellow.

"Littlest and last Van Vrooman, do you come too?"
She knew him, it appeared, would know him better,
The scarlet hulk of hell with a fat bosom,
Pirouetting at the bottom of the forest.
Certainly Max had come, but he was going,
Unequal contests never being commanded
On young knights only armed in innocency.
"When I am a grown man I will come here
And cut your head off!" That was very well;
Not a true heart beating in Christendom
Could have said more, but that for the present would do.
Max went straight home; and nothing chilled him more
Than the company kept him by the witch's laugh
And the witch's song, and the creeping of his flesh.

Max is more firmly domiciliated.
A great house is Van Vrooman, a green slope
South to the sun do the great ones inhabit
And a few children play on the lawn with the nurse.
Max has returned to his play, and you may find him,
His famous curls unsmoothed, if you will call

39| *F*: half-expected
SP63, *SP69*: never imagined
40| *F*: To see a
SP69: A witch's house that would be red and dirty,
41| *SP69*: Or a witch's bosom wide and yellow
42| *SP63*, *SP69*: Or one that combed so
49| *SP63*, *SP69*: bosom
51| *F*: going;
SP63: come. But < > going;
SP69: going;
52| *F*: never were commanded
53| *SP69*: in innocence.
55| *F*: well,
SP63, *SP69*: well.
57–58| *SP63*: #stanza break#
58| *SP63*, *SP69*: home, and
60| *F*: the creep of his own flesh.
61| *F*: Now Max is firmly
63| *SP63*, *SP69*: inhabit,
64| *F*: with a nurse.

Where the Van Vroomans live; the tribe Van Vrooman
Live there, at least, when any are at home.

Grandgousier

Dry bones,
Dry brains,
And priest to pray;
Belly that groans
Of its long thirst-pains,
It is all that remains
Of the Grandgousier.

You fitted his muzzle,
Bishop Bamboozle;
Bishop Bamboozle,
You voided his guzzle.
You shall have crowns
And angel gowns.

Your delicate snout
Had nigh snuffed out
When the member observed 'em—
Bitters and stout
And cider at spout,
And the wenches that served 'em—
Each spidery chink
Was a freshet of drinkables,
Clink-clink-clink
Was a sound of unthinkables,
Your clerical ear
Went crack to hear.

68| *SP63*, *SP69*: there at least when

3| *F*: pray— #line indented#
7| *F*: #line indented#
13| *F*: angel's
16| *F*: #line indented# 'em:
19| *F*: 'em. #line indented#
21| *F*: #line indented#
22| *F*: Clink—clink—clink
23| *F*: #line indented#
25| *F*: Crack-cracked to

Take water and ice it,
And give him, you say?
Lemon, and slice it,
Sugar, and spice it,
For Grandgousier?

Weary is weary,
Doctor O'Dreary,
Says Grandgousier;
But O man, to be beery,
Mirth-mad-merry,
At the finish of day!

Will you give him to guzzle,
Bishop Bamboozle,
A sponge from a jar
Of the rank vinegar?

For to sip where he lies
Till he ups and dies—
And this is his day—
Till the pink puffed eyes
See the old Paradise
Of the Grandgousier.

Miss Euphemia

Out of her house she crept,
Which was her winger's jail,
Hearing the rumor that now
Was the birds' common tale—
Birds for all the ladies,
And husbands at church-door—
In fine, a spring was promised
As fifty years before.

26| *F*: Get water, and
27| *F*: #line indented#
30| *F*: #line indented#
33| *F*: #line indented#
34| *F*: But it's O to
36| *F*: #line indented# And rolling away!
41| *F*: lies,
43| F: #line indented#
45| *F*: paradise
46| *F*: #line indented#

A phase of green and tender
Was on the mortal clay,
But white upon her stick went
Miss Euphemia,
To count up all her tulips
That celebrated March,
Out of the frore escaping
To the blue upper arch.

Into her house she fled,
Buffeted back to prison,
And sought the very great-chair
From which she had arisen;
Down sat in her whiteness—
Bitter how she laughed—
Opening doors to March, yet
Quaking in his draught.

Nor scarcely can she, dwindling,
Throw down a bridge of dream
For a broken lady's traverse,
Neat-footing on the beam;
She had too much of winter,
And all her ways were lost,
And she sits with us only
Till next Pentecost.

Winter's Tale

Now the winter's frosty freight
Bows the tree and crowns the stump,
Yet sits poor Drury lone and late,
Watching his great cats jump.

Man of oak, is this your honor,
Buried in a mighty house,
To give your seven cats their humor,
Like a plaything, or a mouse?

Never your brethren toiled so hard,
Under the summer skies;
But now they use their long reward,
Wintering not so foolishwise.

Here's winter's ease, nor yet are any
Ladies laughing through his house;
Only truant thoughts of Jenny
Scampering through him like a mouse,

Jenny tripping through his head
As he met her in the wood;
But Drury wonders, is afraid,
If he could, or if he should;

And nods, while pay and claw and fang
Are flashing by the ingle—
Truly these be tiger's young
In this Kilkenny tangle.

But Tom the Tawny gave a cry!
And he took a mighty spring
To the oaken ledge, and by,
Like a mad, free thing;

And then, on seeing him go,
Old Drury started after,
In a good three-inch of snow,
And a winter-wind laughter.

Look at Drury's black coat,
And the kit's red jacket!
Listen, Drury's great throat
In the hell-cat's racket!

Will you rhyme us their whither?
Oh, skipping and skating
To the bricks in the weather
Where the woman was waiting.

She cracked open her door
To the cat of Kilkenny:
Here is Tom on your floor,
Here is Drury, good Jenny.

What became of all those?
Well, Jenny she cried;
Tom vanished—God knows
If he lived or he died;

And Drury was corrected
Of being long a ninny,
When his wander-wits contracted,
And his arms took hold of Jenny.

Emily Hardcastle, Spinster

We shall come tomorrow morning, who were not to have her love;
We shall bring no face of envy, but a gift of praise and lilies
To the stately ceremonial we are not the heroes of.

Let the sisters now attend her, who are red-eyed, who are wroth;
They were younger, she was finer, for they wearied of the waiting
And they married them to merchants, being unbelievers both.

I was dapper when I dangled in my pepper-and-salt;
We were only local beauties, and we beautifully trusted
If the proud one had to tarry we would take her by default.

But right across her threshold has the Grizzled Baron come;
Let them wrap her as a princess, who would patter down a stairway
Where the foreigner may take her for his gloomy halidom.

LR: #alternate lines indented#
1| *LR*, MS*SP45*, *SP45*, *PE*, *SP63*, *SP69*: love,
2| *LR*: Bringing not the face
MS*SP45*, *SP45*, *PE*, *SP63*, *SP69*: envy but
8| *LR*: were proper local
9| MS*SP45*, *SP45*, *PE*, *SP63*, *SP69*: would have her
10| *LR*, *SP69*: across the threshold
LR, *PE*, *SP63*, *SP69*: has her Grizzled
MS*SP45*, *SP45*: come.
11| *LR*: who will patter < > stairway,
SP63: who'd go softly down
SP69: them robe her, Bride and Princess, who'll go down a leafy archway
12| *PE*, *SP69*: And seal her to the stranger for his castle in the gloom.
SP63: And seal her to a stranger for his castle in the gloom.

Number Five

"Come in out of the night," said the landlord.
"Hang up your caps, men, and I will pass the gin."
And what for us thirsty pirates but walk right in,
Me with my lips locked tight, saying not a word?

Five hang-dog men, and I was number five.
"Give us a drink then, mate. It's terrible loud
And it's terrible bitter under the storm-cloud,
And we be blown to deader than alive."

God bless strong drink that's given to the weak.
Five of us sat to the bottle, but I was one,
For thinking of what so desperate had been done,
I couldn't drink to my mates, lest I might speak.

"Here's one won't take his drink. Now is he proud?
This is a rummy lad," says the proprietor.
Says he, "I've not seen this young beauty quieter."
Thinks I, "Now it is going to come out loud."

And here comes the girl, and looks us in the face—
Never she'd seen us faces more in evil
Nor us great hulks with more power of the devil—
But finally she sits down in the sixth place,

And presses my hand. But I turn like a hare,
I run to the window over the black water,
Thinking if I may tell them what's the matter;
Happen it's dark, but I know what is down there.

But open field is better. And I slide down
And howl in the storm, with let for my slippery tongue
That never to girls nor priests may tell the wrong—
And I run by the river where the dead things drown.

3| *F*: us thirsted pirates
6| *F*: drink, then
10| *F*: one
16| *F*: I, "O it
22| *F*: water
27| *F*: Which never < > girls and priests < > wrong.

Good Ships (*SP*45)

Fleet ships encountering on the high seas
Who speak, and then unto the vast diverge,
These hailed each other, poised on the loud surge
Of one of Mrs. Grundy's Tuesday teas,
Nor trimmed one sail to baffle the driving breeze.
A macaroon absorbed all her emotion;
His hue was ashy but an effect of ocean;
They exchanged the nautical technicalities.

It was only a nothing or so, and thus they parted.
Away they sailed, most certainly bound for port,
So seaworthy one felt they could not sink;
Still there was a tremor shook them, I should think,
Beautiful timbers fit for storm and sport
And unto miserly merchant hulks converted.

Youngest Daughter

Who will wed the old dam's youngest daughter?
Not the sailor, filled with ale,
Who moored his expected boat to a stake in the water
And Heave-Ho, unto her halls went up for mating,
But was seduced by her ill-bred lady-in-waiting,
Round of bosom, and not so pale.

Title| MS*SP*45: Fleet Ships
2| *F, CF*: and unto eternity diverge—
MS*SP*45: then into #last word altered to# unto
3| *SP*69: Two hailed
6| MS*SP*45: all his #crossed out and replaced by# her
7| *F, CF*: ashy, but
*SP*69: was ruddy but
9| *F, CF*: parted;
*SP*69: so until they
10| *SP*69: they went, most
11| *F, CF*: seaworthy, one
12| *F, CF*: think—
13| *F*: timbers meant for stormy sport
CF: for stormy sport
13| MS*SP*45: The merry timbers
14| *F, CF*: And into miserly

Title| *SP*69: Romance of a Youngest Daughter
1| *SP*69: the Dowager's youngest daughter,
2| *F*: #line indented#
*SP*69: The Captain? filled < > ale?
4| *F*: went mating,
*SP*69: And stumbled on sea-legs into the Hall for
5| *SP*69: Only to be seduced < > her lady-in-waiting,
6| *F*: #line indented#

Nor the burgher's shiny boots and vest,
His considered views of marriage;
With her tidy scullery maid was he impressed,
Who kept that house from depreciation and dirt,
And (blushing for the wretched state of his undershirt)
He rode her home in his carriage.

Nor even the grim shanks of the scholar antiquary
Who was her last resort;
They set him humble down in the great library,
Then found him compromised with a musty tome,
And crying his Truelove therein had her home
And made him sweet disport.

Heart's Desire (so her mother named her) never will wed,
Fairest (she swore) in her time;
For "Revenge on these!" the passionate carline said;
"Henceforth the tightest nunnery be thy tomb;
Thy face a fever shall burn in every head;
Against thy walls incessant man shall come
And claw, but may not climb!"

SP69: Round-bosomed, and
7| *SP69*: Or the thrifty burgers in < > fancy vest
8| *F*: #line indented# views on marriage;
SP69: With considered < > marriage?
9| *SP69*: By the tidy < > maid he was impressed
11| *SP69*: But wife does double duty and takes no hurt,
12| *F*: #line indented# He asked her
SP69: So he rode
13| *F*: #line indented# Nor the grim
SP69: Never the spare young scholar
14| *SP69*: was their next resort;
15| *F*: When her mother fetched her into the < > library
SP69: him wait in the crypt of the Old Library
16| *SP69*: And found < > a Saxon book,
17| *F*: Wherein (he claimed) his Truelove had
SP69: Claiming his truelove Learning kept that nook
18| *F*: #line indented# And gave him
SP69: And promised sweet
19| *SP69*: Desirée (of a mother's christening) never shall wed
20| *F*: #line indented#
SP69: Though fairest child of her womb;
21| *F*: said,
SP69: "We will have revenge," her injured Ladyship said,
22| *F*: tomb,
23| *F*: head.
23–25| *SP69*: By the topmost stair! When the ill-bred lovers come / We'll say, She is not at home."
24| *F*: Thy walls
25| *F*: #line indented#

Necrological (*SP*45)

The friar had said his paternosters duly
And scourged his limbs, and afterwards would have slept;
But with much riddling his head became unruly,
He arose, from the quiet monastery he crept.

Dawn lightened the place where the battle had been won.
The people were dead—it is easy he thought to die—
These dead remained, but the living all were gone,
Gone with the wailing trumps of victory.

The dead men wore no raiment against the air,
Bartholomew's men had spoiled them where they fell;
In defeat the heroes' bodies were whitely bare,
The field was white like meads of asphodel.

Not all were white; some gory and fabulous
Whom the sword had pierced and then the grey wolf eaten;
But the brother reasoned that heroes' flesh was thus,
Flesh fails, and the postured bones lie weather-beaten.

The lords of chivalry lay prone and shattered,
The gentle and the bodyguard of yeomen;
Bartholomew's stroke went home—but little it mattered,
Bartholomew went to be stricken of other foemen.

Beneath the blue ogive of the firmament
Was a dead warrior, clutching whose mighty knees
Was a leman, who with her flame had warmed his tent,
For him enduring all men's pleasantries.

F: #lines are alternately indented#
1| *F*: duly,
5| *F*: won,
6| *F, CF, FA*: easy, he thought, to
9| *SP*63: dead wore no rainment against
10| *F*: men despoiled them
11| *F, CF, FA*: heroes' bosoms were
14| *F*: eaten,
15| *PE, SP*63: thus.
*SP*69: thus;
17| *F, CF, FA,* MS*SP*45: chivalry were prone
*PE, SP*63: shattered.
20| *F*: The conqueror went
21| *F*: The monastic strode beneath the
22| *F*: And found a warrior
23| *F*: who in her

Close by the sable stream that purged the plain
Lay the white stallion and his rider thrown,
The great beast had spilled there his little brain,
And the little groin of the knight was spilled by a stone.

The youth possessed him then of a crooked blade
Deep in the belly of a lugubrious wight;
He fingered it well, and it was cunningly made;
But strange apparatus was it for a Carmelite.

Then he sat upon a hill and hung his head,
Riddling, riddling, and lost in a vast surmise,
And so still that he likened himself unto those dead
Whom the kites of Heaven solicited with sweet cries.

Armageddon (*SP*45)

Antichrist, playing his lissome flute and merry
As was his wont, debouched upon the plain;
Then came a swirl of dust, and Christ drew rein,
Brooding upon his frugal breviary.

Now which shall die, the roundel, rose, and hall,
Or else the tonsured beadsman's monkery?
For Christ and Antichrist arm cap-a-pie,
The prospect charms the soul of the lean jackal.

But Antichrist got down from the Barbary beast
And doffed his plume in courteous prostration;
Christ left his jennet's back in deprecation
And raised him, his own hand about the waist.

26| *F*: thrown;
CF, FA: thrown.
30| *F*: wight,
CF: lugubrious knight;
31| *F*: well and found it cunningly made—
33| *PE, SP63*: and bowed his head
SP69: He sat < > and bowed his head
34| *PE, SP63, SP69*; As under a riddle, and in a deep surmise
35| *F, SP63, SP69*: So

6| MS*SP45*: the tonsured #last word crossed out and then same word inserted above#
11| *Arma, CF*: deprecation,
12| MS*SP45*: raised him, #*m* and comma added by hand# his
CF: about his waist

And then they fingered chivalry's quaint page,
Of precedence discoursing by the letter.
The oratory of Antichrist was better,
He invested Christ with the elder lineage.

He set Christ on his own Mahomet's back
Where Christ sat fortressed up like Diomede;
The cynical hairy jennet was his steed,
Obtuse, and most indifferent to attack.

The lordings measured lances and stood still,
And each was loath to let the other's blood;
Originally they were one brotherhood;
There stood the white pavilion on the hill.

To the pavilion went then the hierarchs,
If they might truce their honorable dispute;
Firm was the Christian's chin and he was mute,
And Antichrist ejected scant remarks.

Antichrist tendered a spray of rosemary
To serve his brother for a buttonhole;
Then Christ about his adversary's poll
Wrapped a dry palm that grew on Calvary.

Christ wore a dusty cassock, and the knight
Did him the honors of his tiring-hall,
Whence Christ did not come forth too finical,
But his egregious beauty richly dight.

13| *Arma*: At first they
PE, SP63: Then next they
SP69: Then they must finger
14| *Arma*: letter;
19| *Arma*: cynical, hairy
SP69: cynical jennet was the other steed,
20| *Arma*: Obtuse and most untoward for attack.
CF: indifferent in attack.
24| MS*SP45*: the white #last word crossed out# pavilion
24–25| *Arma, CF*: hill; / Nor were they hacked and harried to their boot; / Men die when wounds insufferable are got; / These, plagued with immortality, could not, #no commas in *CF*# / When grim Lord Ares trod them underfoot. / To the white pavilion went the hierarchs #*CF* has a comma#
27| *Arma*: chin, and < > mute;
28| *Arma*: But Antichrist ejected small remarks.
32| *Arma*: palm inscribed Mount Calvary.
CF: palm inscribed "Mount Calvary."
33| *Arma*: cassock, till the
35–36| *SP69*: finical / In his

With feasting they concluded every day,
And when the other shaped his phrases thicker
Christ, introducing water in the liquor,
Made wine of more ethereal bouquet.

At wassail Antichrist would pitch the strain
For unison of all the retinue;
Christ beat the time, and hummed a stave or two,
But did not say the words, which were profane.

Perruquiers were privily presented,
Till, knowing his need extreme and his heart pure,
Christ let them dress him his thick chevelure,
And soon his beard was glozed and sweetly scented.

And so the Wolf said Brother to the Lamb,
The True Heir keeping with the poor Impostor,
The rubric and the holy paternoster
Were jangled strangely with the dithyramb.

It could not be. There was a patriarch,
A godly liege of old malignant brood,
Who could not fathom the new brotherhood
Between the children of the light and dark.

He sought the ear of Christ on these mad things,
And in the white pavilion when he stood
And saw them featured and dressed like twins at food,
He poured in the wrong ear his misgivings.

38| *Arma, CF*: thicker,
46| *CF*: Till knowing < > extreme, and
49| *Arma*: wolf < > brother < > lamb,
50| *Arma*: true < > the rank imposter;
52| *Arma*: Were strangely jangled with
53| *Arma*: be; there
54| *SP69*: brood
56| *Arma*: Betwixt
57| *PE, SP63*: these strange things, *SP69*: these doings
58| *Arma*: And, in *CF, PE, SP63*: stood, *PE, SP63, SP69*: But in
59| *PE, SP63, SP69*: them favored and
60–61| *PE, SP63, SP69*: Profound and mad became his misgivings. // The voices, and their burdens, he must hear, / But equal between the pleasant Princes flew / Theology, the arts, #*SP69* has for last two words *art*# the old customs and the new; #*SP69* omits last *the*#/ Hoarsely he ran and hissed in the wrong ear. #*SP69* adds dash after *hissed*#// He

He was discomfited, but Christ much more.
Christ shed unmannerly his devil's pelf,
Took ashes from the hearth and smeared himself,
Called for his smock and jennet as before.

His trump recalls his own to right opinions,
With scourge they mortify their carnal selves,
With stone they whet the ax-heads on the helves
And seek the Prince Beelzebub and minions.

Christ and his myrmidons, Christ at the head,
Chanted of death and glory and no complaisance;
Antichrist and the armies of malfeasance
Made songs of innocence and no bloodshed.

The immortal Adversary shook his head:
If now they fought too long, then he would famish;
And if much blood was shed, why, he was squeamish:
"These Armageddons weary me much," he said.

Epitaph

Napoleon took many captures and is dead,
Julius brought unto Rome many victories,
Nor did Alexander expire on a wastrel's bed;
But this was a somewhat greater captain than these.

He took a city too, O Eminences.
It was a city reared stubborn against a foe,
Furnished it was with no frail few defenses,
But it fell to the intrepid Generalissimo.

61| *Arma*: discomfited; but < > more,
CF: discomfited; but < > more;
62| *PE, SP63, SP69*: sheds
63| *PE, SP63, SP69*: Takes < > smears
64| *PE, SP63, SP69*: Calls
65| *Arma*: opinions;
67| *Arma*: stones < > axe-heads < > helves,
71| *Arma*: and his armies
73| *Arma, SP69*: head;
74| *SP69*: long, why, he
75| *Arma*: squeamish;
SP69: shed he would be squeamish.
76| *SP69*: "These Armageddons!" he said;
and later bled.

F: #alternate lines indented#
5| *F*: city, too, O Eminences;

Its two towers compacted of a tough masonry,
The right tower squat against the thunderbolts of Heaven,
The left tower sheer on the brink like a mighty tree
From the bottom of Hell, and terrible to the craven.

He was a lone besieger of a grim defense,
He was scarred, and weary of circling it round after round,
He battered incessantly upon its fundaments,
At last he bestrode it thundering to the ground.

A lone besieger, so Caesar's ghost had said,
Leading no soldiers; but he had known black magic,
And mustered invisible regiments to his aid,
For he triumphed; and the envious Caesars took it as tragic.

Judith of Bethulia

Beautiful as the flying legend of some leopard,
She had not yet chosen her great captain or prince
Depositary to her flesh, and our defense;
And a wandering beauty is a blade out of its scabbard.
You know how dangerous, gentlemen of threescore?
May you know it yet ten more.

Nor by process of veiling she grew the less fabulous.
Grey or blue veils, we were desperate to study
The invincible emanations of her white body,
And the winds at her ordered raiment were ominous.
Might she walk in the market, sit in the council of soldiers?
Only of the extreme elders.

But a rare chance was the girl's then, when the Invader
Trumpeted from the south, and rumbled from the north,
Beleaguered the city from four quarters of the earth,

18| *F*: he must have known

1| MS*SP45*, *SP45*, *PE*, *SP63*, *SP69*: leopard
2| *SP69*: not chosen yet her
4| *SP69*: A wandering
7| *SP69*: grew less
8| *F*: veil
10| *F*: And each wind < > was
11| *F*: in her council
14| *F*, *SP69*: South < > North,

Our soldiery too craven and sick to aid her—
Where were the arms could countervail his horde?
Her beauty was the sword.

She sat with the elders, and proved on their blear visage
How bright was the weapon unrusted in her keeping,
While he lay surfeiting on their harvest heaping,
Wasting the husbandry of their rarest vintage—
And dreaming of the broad-breasted dames for concubine?
These floated on his wine.

He was lapped with bay-leaves, and grass and fumiter weed,
And from under the wine-film encountered his mortal vision.
For even within his tent she accomplished his derision;
She loosed one veil and another, standing unafraid;
And he perished. Nor brushed her with even so much as a daisy?
She found his destruction easy.

The heathen are all perished. The victory was furnished,
We smote them hiding in our vineyards, barns, annexes,
And now their white bones clutter the holes of foxes,
And the chieftain's head, with grinning sockets, and varnished—
Is it hung on the sky with a hideous epitaphy?
No, the woman keeps the trophy.

May God send unto the virtuous lady her prince.
It is stated she went reluctant to that orgy,
Yet a madness fevers our young men, and not the clergy
Nor the elders have turned them unto modesty since.
Inflamed by the thought of her naked beauty with desire?
Yes, and chilled with fear and despair.

16| *F*: her;
17| MS*SP45*, *SP45*, *PE*, *SP63*: countervail this horde?
21| *SP69*: heaping
26| MS*SP45*, *SP45*, *PE*, *SP63*, *SP69*: vision,
27| *F*: derision:
SP69: derision,
28| *F*: unafraid,
SP69: Loosing one < > another, she stood unafraid;
31| *F*: perished, the
SP69: heathen have all < > furnished.
32| *SP69*: in vineyards
34| *F*: varnished,
37| MS*SP45*, *SP45*, *PE*, *SP63*, *SP69*: unto our virtuous
SP69: her Prince!
41| *SP69*: her nakedness with

Conrad Sits in Twilight

Conrad, Conrad, aren't you old
To sit so late in your mouldy garden?
And I think Conrad knows it well,
Nursing his knees, too rheumy and cold
To warm the wraith of a Forest of Arden.

Neuralgia in the back of his neck,
His lungs filling with such miasma,
His feet dipping in leafage and muck:
Conrad! You've forgotten asthma!

Conrad's house has thick red walls
And chips on Conrad's hearth are blazing,
Slippers and pipe and tea are served,
Butter and toast, Conrad, are pleasing!
Still Conrad's back is not uncurved
And here's an autumn on him, teasing.

Autumn days in our section
Are the most used-up thing on earth
(Or in the waters under the earth),
Having no more color nor predilection
Than cornstalks too wet for the fire,
A ribbon rotting on the byre,
A man's face as weathered as straw
By the summer's flare and the winter's flaw.

Title| *F, SP*69a: Conrad at Twilight
MS*SP*45, *SP*45, *SP*63, *PE*: Conrad in Twilight
2| *F*: in a mouldy
9| *F*, MS*SP*45, *SP*45, *PE*, *SP*63: asthma.
*SP*69a: Conrad, you've < > asthma.
10| *PE*, *SP*63: walls,
11| *PE*, *SP*63: The log on < > hearth is blazing,
13| *F*, *SP*69a: Anchovy toast, Conrad! 'Tis pleasing,
PE, *SP*63: toast are meant for pleasing!
14| *F*, *SP*69a: uncurved,
17| *F*, *SP*69a: earth,
18| MS*SP*45, *SP*45, *PE*, *SP*63: earth)
23| MS*SP*45, *SP*45, *PE*, *SP*63: and winter's
F, *SP*69a #contain the following additional stanza#

Conrad, rise up and steel your soul
And smite an anvil, draw a sword
(See William James and Henry Ford)
And point you to a mightier goal!
But Conrad has not answered a word.

Nocturne

Where now is the young Adam, sultry in his Aiden?
And where is the goat-footed, pursuing his naked maiden?
Our man shall cut few capers in his dark seersucker coat,
His grave eye subduing the outrageous red tie at his throat,
Considering if he should carry his dutiful flesh to the ball,
Rather than open his book, which is flat, and metaphysical.

The centuries have blown hard, and dried his blood
Unto this dark quintessence of manhood;
Much water has passed the bridges, fretfully,
And borne his boats of passion to the sea;
There is no storm in this dusk, but a distant flash
Over the foamy sea where the great floods wash.

But still the plum-tree blooms, despite the rocks at its root,
Despite that everyone knows by now its wizened and little fruit,
And the white moon plunges wildly, it is a most ubiquitous ghost,
Always seeking her own old people that are a long time lost—
Till he is almost persuaded, and perhaps he would go to the ball,
If he had the heart, and the head, for a furious antique bacchanal.

Blackberry Winter

If the lady hath any loveliness, let it die.
For being drunken with the steam of Cuban cigars,
I find no pungence in the odor of stars,
And all my music goes out of me on a sigh.

But still would I sing to my maidenly apple-tree,
Before she has borne me a single apple of red;

2| *F*: goat-footed pursuing
9| *F*: has flowed beneath him fretfully,
10| *F*: sea.
14| *F*: fruit—
15| *F*: ghost

1| *SP69*: If there be a power of sweetness, let it lie,
2| *SP69*: cigars
3| *SP69*: He takes < > pungence from the
4| *SP69*: And even his music stops on one long sigh.
5| *F*: Still
SP69: Still he must sing to his virgin apple-tree
6| *F*: red.
SP69: Who has not borne him a winey beauty of

The pictures of silver and apples of gold are dead;
But one more apple ripeneth yet maybe.

The garnished house of the Daughter of Heaven is cold.
I have seen her often, she stood all night on the hill,
Fiercely the pale youth clambered to her, till—
Hoarsely the rooster awakened him, footing the mold.

The breath of a girl is music—fall and swell—
The trumpets convolve in the warrior's chambered ear,
But I have listened, there is no one breathing here,
And all of the wars have dwindled since Troy fell.

But still I will haunt beneath my apple-tree,
Heedful again to star-looks and wind-words,
Anxious for the flash of whether eyes or swords,
And hoping a little, a little, that either may be.

Lichas to Polydor,

WHO REGRETTED ALL HIS YEARS OF SERVING CYTHEREA

Her huge affirmative emblazed thy sodden skies,
It was a sign had puffed up great the mortalest worm that dies;
But now thou knowest her sworn a spinster, and her true-tokens lies.

Rained her endearments thick as snow and covered thee,
Thy prayer was not appeased; naked and unrewarded must thou flee.
Not so had served thee Thalia, Charis, or Melpomene.

7| *F*: dead,
SP69: The silver blooms and bronzy nubs drop dead
8| *F*: But ripeneth one < > apple yet for me.
SP69: But the nonpareil may ripen yet, maybe.
9| *SP69*: Bestarred is the < > Heaven's house, and cold,
10| *F*: often—she
SP69: He has seen < > she sat all
11| *SP69*: Unseemly the < > clambered toward her, till
12| *SP69*: Untimely the peacock screamed, and he awakened old.
13| *SP69*: music of fall < > swell.
14| *SP69*: Trumpets
15| *SP69*: But he has listened; none is resounding here,
16| *SP69*:#ends with this line# So much the

Much better marriages thou hadst becoming to thy station:
Remember the Powerful Ladies, unreluctant to thy passion,
Thou less than the bandy-legged of the heathen congregation!

Spiel of the Three Mountebanks

THE SWARTHY ONE—
Villagers who gather round,
This is Fides, my lean hound.
Bring your bristled village curs
To try his fang and tooth, sweet sirs!
He will rend them, he is savage,
Thinking nothing but to ravage,
Nor with cudgel, fire, rope,
May ye control my misanthrope;
He would tear the moon in the sky
And fly at Heaven, could he fly.
And for his ravening without cease
I have had of him no peace;
Only once I bared the knife
To quit my devil of his life,
But listen, how I heard him say,
"Think you I shall die today?
Since your mother cursed and died,
I am keeping at your side,
We are firmly knit together,
Two ends tugging at one tether,
And you shall see when I shall die
That you are mortal even as I."
Bring your stoutest-hearted curs
If ye would risk him, gentle sirs.

7| *F*: station;
8| *F*: Remember those Powerful < > passion:
9| *F*: congregation.

Title| *SP69*: Spiel of Three Mountebanks

1| *F*: #identification of speaker is centered and without dash#
5| *F*: sirs,
9| *SP69*: May you control
11| *F*: at Heaven could
16| *F*: say:
25| *F*: If you would < > him then, good sirs.

THE THICK ONE—

Countrymen, here's a noble frame,
Humphrey is my elephant's name.
When my father's back was bent
Under steep impediment,
Humphrey came to my possession,
With patient strength for all his passion.
Have ye a mountain to remove?
It is Humphrey's dearest love.
Pile his burden to the skies,
Loose a pestilence of flies,
Foot him in the quick morass
Where no laden beast can pass:
He will staunch his weariless back
And march unswerving on the track.
Have ye seen a back so wide,
So impenetrable hide?
Nor think ye by this Humphrey hill
Prince Hamlet bare his fardels ill?
Myself I like it not for us
To wear beneath an incubus,
I take offence, but in no rage
May I dispose my heritage;
Though in good time the vast and tough
Shall sink and totter soon enough.
So pile your population up,
They are a drop in Humphrey's cup;
Add all your curses to his pack
To make one straw for Humphrey's back.

THE PALE ONE—

If ye remark how poor I am,

26| *F*: #identification of speaker is centered and without dash#
38| *F*, *SP*45, *PE*, *SP*63, *SP*69: pass,
MS*SP*45: pass: #colon marked out and replaced by comma#
43| *SP*69: think you by
45| *F*: Betimes I
*SP*69: Myself, I
47| *F*: but by no
50| *F*: May sink
MS*SP*45, *SP*45: totter fast enough.
52| *F*: You are < > cup,
53| *F*: And all your goods and idols pack,
MS*SP*45: All all [*sic*] your
54| *F*: They are a straw on Humphrey's
55| *F*: #identification of speaker is centered and without dash#
56| *SP*69: If you remark

Come, citizens, behold my lamb!
Have ye a lion, ounce, or scourge,
Or any beast of dainty gorge?
Agnus lays his tender youth
Between the very enemy's mouth,
And though he sniff his delicate meat,
He may not bruise that flesh nor eat,
He may not rend him limb from limb,
If Agnus do but bleat on him.
Fierce was my youth, but like a dream
I saw a temple, and a stream,
And where I knelt and washed my sore,
This infant lamb stood on the shore,
He mounted with me from the river,
And still he cries, as brave as ever,
"Lay me down by the lion's side
To match my frailty with his pride!
Fain would I welter in my blood
To teach these lions true lionhood."
So daily Agnus would be slain
But daily is denied again,
And still the hungry lions range
While Agnus waits upon a change;
Only the coursing lions die
And in their deserts mortify.
So bring us lion, leopard, bear,
To try of Agnus without fear,
And ye less gentle than I am,
Come, be instructed of my Lamb.

57| *F*: lamb.
58| *SP69*: Have you a
59| *F*: beast with dainty
61| *PE, SP63, SP69*: mouth.
62| *F*, MS*SP45*, *SP45*, *PE*, *SP63*, *SP69*: meat
63| *PE, SP63*: eat.
64| MS*SP45*, *SP45*, *PE*, *SP63*, *SP69*: limb
67| *PE, SP63, SP69*: temple and
68| *F*: sore
71| *F*, MS*SP45*, *SP45*, *PE*, *PS63*, *SP69*: ever:
73| *F*: pride;
MS*SP45*, *SP45*, *PE*, *SP63*, *SP69*: pride.
75: *F*: To show these
76| *F*: slain,
82| *F*: us leopard, tiger, bear,
84| *SP69*: And you less
85| *F*: lamb.

Night Voices

By night and inky fog,
Unseen they hoped of all the synagogue,
Two pale high-fronted youths withdrew apart
Upheaving each his bitterness of heart
In a dark duologue.

"I have the whole hearsay,
They titled thee a little God today.
But didst thou promise to annul the tomb,
Complaisant with that frighted breed to whom
Thou fellowest in clay?"

"I sped their tremulous hope
For pity of their darkling horoscope.
For thou art Nicodemus, and thy sect
Hath schooled them so funereal, O stiff-necked,
Ye stinted all their scope."

"Our order doth not use
To ease them with false tidings of good news.
Our fashion is a jealous elder God
Who tempereth sometimes his chastening rod
But raiseth no dead Jews."

"Ye slay the cripples' hope,
Who would but slough their warty envelope,
The meek laborious who would mirth and play,
The tight-lipped righteous travailing for that day
When rock-bound graves may ope."

"Friend, these lies profit not
When carcasses so visibly do rot.
As well run forth and cry there is no Rome!

F: #contains the following epigraph#
Nicodemus . . . came to Jesus by night.
1| *F*: Upon a night of fog,
5| *F*: duologue:
7| *F*: god
9| *F*: that frightened breed
19| *F*: rod,
20| *F*: dead Jews!"
24| *F*: travailing to that
28| *F*: no Rome,

Still would the legionaries scourge them home,
Though they had fain forgot."

"Nay, this hope lasteth more,
And maketh the mortal mark bite not so sore.
Our Jewry is fanatic, and I said,
In three days must each tomb unclasp his dead!
Nor heard such joy before."

"Take heed, high-hearted youth,
For they will kill thee save thou speak them sooth,
And they will say attentive to thy grave,
The little carpenter's promises were brave,
But carrion telleth truth!"

"O dogma'd Pharisee,
The hope I startle flitteth wide of me;
Suppose in thy turn thou shouldst firmly swear
That I had cleft the tomb and breathed the air,
Would it not flutter free?"

And further on they walked,
Out of old passion in the heart they talked,
And when the grey morn glimmered overhead,
They found they trod the gardens of the dead,
And specter-white they stalked.

Adventure This Side of Pluralism

Angered with a braggart kind
Prescribing others to its yoke
And seeming jauntily designed,
I rent my smooth locks and I spoke:
—Lordly, have ye intimations

29| *F*: the legionary scourge < > home
30| *F*: Whom they
31| *F*: this lie lasteth
34| *F*: 'In < > dead!'
36| *F*: youth!
37| *F*: thee, save
39| *F*: 'This
40| *F*: truth.'"
43| *F*: Shouldst thou and some one other then make oath
44| *F*: and met you both,
49| *F*: 'Twas found

Of more excellent pedigree,
That ye taint the other stations
With the limp of bastardy?

Can ye outscream the peahen,
Or outspring the springbok,
Or scare away the wind and rain
With Shibboleth or Fokmafok?

Rear ye prouder than a stallion,
Creep ye lower than a snail,
As ye tread your suave cotillion,
Satyrs in a swallowtail?

But likest brethren fall apart,
And who can tie the miscellany,
Plato, Scythian, dog, and wart?
One is One, but these be Many.

There was an ancient man withal,
Doctor of Genealogy,
With wisdom on his red eyeball,
Who heard and answered me;

His daughters wedded with the plague,
His pigeons wiven of the fox,
All the jewels in his bag
Gone in shipwreck on the rocks;

With none to mind or mourn,
He sat beneath his locust-tree,
But he saw my visage torn
And lifted up his voice to me:
—Aforetime there was one God only,
Simplex was his name, none other,
Ah, but Simplicity was lonely,
Nothing saying Father.

27| *F*: the treasures in
29| *F*: mourn
32| *F*: me.

Feudal Heart without a fief,
Empty Imperator, Rex,
Jahveh, Allah, Indian Chief,
Pontiff, Mandarin, Multiplex.

Where were the singers of his state,
Who were the largess of his loins,
Unless he mightily begat
Other Gods, many sons?

The vague moon and the fierce sun,
Lampless in the deathy quiet,
Pricked his continence, waiting on
The whisper of the Fiat;

The fir-tree quivering in her vase,
And the hop-toad in his kettle,
And a lady's lovely face,
And the tight-suited beetle.

Out of joy they took their form,
Joyous they came forth and sped,
Both the able-bellied worm
And immaculate biped.

They were patterned prettily,
And of love; and even so,
Their young mouths cried terribly,
Ego, Ego, Ego!

If he wrought them for obeisance,
Simplicissimus missed his mark,
Too promiscuous of his essence,
Obsolescent Hierarch.

For the Stark, Prime, Simple,
When he multiplied his One,

41| *F*: state?
42| *F*: loins?
44| *F*: sons.

Shared the holies of his temple
And conveyed his throne.

Some may have returned him praise:
I, who bended a good knee
As a novice in those days
To my mad Aunt Piety!

Have you heard the Ave sung?
Here's the cuckoo, bull, and fife,
Lark's bill and Cicero's tongue,
Loud of lustihood and strife.

And his messengers the suns,
Perfect clerks and bibliophiles,
Are stubborn hot automatons,
Running out their rebel wills.

Phoebe vibrant in the tree,
Running water, April pigments,
Mirrors changing endlessly:
"We are wholes and not fragments."

Man was the youngest child,
And knew the son then its own father?
It was thoroughly beguiled
Of its own image rather.

And the mere spied weed
With its red heart perfect centred:
"I am ultimate indeed,
And a God, well accoutred."

The free hearts and free lances,
Man and Beast and Thingdom:
"We unnatural Princes
Will parcel out his kingdom."

69| *F*: And if some return him praise—
72| *F*: mad Aunt Piety—
79| *F*: automatons
91| *F*: indeed

My son, the motley and the pied,
The swarming and oblivious brood,
Are swimming deep in fratricide,
Being brother-and-sisterhood.

So tell those Dignities Respective,
Noses counted to four hundred,
Tribes and orators invective!
Whom they slay are kindred!

On the Road to Wockensutter

"Sahara doth not keep her livid hell
Wholly unto herself," writes Herodote;
"Sirocco scourgeth even the greenlands well,
The pulver of her brimstone scratched my throat."

Brady had little Latin and less Greek,
Not his to verify the obscure quotation,
But Brady knew, no waterfall nor creek
Nor arctic tremor stayed his oxidation.

By sixty fiery miles they call a trail,
Red Hole communicates with Wockensutter.
Here Brady, who had started on a rail,
Pursued his march diminishing like butter.

For Brady had deployed the manifold
Beneath the sacred Principle of Venus.
But desert ladies named him greasy and old,
And the impaneled peers pronounced it heinous. . . .

103| *F*: invective,
104| *F*: kindred.

Title| *SP69*: On the Road to Wockensutter / *(a Western)*
2| *SP69*: herself," said Herodote;
4| *DD*: brimstone itched my
SP69: of his brimstone
6| *SP69*: obscure citation,
7| *SP69*: knew no
9| *DD, SP69*: trail
10| *SP69*: Red Rock communicates < > Wockensutter,
11| *SP69*: And Brady
14| *DD*: of Venus;
SP69: the holy principle of Venus,
15| *SP69*: Till desert
16| *DD*: #line indented in error# heinous.
SP69: heinous.

"She is a verity, else all is nit,"
Cried Brady, his faith quivering with outrage,
And saw the yellow-feathered pert pewit
Who flashed upon the acrid sea of sage.

Noon of the second day made his ascension,
The Brady marched emblistered at the goal
And to the pewit made offensive mention
Of words that scored the tablets of her soul.

"A simple shotgun with a choke were best,"
Says Brady, looking for a place to sit;
But, as long eluded of Burd Helen's breast,
He adds, "Could any human engine hit;

"For you again are Venus, I suppose;
I have your evidences of shape and feather;
And no man more impatient ever rose
To see you turn to nothing altogether;

"And though I had a miracle of salt
To sprinkle on your saucy tilt of tail,
I think I'd rather loose you in default
Than catch another mere obscene female."

17| *SP69*: "She was my Star, and now forbidden me?"
18| *SP69*: outrage;
19| *SP69*: Then heard and < > yellow pert pewee
20| *SP69*: flashed across the
22| *DD*: goal,
SP69: emblistered for the goal,
23| *SP69*: the pewee made
24| *DD*: of his soul.
26| *DD*: sit,
SP69: a spot to
27| *DD*: But as
SP69: But now eluded < > breast
28| *DD*: hit!
SP69: hit.
29| DD: suppose.
30| *DD*: evidence <> feather,
32| *DD*: altogether.
29–36| *SP69*: #contains the following three stanzas, replacing copy-text's final two stanzas#

"Venus you are, and we are long acquainted,
I know your signs in any shape and weather,
And even if mortal dared, I have not wanted
To harm a little bird that's false of feather.

"And look, Transfigured! How rightly you betray
To a right man your woman's beauty and bounty.
But I have given my oath. 'Tis sad to say,
My Wockensutter lies in Christian County.

"You smile? I melt—by virtue of my hot rock.
Hadn't we best say farewell altogether?
I'm balancing my years against my luck
Hoping I'll never wonder which or whether."

Prometheus in Straits

Garrulous gentlemen on a veranda,
Bibbers or non-bibbers of illicit potations,
Rehearsing the acta and the agenda
Of Republican or Democratic administrations,
I am not committed to taking memoranda
Culled from the lacunae of your cerebrations.

And now approaches the radiant band, all spinster,
White spirits weaving a delirious rhythm of chatter
Of picture galleries and of Westminster—
But my sad, alas, insensitivity is too utter,
I attend you as some tired jungle monster,
The parrots' bonnets are annulled by the tedium of their twitter.

To the library then and the masterpieces?
Not now, though I risk the damage of your inference;
For before your alterations respect ceases,
The glowing centers you have laid over with absurd circumference;

1| *SP63*, *SP69*: Windy gentlemen wreathing a long verandah,

2| *SP63*: With tongues at the moments between illicit potations
SP69: With tongues busy between illicit potations

3| *SP63*, *SP69*: Assailing all the acta and/or agenda

4| *SP63*, *SP69*: Of previous and/or present administrations:

5| *SP63*: Observe me carefully jotting no memoranda
SP69: Observe that I'm carefully jotting no memoranda

6| *SP63*, *SP69*: Lest I seem to identify your wits with your nation's. #*your* in italics in *SP63*#

7| *SP63*, *SP69*: But now approaches a radiant band all spinster #*SP69* has "the" for "a"#

8| *SP63*: Of spirits weaving delirious
SP69: Of spirits weaving delirious rhythms

9| *SP63*, *SP69*: About old picture < > and Westminster;

10| *SP63*, *SP69*: My sensitivity's out of this world, it is utter;

11| *F*: monster:
SP63, *SP69*: I wish I were a patriarch jungle monster;

12| *F*: their chatter.
SP63, *SP69*: bonnets, yes; but stop the twitter.

13| *F*: then to view the
SP63: the colleges then < > the modern masterpieces?
SP69: the colleges then, and the modern masterpieces?

14| *F*: inference,
SP63, *SP69*: now though

15| *F*: before their alterations < > ceases:
SP63, *SP69*: Before your explications respect ceases

16| *F*: The glowing < > circumference,
SP63: For the centers lost in so absurd
SP69: For centers lost in so absurd

Indeed you have undone them with exegesis,
And provoke me to a gesture not of deference.

Though I be Prometheus, my wits wandered
To bring my pious offices unto this people.
Where all must be the teachers, nullity is engendered,
My doctrine perishes crying for an ear that is simple,
The prophet is solicited before he has well thundered
And escapes with credit if he do not turn disciple.

My function concerns itself, however, with this planet,
My act is simple as an incident of vegetation,
I will go, then, to a streamside abounding with granite
Or gaunt place with no history nor human condition,
And, having unbuttoned myself, erect an altar on it
And comfort my knees with red bruises of prostration.

Plea in Mitigation

You have heard something muttered in my scorn:
"A little learning addleth this man's wit,
He crieth on our dogmas, Counterfeit!
And no man's bubble 'scapeth his sharp thorn.

17| *SP63*, *SP69*: You have only betrayed them by your exegesis
18| *SP63*, *SP69*: to gestures
19| *F*: be Prometheus my
SP63, *SP69*: be Prometheus my mind may have wandered
20| *SP63*: offices to this people;
SP69: In bringing my < > offices to this people;
21| *F*: teachers nullity
SP63: be teachers nullity < > engendered
SP69: be teachers < > engendered
22| *SP63*, *SP69*: ear which is simple;
25| *F*: itself however with
SP63: At least my < > itself with < > planet
SP69: At least my < > itself with your planet
26| *SP63*, *SP69*: And the due distinctions of faith and fact and fiction; #*SP69* omits *the*#
27| *F*: go then to
SP63, *SP69*: go somewhere by a
28| *SP63*, *SP69*: And but little human history and dereliction;
29| *F*: And having < > myself erect
SP63: To the Unknown Man I will raise < > altar upon it
SP69: To the Man Unknown I will raise < > altar upon it
30| *SP63*: with bruises < > genuflection.
SP69: And practice my < > with bruises of genuflection.

Title| *F*: Ego
3| *F*: dogmas Counterfeit!
4| *F*: thorn;

"Nor he respecteth duly our tall steeple,
But solitary poring on his book,
Heareth our noise and hardly offereth look,
Nor liveth neighborly with these the people."

With reason, friends, I am complained upon,
Who am a headstrong man, sentenced from birth
To love unusual gods beyond all earth,
And the easy gospels bruited hither and yon.

So I bring hurt upon mine own sweet kin,
And on my scholars, the young simple snails,
Treading their tumuli to holy grails;
I make reproach, then my deep grief sets in.

But, friends! acquit me of that stain of pride:
Much has been spoken solemnly together,
And you have heard my heart, so answer whether
I am so proud a fool, and godless beside.

Sages and friends, too often have you seen us
Deep in the midnight conclave as we used;
For my part, reverently were you perused;
No rank and primacy being hatched between us;

For my part, much beholden to you all,
Giving a little and receiving more;
Learning had stuffed this head with but lean lore
Betwixt the front bone and the occipital;

Anatomy, that doled my dubious features,
Had housed within me, close to my breastbone,
My demon, always clamoring, Up, Begone,

6| *F*: But in his pride turning from book to book
11| *F*: earth
15| *F*: grails:
16–17| *F*: reproach, and then these griefs begin. // For no man loves to seem so small of grace, / And I could wish me too born dull, born blind, / If I might not estrange my gentle kind, / Nor brag, nor run a solitary race. // But
17| *F*: Friends! come acquit
19| *F*: heart; so
24| *F*: rank or primacy
31| *F*: clamoring Up

Pursue your gods faster than most of creatures!

And if an alien, hideously at feud
With those my generation, I have reason
To think to salve the fester of my treason:
A seven of friends exceeds much multitude.

Tom, Tom, the Piper's Son

Grim in my little black coat as the sleazy beetle,
And gone of hue,
Lonely, a man reputed for softening little,
Loving few—

Mournfully going where men assemble, unfriended, pushing
With laborious wares,
And glaring with little grey eyes at whom I am brushing,
Who would with theirs—

Full of my thoughts as I trudge here and trundle yonder,
Eyes on the ground,
Tricked by white birds or tall women into no wonder,
And no sound—

Yet privy to great dreams, and secret in vainglory,
And hot and proud,
And poor and bewildered, and longing to hear my own story
Rehearsed aloud—

How I have passed, involved in these chances and choices,
By certain trees

32–33| *F*: creatures; // So I take not the vomit where they do, / Comporting downwards to the general breed; / I have run further, matching your heat and speed, / And tracked the Wary Fugitive with you; // And
33| *F*: alien, miserably at

6| *F, SP69a*: To sell my wares,

10| *PE*: ground
11| *F, SP69a*: wonder
MS*SP45*: Tricked even #last word crossed out# by white #last word inserted above# birds < > women to no wonder
SP45: #identical to MS reading#
PE: by bird-flights or women to no wonder
17| *F*: How I passed

Whose tiny attent auricles receive the true voices
Of the wordless breeze—

And against me the councils of spirits were not then darkened
Who thereby house,
As I set my boots to the path beneath them, and hearkened
To the talking boughs—

How one said, "This ambulant worm, he is strangely other
Than they suppose"—
But one, "He was sired by his father and dammed by his mother,
And acknowledges those"—

And then: "Nay, nay—this man is a changeling, and knows not—
This was a Prince
From a far great kingdom—and should return, but goes not—
Long years since"—

But like a King I was subject to a King's condition,
And I marched on,
Not testing at eavesdrop the glory of my suspicion,
And the talkers were gone—

And duly appeared I on the very clock-throb appointed
In the litten room,
Nor was hailed with that love that leaps to the Heir Anointed:
"Hush, hush, he is come!"

Old Man Playing with Children

A discreet householder exclaims on the grandsire
In warpaint and feathers, with fierce grandsons and axes,
Dancing around a backyard fire of boxes,
"Watch grandfather, he'll set the house on fire."

21| MS*SP*45, *SP*45, *PE*: council
27| MS*SP*45, *SP*45, *PE*: mother
29| MS*SP*45, *SP*45, *PE*: changeling and
37| MS*SP*45, *SP*45, *PE*: appeared I at the
39| *F*: leaps for the
40| MS*SP*45: hush #comma inserted following last word#

1| *F*: The discreet
2| MS*SP*45, *SP*45, *PE, SP*63, *SP*69: axes
3| *F*: boxes:
MS*SP*45, *SP*45, *PE, SP*63, *SP*69: round < > boxes:

But I will unriddle for you the thought of his mind,
An old one you cannot open with conversation.
What animates those thin legs in risky motion?
Mixes the snow on the head with snow on the wind?

"Grandson, grandsire. We are equally boy and boy.
Do not offer me your reclining-chair and slippers
With tedious old women talking in wrappers.
This life is not good but in danger and in joy.

"It is you who are elder to these and younger to me
That are penned as slaves by your properties and causes
And never walk out of your shaped insupportable houses,
And shamefully, when boys shout, go in and flee.

"God forgive me, I know too well your middling ways,
Having taken care and performed ignominies unreckoned
Between the first brief childhood and the brief second,
But I will be more honorable in these days."

Captain Carpenter

Captain Carpenter rose up in his prime
Put on his pistols and went riding out
But had got wellnigh nowhere at that time
Till he fell in with ladies in a rout.

It was a pretty lady and all her train
That played with him so sweetly but before

7| MS*SP*45, *SP*45, *PE*, *SP*63, *SP*69: animates the thin
10| MS*SP*45, *SP*45, *PE*, *SP*63, *SP*69: offer your reclining-chair
11| MS*SP*45: women #followed by two or three words illegibly blotted out# talking
12| *F*: is too good but for danger and for joy.
13| MS*SP*45, *SP*45, *PE*, *SP*63, *SP*69: you the elder
14| MS*SP*45, *SP*45, *PE*, *SP*63, *SP*69: by properties
15| *F*: houses
MS*SP*45, *SP*45: walk from your < > houses
PE, *SP*63: walk from your insupportable houses
*SP*69: walk from your insupportable houses.
16| *SP*69: Shamefully < > shout, you turn and
17| MS*SP*45, *SP*45, *PE*, *SP*63, *SP*69: "May God < > know your

F: #alternate lines indented#

An hour she'd taken a sword with all her main
And twined him of his nose for evermore.

Captain Carpenter mounted up one day
And rode straightway into a stranger rogue
That looked unchristian but be that as may
The Captain did not wait upon prologue.

But drew upon him out of his great heart
The other swung against him with a club
And cracked his two legs at the shinny part
And let him roll and stick like any tub.

Captain Carpenter rode many a time
From male and female took he sundry harms
He met the wife of Satan crying "I'm
The she-wolf bids you shall bear no more arms."

Their strokes and counters whistled in the wind
I wish he had delivered half his blows
But where she should have made off like a hind
The bitch bit off his arms at the elbows.

And Captain Carpenter parted with his ears
To a black devil that used him in this wise
O Jesus ere his threescore and ten years
Another had plucked out his sweet blue eyes.

Captain Carpenter got up on his roan
And sallied from the gate in hell's despite
I heard him asking in the grimmest tone
If any enemy yet there was to fight?

8| *F*: forevermore
9| *F*: mounted another day
10| *F*: And straightway rode into a surly rogue
14| MS*SP*45: other #next word crossed out and replaced above by# swung
19| *F*: And met
22| *F*: I would he
25| F: Captain
26| *F*: a surly rogue that
28| *F*: had pinched out
30| *F*: gate for hell's
32| *F*: enemies < > there were to

"To any adversary it is fame
If he risk to be wounded by my tongue
Or burnt in two beneath my red heart's flame
Such are the perils he is cast among.

"But if he can he has a pretty choice
From an anatomy with little to lose
Whether he cut my tongue and take my voice
Or whether it be my round red heart he choose."

It was he neatest knave that ever was seen
Stepping in perfume from his lady's bower
Who at this word put in his merry mien
And fell on Captain Carpenter like a tower.

I would not knock old fellows in the dust
But there lay Captain Carpenter on his back
His weapons were the old heart in his bust
And a blade shook between rotten teeth alack.

The rogue in scarlet and grey soon knew his mind
He wished to get his trophy and depart
With gentle apology and touch refined
He pierced him and produced the Captain's heart.

God's mercy rest on Captain Carpenter now
I thought him Sirs an honest gentleman
Citizen husband soldier and scholar enow
Let jangling kites eat of him if they can.

But God's deep curses follow after those
That shore him of his goodly nose and ears
His legs and strong arms at the two elbows
And eyes that had not watered seventy years.

The curse of hell upon the sleek upstart
Who got the Captain finally on his back

33| *F*: "Is there an adversary drunk with fame
34| *F*: Who will risk
36| *F*: These are
43| *F*: Who on this
47| *F*: the stout heart
62| *F*, MS*SP45*, *SP45*, *PE*, *SP63*, *SP69*: That got

And took the red red vitals of his heart
And made the kites to whet their beaks clack clack.

These Winters

Time was when the gods we gentlemen deride
Visited us with winters that were cold;
And I could assist at a thousand stories told
Of black turned white, and flood solidified
(All but the red, which was at early tide),

And of our smoky breath that stained the air
As we slipped like roes between the earth and the sky
And, out of ourselves with glory, made outcry;
But the little devils of sense were frozen where
There was such purity of atmosphere.

And were we ever driven into house?
We were the brave who would be purified
And a great weather was emptied on our pride;
But weather or we have changed; for we make mows
At the present gods, and say Where Nows, Where Nows,

And are diverted in our tepid ease
With asking if the gods, as were are told,
Will blot the sun with such a pall of cold
That gentlemen pink and slippered even as these
Shall dance like locusts on the winter breeze.

Old Mansion (*SP*45)

As an intruder I trudged with careful innocence
To mask in decency a meddlesome stare,
Passing the old house often on its eminence,
Exhaling my foreign weed on its weighted air.

Subtitle| *SP*69: (*After Henry James*)
2| *F*, *CF*: mask decently a quite meddlesome
MS*SP*45: mask decently #last word crossed out and replaced above by two words# in decency a quiet #last word crossed out# meddlesome

Here age seemed newly imaged for the historian
After his monstrous chateaux on the Loire,
A beauty not for depicting by old vulgarian
Reiterations which gentle readers abhor.

Each time of seeing I absorbed some other feature
Of a house whose annals in no wise could be brief
Nor ignoble; for it expired as sweetly as Nature,
With her tinge of oxidation on autumn leaf.

It was a Southern manor. One need hardly imagine
Towers, white monoliths, or even ivied walls;
But sufficient state if its peacock *was* a pigeon;
Where no courts kept, but grave rites and funerals.

Indeed, not distant, possibly not external
To the property, were tombstones, where the catafalque
Had carried their dead; and projected a note too charnel
But for the honeysuckle on its intricate stalk.

Stability was the character of its rectangle
Whose line was seen in part and guessed in part
Through trees. Decay was the tone of old brick and shingle.
Green blinds dragging frightened the watchful heart

To assert, "Your mansion, long and richly inhabited,
Its exits and entrances suiting the children of men,
Will not for ever be thus, O man, exhibited,
And one had best hurry to enter it if one can."

6| *F*: the Loire;—
8–13| *SP63*, *SP69*: Reiterations that gentle < > abhor. // It < > One hardly imagines
9| *CF*: seeing, I
11| *F*: ignoble. For
14| *SP63*, *SP69*: Towers, arcades, or forbidding fortress walls;
15| *SP63*, *SP69*: state though its peacocks now were pigeons;
16| *F*: courts held, but
17| *F*, *CF*: (Indeed
20| *F*, *CF*: stalk.)
24| *CF*: blinds, dragging, frightened
SP63, *SP69*: Green shutters dragging
25| *F*: assert: "Your
SP63, *SP69*: assert: Your
26| *F*: man,
SP63, *SP69*: Its porches and bowers suiting
28| *SP63*, *SP69*: if one can.

And at last, with my happier angel's own temerity,
Did I clang their brazen knocker against the door,
To beg their dole of a look, in simple charity,
Or crumbs of legend dropping from their great store.

But it came to nothing—and may so gross denial
Which has been deplored with a beating of the breast
Never shorten the tired historian, loyal
To acknowledge defeat and discover a new quest—

The old mistress was ill, and sent my dismissal
By one even more wrappered and lean and dark
Than that warped concierge and imperturbable vassal
Who bids you begone from her master's Gothic park.

Emphatically, the old house crumbled; the ruins
Would litter, as already the leaves, this petted sward;
And no annalist went in to the lords or the peons;
The antiquary would finger the bits of shard.

But on retreating I saw myself in the token,
How loving from my foreign weed the feather curled
On the languid air; and I went with courage shaken
To dip, alas, into some unseemlier world.

Inland City

She lies far inland, and no stick nor stone of her
Ever has looked on the sounding sea,

29| *F*: last with < > temerity
CF: temerity
30| *F*: door
32| *F*: of history dropping
SP63, *SP69*: of wisdom dropping
33| *F*: may such gross denial,
CF: may such gross
34| *F*: deplored duly with < > breast,
CF: deplored duly with
36| *F*: quest.—
SP63, *SP69*: quest.
40| MS*SP45*: from his master's
P*SP45*: from his #last word crossed out and replaced above by# her master's
SP63, *SP69*: Who had bid me begone
43| *F*: lord
CF: But no < > lord
MS*SP45*: But #first word crossed out and replaced above by# And no
44| *F*: would gather the
45| *F*, *CF*: retreating, I
46| *SP63*, *SP69*: my dying weed

F: #alternate lines indented#

And how should she speak of her swift barks and roadways
And white sloops crowding to lift and be free?

"Ye towers and steeples, and belfries and crosses,
Toll for the doomed ships passing to sea.
But ye walls and gateposts, and ye halls and gardens,
Moor in my little boats vigilantly!"

Philomela

Procne, Philomela, and Itylus,
Your names are liquid, your improbable tale
Is recited in the classic numbers of the nightingale.
Ah, but our numbers are not felicitous,
It goes not liquidly for us.

Perched on a Roman ilex, and duly apostrophized,
The nightingale descanted unto Ovid;
She has even appeared to the Teutons, the swilled and gravid;
At Fontainebleau it may be the bird was gallicized;
Never was she baptized.

To England came Philomela with her pain,
Fleeing the hawk her husband; querulous ghost,
She wanders when he sits heavy on his roost,
Utters herself in the original again,
The untranslatable refrain.

Not to these shores she came! this other Thrace,
Environ barbarous to the royal Attic;
How could her delicate dirge run democratic,
Delivered in a cloudless boundless public place
To an inordinate race?

3| *F*: her sails in harbor,
5| *F*: "Ye steeples and towers, and
6| *F*: sea;

#MS*SP*45 does not contain this poem#
4| *F*: (Ah < > are less felicitous,
5| *F*: us.)
6| *F*: ilex and < > apostrophized
8| P*SP*45: swelled #altered to# swilled
12| *F*: husband. Querulous
20| *F*: To a hypermuscular race?

I pernoctated with the Oxford students once,
And in the quadrangles, in the cloisters, on the Cher,
Precociously knocked at antique doors ajar,
Fatuously touched the hems of the hierophants,
Sick of my dissonance.

I went out to Bagley Wood, I climbed the hill;
Even the moon had slanted off in a twinkling,
I heard the sepulchral owl and a few bells tinkling,
There was no more villainous day to unfulfil,
The diuturnity was still.

Up from the darkest wood where Philomela sat,
Her fairy numbers issued. What then ailed me?
My ears are called capacious but they failed me,
Her classics registered a little flat!
I rose, and venomously spat.

Philomela, Philomela, lover of song,
I am in despair if we may make us worthy,
A bantering breed sophistical and swarthy;
Unto more beautiful, persistently more young
Thy fabulous provinces belong.

26| *F*: hill,
31| *F*: sat
SP69: Out of the darkness where
32| *F*: issued—what
33| *F*: ears called
37| *F*: I have despaired if
38| *F*: This bantering < > and earthy;
39| *SP45*, *PE*, *SP63*, *SP69*: young,

TWO GENTLEMEN IN BONDS

The Innocent Doves

Vision by Sweetwater

Go and ask Robin to bring the girls over
To Sweetwater, said my Aunt; and that was why
It was like a dream of ladies sweeping by
The willows, clouds, deep meadowgrass, and the river.

Robin's sisters and my Aunt's lily daughter
Laughed and talked, and tinkled light as wrens
If there were a little colony all hens
To go walking by the steep turn of Sweetwater.

Let them alone, dear Aunt, just for one minute
Till I go fishing in the dark of my mind:
Where have I seen before, against the wind,
These bright virgins, robed and bare of bonnet,

Flowing with music of their strange quick tongue
And adventuring with delicate paces by the stream—
Myself a child, old suddenly at the scream
From one of the white throats which it hid among?

Eclogue (*SP*45)

JANE SNEED BEGAN IT: My poor John, alas,
Ten years ago, pretty it was in a ring
To run as boys and girls do in the grass—
At that time leap and hollo and skip and sing
Came easily to pass.

4| *SP*69: and river.
6| VMS: tinkled light #last word inserted#

#speaker identifications in *LD* are not in uppercase#

1| *F, LD, TGB*: alas!
3| MS*SP*45: run and #last word crossed out#
4| *F, LD, TGB*: time, leap
5–11| *SP*69: pass. // JOHN

And precious little innocents were we.
Said a boy, "Now shall we let her be the fox?"
Or a girl, "Now which of you will climb the tree?"
We were quick-foot the deer, strong-back the ox,
We were the busy bee.

JOHN BLACK SAID: I'll interpret what you mean.
Our infant selves played happily with our others,
The cunning me and mine came not between
Which like a sword is, O sweethearts and brothers
Numberless, who have seen.

JANE SNEED: I tell you what I used to do.
For joy I used to run by river or wood
To see with what speed all came trooping too;
Those days I could not quit you if I would,
Nor yet quit me could you.

JOHN BLACK RETURNED: But now, Jane, it appears
We are sly travelers, keeping good lookout
Against the face whose ravage cries for tears;
Old friends, ill met; and supposing I call out,
"Draw nigh, friend of these years"—

Before he think of any reason why,
The features of that man resolve and burn
For one long look—but then the flame must die.
The cold hearts in us mortally return,
We must not fructify.

JANE SNEED SAID BITTERLY: Why, John, you are right.
We were spendthrifts of joy when we were young,
But we became usurious, and in fright
Conceived that such a waste of days was wrong
For marchers unto night.

6| *F, LD*: we!
9| *F, LD, TGB*: deer, strong-heart the
10| *F, LD, TGB*: Business-man the bee.
13| *F, LD*: between,
19| *F, LD*: days, I < > would!
TGB: days, I < > would;
20| *F, TGB*: me, could
21| *F, LD*: appears,
25| *F, LD*: Draw < > years!—
SP69: of those years"—
30| *F, LD, TGB*, MS*SP45*: We may not

JOHN BLACK SAID: Yes, exactly, that was when
It happened. For Time involved us: in his toils
We learned to fear. And every day since then
We are mortals teasing for immortal spoils,
Desperate women and men.

JANE SNEED CONSENTED: It was nothing but this.
Love suffereth long, is kind—but not in fear.
For boys run banded, and simple sweethearts kiss,
Till in one day the dream of Death appear—
Then metamorphosis.

JOHN BLACK SAID: To explain mistrust and wars,
Theogony has a black witch with hell's broth;
Or a preposterous marriage of fleshless stars;
Or the Fiend's own naked person; or God wroth
Fingering his red scars.

And philosophy, an art of equal worth,
Tells of a flaw in the firmament—spots in the sun—
A Third Day's error when the upheaving earth
Was young and prime—a Fate reposed upon
The born before their birth.

JANE SNEED WITH GRIM LIPS MOCKED HIM: Who can tell—
Not I, not you—about those mysteries!
Something, John Black, came flapping out of hell
And wrought between us, and the chasm is
Digged, and it digged it well.

JOHN BLACK IN DEPRECATION SAID: Be sure
That love has suffered a most fatal eclipse;
All brotherhoods, filialities insecure;
Lovers compounding honey on their lips
With deep doubts to endure.

44| *F, LD*: Till, on one day, the face of < > appear,
TGB: Till on one
45| *F, LD*: metamorphosis!
55| *F, TGB*: born, before
57| *F*: about these mysteries!
60| *F*: Digged—and

JANE SNEED SIGHED SLOWLY: I suppose it stands
Just so. Yet I can picture happiness—
Still faithful lovers wander in some lands
Who when Night stalks, the dark and fathomless,
Consort their little hands;

And well, John Black, those darkened lovers may,
For hands hold much of heat in little storage,
And eyes are flickerless torches good as day;
The flame of each to the other's flame cries Courage!
Soon heart to heart slide they;

So unafraid they keep the whole night through,
Till the sun of a sudden glowing through the bushes
They wake and laugh, their eyes again are blue,
They run to the fields, and beautiful the thrushes,
Fabulous the dew.

JOHN BLACK'S THE LAST SAY THEN: O innocent dove,
This is a dream. We lovers mournfully
Exchange our bleak despairs. We are one part love
And nine parts bitter thought. As well might be
Beneath ground as above.

66| *F, TGB*: SNEED SAID SLOWLY
MS*SP*45: SNEED SAID SLOWLY #last two words crossed out and replaced by two words# SIGHED SLOWLY
68| *F, TGB*: Still wander lovers in the fairy lands
*PE, SP*63: Perhaps there wander lovers in
69| *F, TGB*: Who, when stalks Night the
MS*SP*45: Who, when < > stalks the
*PE, SP*63, *SP*69: when Night comes, when it is fathomless,
71| *PE, SP*63: well, John Black the darkened
*SP*69: well, John Black, the
73| *PE, SP*63, *SP*69: The eyes are almost torches < > day,
74| *PE, SP*63, *SP*69: And one flame to the other flame < > Courage,
75| *F*: they.
*PE, SP*63, *SP*69: When heart
76| *F, TGB*: Thus unafraid
*PE, SP*63: So they keep unafraid the
75–81| *SP*69: they; // JOHN
77| *F, TGB*: brushes,
79| *F, TGB*: and apprehend the
PE: And listen! Are those not the doves, the thrushes?
80| *F, TGB*: And print the fairy dew.
*PE, SP*63: Look there! the golden dew.

Piazza Piece

—I am a gentleman in a dustcoat trying
To make you hear. Your ears are soft and small
And listen to an old man not at all,
They want the young men's whispering and sighing.
But see the roses on your trellis dying
And hear the spectral singing of the moon;
For I must have my lovely lady soon.
I am a gentleman in a dustcoat trying.

—I am a lady young in beauty waiting
Until my truelove comes, and then we kiss.
But what grey man among the vines is this
Whose words are dry and faint as in a dream?
Back from my trellis, sir, before I scream!
I am a lady young in beauty waiting.

Moments of Minnie

We must not honor girls of Minnie's kind
Whose charms are more endearing than her mind.
We are the Christian moralists we are.

Yet it oppressed me when an evil star
Had thralled so lazy and beautiful a creature
And scared and misshapen her most tender feature.
The mouth-corners were pulled down, and the outleaning
Of her soft lips drew back their gallant meaning.
Pain is hideous—it pinched the vaulted line
To a flatness terrible, yet no doing of mine;
And pain is primitive—it undid words
And left her no more speech than ill-bred birds.

6| *F*: moon—
7| *F*, MS*SP*45, *SP*45, *PE*, *SP*63, *SP*69: soon,

1| *SP*69: honor a girl
2| *F*: mind;
*SP*69: mind,
3–4| *SP*69: If we are the casuists we think we are, / #no stanza break# Yet
6–7| *SP*69: feature. // Mouth-corners
9| *SP*69: hideous; it
10| *SP*69: mine.
11| *SP*69: primitive; it
12| *SP*69: than tuneless birds.
13| *SP*69: She uttered

For she uttered and I heard that which could not
Be foreseen, nor yet afterwards forgot:
Oh, Oh, Oh! Not a word, not a name,
And no tears flowed, yet wry and dry it came
Till I trembled—and I fled—I had to find
Distance for a contagion-catching mind.

Then I washed my mind with its old memories.
For it was better to reconstitute the trees
And the bridegroom scarlet bird of April crying
To his brown one embowered, and the flying
Mirth that bubbled off this woman's mouth
From secret wells abundant as the South
Which spilled their joy too thickly for sharp speech.
Ah, Ah, Ah! she sighed deeply, and each
Breathing was a new Ah! until I heard
What never issues on a lettered word.

Husband Betrayed

And so he called her Pigeon,
Saying to himself, "She flutters walking
And in sweet monotone she twitters talking."
Nothing was said of her religion.

There was wood-wildness in her—say a dove.
For doves are pigeons not domesticated
And whoso catches one is soon frustrated,
Expecting quick return of love.

14| *SP69*: afterward
15| *SP69*: Oh, Oh, Oh! Not a word, and not
17| *SP69*: Till I trembled, and I fled, I
19| *SP69*: I wash my mind of those old
20| *SP69*: Better now to
22| *SP69*: embowered; then the
25| *F*: speech:
SP69: thickly to be speech.
26| *SP69*: she murmured deeply
27| *SP69*: Breath < > Ah! and I had heard

Title| *MQR:* Farmer Husband
1| *F:* He said, "I'll have to call her
MQR: Foremost farmer in his region,
2| *F:* And me the fancier. For she
MQR: He said at once to himself, "She
3| *MQR:* in pure monotone
4| *MQR:* He could not think it was religion.
5| *MQR:* But there was character in her, say a dove,
6| *MQR:* dove is bird not yet domesticated
7| *MQR:* one may be frustrated

At all events she had a snowy bosom
And trod so mincingly that you would say
She only wanted wings to fly away,
Easy and light and lissome.

She pecked her food with ravished cries,
She sunned her bosom by the wall in the morning,
Preening prettily in the sun and turning
In her birdwise.

But there was heavy dudgeon
When he that should have married him a woman
To sit and drudge and serve him as was common
Discovered he had wived a pigeon.

Miller's Daughter

I have seen, O, the miller's daughter
And on her neck a coral necklace lies
And yellow glint of corn is in her eyes
Which are a blue stillwater.

The strange miller hath strange daughter
For he is pink and painfully doth walk
And life demandeth of them little talk
Beside the small millwater.

At candlelight I hear she goes
And on a bed of snow like snow she lies
Yet warmer much and lids her sleepy eyes.
Long lies the tall white tower which uprose.

9| *MQR:* In any event she had her share of bosom
10| *MQR:* And stepped so
11| *MQR:* away
13| *MQR:* with ravished cries
14| *MQR:* And took herself outside the house each morning
17| *MQR:* But never was there dudgeon
18| *MQR:* he, who could have
19| *MQR:* To sew and cook and < > common,
20| *MQR:* Instructed her, and named her "Pigeon."

Title| *F*: The Miller's Daughter

At daylight some vague bird
Tinkles his little bell and she comes down
Coiling her hair as queens would coil a crown.
Yet queens are too absurd.

And so am I, poor bookish hind,
Who come by fabulous roads around the hill
To bring the famous daughter of the mill
No combs to sell, no corn to grind,

But too much pudding in my head
Of learned characters and scraps of love
Which O that she might peck at (dainty dove!)
And words vain to be said.

What then to do but stare—
A learned eye of our most Christian nation
And foremost philosophical generation—
At primary chrome of hair,

Astronomied Oes of eyes
And the white moons I tremble to behold
(More than my books did shake me, or a tale told)
And all her parts likewise.

She dwells beside a water,
She counts the bins and ties the sacks pardee
And cleaves my closest thought, and is to me
A long-dreamt miller's daughter.

Blue Girls

Twirling your blue skirts, traveling the sward
Under the towers of your seminary,
Go listen to your teachers old and contrary
Without believing a word.

16| *F*: absurd,
33| *F*: water
34| *F*: And counts
36| *F*: A most rare miller's

Tie the white fillets then about your lustrous hair
And think no more of what will come to pass
Than bluebirds that go walking on the grass
And chattering on the air.

Practice your beauty, blue girls, before it fail;
And I will cry with my loud lips and publish
Beauty which all our power shall never establish,
It is so frail.

For I could tell you a story which is true:
I know a lady with a terrible tongue,
Blear eyes fallen from blue,
All her perfections tarnished—yet it is not long
Since she was lovelier than any of you.

Her Eyes

To a woman that I knew
Were eyes of an extravagant hue:
Viz., china blue.

Those I wear upon my head
Are sometimes green and sometimes red,
I said.

My mother's eyes are wet and blear,
My little sister's are not clear,
Poor silly dear.

It must be given to but few,
A pair of eyes so utter blue
And new.

5| MS*SP*45, *SP*45, *PE*, *SP*63, *SP*69: your hair
13| *TGB*, MS*SP*45, *SP*45, *PE*, *SP*63, *SP*69: true; #emended to VMS reading# true: #see Emendations#
14| *SP*69: a woman with
16| *TGB*: tarnished—and yet #emended to # tarnished—yet #see Emendations#

2| *SP*69: hue,
3| *SP*69: They were china
12| MS*SP*45, *SP*45, *PE*, *SP*63, *SP*69: new;

Where does she keep them from this glare
Of the monstrous sun and the wind's flare
Without any wear;

And were they never in the night
Poisoned by artificial light
Much too bright;

And had this splendid beast no heart
That boiled with tears and baked with smart
The ocular part?

I'll have no business with those eyes,
They are not kind, they are not wise,
Painted pigsties.

A woman shooting such blue flame
I apprehend will get some blame
On her good name.

Parting, Without a Sequel

She has finished and sealed the letter
At last, which he so richly has deserved,
With characters venomous and hatefully curved,
And nothing could be better.

But even as she gave it
Saying to the blue-capped functioner of doom,
"Into his hands," she hoped the leering groom
Might somewhere lose and leave it.

Then all the blood
Forsook the face. She was too pale for tears,

15| *SP*69: wear,
17| *SP*69:Stricken by
18| *SP*69: bright,
19| *SP*45, *PE*, *SP*63, *SP*69: had the splendid
24| MS*SP*45, *SP*45: They are lies. *PE*, *SP*63, *SP*69: They are two great lies.
26| MS*SP*45: Careful may be, but will get blame

5| *AM*: it,
10| *AM*: face; she < > too white for

Observing the ruin of her younger years.
She went and stood

Under her father's vaunting oak
Who kept his peace in wind and sun, and glistened
Stoical in the rain; to whom she listened
If he spoke.

And now the agitation of the rain
Rasped his sere leaves, and he talked low and gentle
Reproaching the wan daughter by the lintel;
Ceasing, and beginning again.

Away went the messenger's bicycle,
His serpent's track went up the hill forever,
And all the time she stood there hot as fever
And cold as any icicle.

Hilda

I.

The dearest one was she to whom it fell
To walk and wear her beauty as in a play
To be enacted nobly on a great day;
And stormily we approved the bosom-swell
And the tones tinkling. For her touch and smell
I cast bright flowers, till garlanded she stood
Scared with her splendor, as in the sight of God
A pale girl curtseying with an asphodel.

No, No, she answered in the extreme of fear,
I cannot. On the dropping of each petal
Rode one that disrespected both the little

11| *AM*: Beholding the < > years;
18| *AM*: gentle,
20| MS*SP45*, *SP45*, *PE*, *SP63*, *SP69*: Ceasing and

1| *SP63*, *SP69*: dearest was the one to
4| *SP63*, *SP69*: bosom-swell,
6| *SP63*, *SP69*: I brought bright
10| *SP63*, *SP69*: of those petals
11| *SP63*, *SP69*: Rode the Estranger, scorning their sweet mettles,

Bloom and lady; him she was looking at,
Not me the praiser; she was too honest for that,
I was such earth that whispered in her ear.

II.

The loveliest are perished. And now uprise
Ghosts in this garden, that hollow and clamorous
Come as blanched lepers crying, "Do not spurn us,"
Ringing in my ears, wetting my eyes,
The obsequious phantoms and disbodied sighs.
Soon they are frightened, and go fast; a smoke
Which clung about my quincebushes, then broke,
And while I look is smeared upon the skies.

O Hilda, proudest of the ladies gone,
Wreathing my roses with blue bitter dust,
Think not I would reject you, for I must
Weep for your nakedness and no retinue
And leap up as of old to follow you—
But flesh hath monstrous gravity, as of stone.

In Mr. Minnit's House

Mr. Mortimer Minnit
Owned the house and all in it,
Among whose far-famed treasures
Be these our present pleasures:

A poor lady daughter
Who was weak as water,

12| *SP63*, *SP69*: Blossoms and women too; him she looked at,
13| *SP69*: me who praised; she
14| *SP63*, *SP69*: was a clod mumbling, to catch her

Title| *HM*: Ghosts
HM #entire sonnet in italics#
1| *SP63*, *SP69*: The perished were the fairest. And
2| *SP63*, *SP69*: Particular ghosts, who hollow
5| *SP63*, *SP69*: Obsequious
6| *SP63*, *SP69*: frightened and
9| *SP63*, *SP69*: But Hilda! proudest, lingering last alone,
12| *SP63*, *SP69*: retinue,
13| *SP63*, *SP69*: you;
14| *SP63*, *SP69*: But what I wear is flesh; it weighs like stone.

A granddaughter and grandson
And whatever description of fun
They might manage to find
With either matter or mind;
Anne with her bird,
Her bright yellow bird,
And Mortimer III
With a cat that purred.

These children played all mornings; played
But remembered to be afraid
That if their grandfather heard
He might say the sharp word
To stop their running and yelling
And their hurting and telling
And put them to their spelling.

O but he was fierce,
His eyes could pierce.

Whereupon,
In the course of their fun,
They played always very gently
Till one morning—evidently
When the snow came down too whitely
And too thoroughly if politely
Covered the earth and drove them in
And predisposed them unto sin—
They became too rude and naughty,
Not quiet as grown-up folk and haughty,
They made faces, pinched, and balked,
When they might have sat and talked,
And they quarreled,
Not carolled.

Quit touching by bird,
That's my yellow bird,
Quit stroking my cat,
Can't you hear that,
I don't care, I don't care,
Don't you dare, don't you dare.

All that they said we don't repeat
While Anne was stamping on both feet,
Till crimes involved, one after the other,
Bird and Tomcat, sister and brother,
And vile tragedy unrolled
In a progress threefold.

First. Mortimer took his sister's hair,
Which was most beautiful yellow hair,
Grabbed it in both his fists
And turned it with horrible twists,
He pulled it very hard,
The cruel young blackguard,
He gave it such a raking
And he gave her such a shaking
She was aching and aching;
And his little sister Anne
Was still screaming as she ran
For comfort of the pale and sickly
Lady: O Mother, come quickly.

Second. Old Tom was too loyal,
With white whiskers and blood royal,
Eying the yellow bird
That twittered and stirred,
And his master with his hands
In his sister's yellow strands;
He leaped up on the table
As only a cat is able
And swung from the cage
To accomplish an outrage;
Seized that bird in his paws
And with teeth and sharp claws
Made her to sing no more
But to lie upon the floor
With her yellow feathers spattered
And her little pieces scattered.

Third. Mortimer was a proper villain
But young and not completely fallen.

When he saw the bird in slaughter
His eyes oozed with righteous water,
He caught up the hearthbroom
And chased the cat around the room
And through the hall and through the house
Exactly as Tom would chase a mouse,
Running harder and harder
To do a bloody murder
On an unspeakable wretch
Whom he could not catch.

But every quarrel
Must publish its own moral.
Mr. Minnit had an ear,
It could not help itself but hear
So great a noise; and now his roar
Contributed to make it more
Until it made it nothing; all
Must cease from theirs to hear his bawl.
They came listening in the hall,
The boy with broomstick, and his sister,
And his mother with none to assist her,
And climbed dutiful up the stair
To assemble at Mr. Minnit's chair;
Whose face was stern and pale
For all the world to quail.

Mr. Minnit was amazing
With his eyes blazing.

So tightdrawn was his cheek,
His jaws could hardly open and speak
As he heavily and slowly
And with rage and melancholy
Addressed Mortimer III:

What was a cat? What was a bird?
It mattered little as to these,
Their lives and deaths and destinies,
But hang a man as high as Haman

If he abused the smallest woman.
And he had infinitely rather
That both Mortimer and his father
Had not been born, than live till they
Should practice their unchivalry
Upon the slightest yellow hair
Of Anne, or Anne's mother there—
The trembling lady—and must Anne
By the harsh hand of any man
Come to be such another broken
Mouse of a woman, timid-spoken,
And never lift up her poor head
Between the rocking-chair and the bed?
O hideous if the tainted blood
Infect young Mortimer's manhood—
As for his father—

He stopped there
At Mortimer's most wondering stare;
Mortimer twitched and fumed;
Then the old man resumed:

As Mortimer III grew older
He would be both slier and bolder,
He would discover a number of ways
To torment some poor lady's days,
To taunt her with her pain,
To make her salt tears rain
Till the fountain drained itself dry
And scarce amounted to an eye,
And her hands eternally shook
Under the needle or the book,
And she turned color and fled
If a loud word was said,
Hiding herself in the closet
If she should even suppose it;
God help them, there would come no joy
Ever on earth from such a boy!

They expected Mr. Minnit
Would have resources infinite
To use this subject now he was in it.
But the tyrant of the town
Had weakened, and now he broke down;
He was too old to take any courage,
Would they go down and send up his porridge?
His age was on him, his voice not stout,
Would they please just get out?

And it was the first time Mortimer had
Seen the old eyes crying and sad.

Janet Waking (*SP*45)

Beautifully Janet slept
Till it was deeply morning. She woke then
And thought about her dainty-feathered hen,
To see how it had kept.

One kiss she gave her mother,
Only a small one gave she to her daddy
Who would have kissed each curl of his shining baby;
No kiss at all for her brother.

"Old Chucky, old Chucky!" she cried,
Running across the world upon the grass
To Chucky's house, and listening. But alas,
Her Chucky had died.

It was a transmogrifying bee
Came droning down on Chucky's old bald head
And sat and put the poison. It scarcely bled,
But how exceedingly

2| *F*: woke them
5| *PE*, *SP*63, *SP*69: mother.
10| *F*, *TGB*: Running on little pink feet upon
MS*SP*45: world #followed by word illegibly crossed out, possibly *on*#
14| *F*: on Chucky's bald old head
MS*SP*45: droning out #crossed out and replaced by# down

And purply did the knot
Swell with the venom and communicate
Its rigor! Now the poor comb stood up straight
But Chucky did not.

So there was Janet
Kneeling on the wet grass, crying her brown hen
(Translated far beyond the daughters of men)
To rise and walk upon it.

And weeping fast as she had breath
Janet implored us, "Wake her from her sleep!"
And would not be instructed in how deep
Was the forgetful kingdom of death.

Little Boy Blue

He rubbed his eyes and wound the silver horn.
Then the continuum was cracked and torn
With tumbling imps of music being born.

The blowzy sheep lethargic on the ground
Suddenly burned where no fire could be found
And straight up stood their fleeces every pound.

The old bellwether rose and rang his bell,
The seven-days' lambs went skipping and skipped well,
And Baa Baa Baa, the flock careered pellmell.

The yellow cows that milked the savory cud
Propped on the green grass or the yellow mud
Felt such a tingle in their lady blood,

19| *F*: rigor. Now
23| *F*: the prayers of

7| *NR*: The grim bellweather
10| *NR*: cud,
11| *NR*: mud,
12| *NR*: blood

They ran and tossed their hooves and horns of blue
And jumped the fence and gamboled kangaroo,
Divinely singing as they wandered Moo.

A plague on such a shepherd of the sheep
That careless boy with pretty cows to keep!
With such a burden I should never sleep.

But when his notes had run around the sky,
When they proceeded to grow faint and die,
He stuffed his horn with straw and put it by.

And when the legs were tired beneath the sheep
And there were spent and sleepy cows to keep,
He rubbed his eyes again and went to sleep.

Lady Lost

This morning, flew up the lane
A timid lady bird to our birdbath
And eyed her image dolefully as death;
This afternoon, knocked on our windowpane
To be let in from the rain.

And when I caught her eye
She looked aside, but as the clapping thunder
And sight of the whole earth blazing up like tinder
Looked in on us again most miserably,
Indeed as if she would cry.

So I will go out into the park and say,
"Who has lost a delicate brown-eyed lady

14| *NR*: kangaroo
15| *NR*: wandered, Moo.
16| *NR*: sheep,
19| *NR*: After his < > sky
20| *NR*: And then proceeded
21| *NR*: by;

1| MS*SP*45: morning flew
P*SP*45: morning, #comma inserted# flew
8| *F, LD*: tinder,
MS*SP*45, *SP*45, *PE*, *SP*63, *SP*69: whole world blazing
9| *SP*69: again so miserably
10| *SP*69: It was as

In the West End section? Or has anybody
Injured some fine woman in some dark way
Last night, or yesterday?

"Let the owner come and claim possession,
No questions will be asked. But stroke her gently
With loving words, and she will evidently
Return to her full soft-haired white-breasted fashion
And her right home and her right passion."

15| *F, LD*: night or
18| *F, LD*: words and
19| *F, LD*: Resume her

The Manliness of Men

Our Two Worthies (*SP*45)

All the here and all the there
Ring with the praises of the pair:
Jesus the Paraclete
And Saint Paul the Exegete.

Jesus proclaimed the truth.
Paul's missionary tooth
Shredded it fine, and made a paste,
No particle going to waste,
Kneaded it and caked it
And buttered it and baked it
(And indeed all but digested
While Jesus went to death and rested)
Into a marketable compound
Ready to lay on any wound,
Meet to prescribe to our distress
And feed unto our emptiness.

When the great captains die,
There is some faithful standing by
To whom the chieftain hands his sword.
Proud Paul received—a Word.

Title| *F*: The Two Worthies
2| *F*: pair,
9–11| MS*SP*45: caked it / (And indeed
16–17| *F*: feed into our emptiness. // And
this is how the pure Idea
Became our perfect panacea,
Both supernal and infernal
And external and internal.
What would the Originator have done
Without his Assisting One?
Would his truth have penetrated
If Paul had not fabricated? // When
TGB, FA, MS*SP*45:
And this is how the pure Idea
Became our perfect panacea,
Both external and internal
And supernal and infernal.
#the second quatrain is identical to *F*#
*PE, SP*63, *SP*69:
And this is how the Pure Idea
Became our perfect panacea,
Both external and internal
And supernal and infernal.
#the second stanza that is in *TGB, FA,* and
MS*SP*45 is not included# // When
17| *F, TGB, FA*: die

This was the man who, given his cause,
Gave constitution and by laws,
Distinguished pedagogue
Who invaded the synagogue
And in a little while
Was proselyting the Gentile.

But what would there have been for Paul
If the Source had finished all?
He blessed the mighty Paraclete
For needing him, to miss defeat,
He couldn't have done anything
But for his Captain spiriting.

He knew that he was competent
For any sort of punishment,
With his irresistible urge
To bare his back unto the scourge,
Teasing his own neck
In prodigious shipwreck;
Hunger and rats and gaol
Were mere detail.

Paul was every inch of him
Valiant as the Seraphim,
And all he went among
Confessed his marvelous tongue,
And Satan fearing the man's spell
Embittered smote the gates of Hell.

So he finished his fight
And he too went from sight.

And this is how the Pure Idea
Became our perfect panacea,
Both external and internal
And supernal and infernal.

29| *F*: the Paraclete
30–31| *F*: him to < > defeat. // He
46| *F*: hell
46–47| *TGB, SP63, SP69*: of Hell. #no stanza break# So
48–53| *F, TGB, FA*, MS*SP45*, *PE, SP63, SP69*: sight. / Then

Then let no cantankerous schism
Corrupt this our catechism
But one and all let us repeat:
Who then is Jesus?
He is our Paraclete.
And Paul, out of Tarsus?
He is our Exegete.

Dead Boy (*SP*45)

The little cousin is dead, by foul subtraction,
A green bough from Virginia's aged tree,
And none of the county kin like the transaction,
Nor some of the world of outer dark, like me.

A boy not beautiful, nor good, nor clever,
A black cloud full of storms too hot for keeping,
A sword beneath his mother's heart—yet never
Woman bewept her babe as this is weeping.

A pig with a pasty face, so I had said,
Squealing for cookies, kinned by poor pretense
With a noble house. But the little man quite dead,
I see the forebears' antique lineaments.

The elder men have strode by the box of death
To the wide flag porch, and muttering low send round

56–59| *F*: repeat:/ *Now is our Edifice complete./Who was the Architect?/Jesus the Paraclete./Who gave the plan effect?/Saint Paul the Exegete.*

Title| *SR*: The Dead Boy #alternate lines indented#
1| *SR*: is gone, by sad subtraction,
3| *SR*: And the county kin sit glowering on the
TGB: And neither the < > kin love the transaction
4–9| *SR*: And some < > me. // A pig < > face, I had long said,
5| *TGB*: He was not a beautiful boy, nor
9| *TGB*: face, I had always said.
10| *SR*: for cakes, and fixing his base pretense
11| *SR*: On a < > But here is the < > man dead,
MS*SP*45: dead, #comma inserted#
12| *SR*: And these are the very forbears' lineaments.
TGB: I can see

The bruit of the day. O friendly waste of breath!
Their hearts are hurt with a deep dynastic wound.

He was pale and little, the foolish neighbors say;
The first-fruits, saith the Preacher, the Lord hath taken;
But this was the old tree's late branch wrenched away,
Grieving the sapless limbs, the shorn and shaken.

Puncture (*SP*45)

Darkness was bad as weariness, till Grimes said,
"We've got to have a fire." But in that case
The match must sputter and the flame glare red
On nothing beautiful, and set no seal of grace
On any dead man's face.

And when the flames roared, when the sparks dartled
And quenched in the black sea that closed us round,
I looked at Grimes my dear comrade and startled
His look, blue-bright—and under it a wound
Which bled upon the ground.

"They got you? I have only lost a hat,
I would have sold the affair for three thin dimes,
But they have stuck your side. It must be looked at
And mended." "No, it's an old puncture," said Grimes,
"Which takes to bleeding sometimes."

"Why, Grimes, I never knew your mortal blood
Had wasted for my sake in scarlet streams,
And no word said. A curse on my manhood
If I knew anything! This is my luck which seems
Worse than my evillest dreams."

But when I would have comforted his white flesh
With ointment and flowing water, he said then,

15| *SR*: day;—O
MS*SP*45: the dead #last word crossed out and replaced by# day

20| *SR*: Aggrieving the < > limbs, all shorn
TGB: Aggrieving the

"Get away. Go work on the corpses if you wish,
Prop their heads up again, wrap their bones in,
For they were good pious men.

"But as for me I have the devil's desire
For delicate tobacco in my pipe, and leisure
To stretch my toes in comfort by this fire.
Amuse yourself then some way, find some pleasure
Sleeping, or digging a treasure."

I could not find it. It was too melancholy
Sitting by Grimes my fortress who reared his head
Breached in the left wall, and subsiding slowly
To the defunctive posture of the stained dead
That now not even bled.

I, not to weep then, like a desperado
Kicked on the carcasses of our enemies
To heave them into the darkness; but my bravado
Quailed in the scorn of Grimes; for even these
Were fit for better courtesies.

Blue blazed the eyes of Grimes in the old manner—
The flames of eyes which jewel the head of youth
Were strange in the leathery phiz of the old campaigner—
Smoke and a dry word crackled from his mouth
Which a cold wind ferried south.

Semi-Centennial

When the green army battled and drove North
The black army, one old fugitive crept forth
From his hole beside the hearth, wearied a little
With fixing his blue eye on ash and spittle.

23| *PE, SP63, SP69*: corpses, if
24| MS*SP45*: their #next two words, *bone is,* blotted out and replaced by next two words and comma# bones in,
25| *PE, SP63*: They were
25–36| *SP69*: They were < > men." // I, not
26| *TGB*: me, I
36| *TGB*: I would not weep, and like
45| *TGB*: And the wind ferried them South.

He hopped outdoors stifflegged on his stave
To quiz the spring and see if it would grave
Bright images on a mind so weathered and hard
It scarcely received the print of his backyard.

He was a small man with head larger than most,
And so much it had kept, and so much lost,
It could not buzz and spin with giddy mirth
At these quick salad hues that gauded earth.

Business brighter than that had been enacted
Day after day within the curled compacted
Grey hemispheres—music and histories
Enveloping more than April novelties.

If the grey cloud of thought for once was stilled
At the great cycle fifty times fulfilled,
Yet it was feathers that quivered, grass, the bee,
The foal, the firstling yellow bloom—not he.

He leaned upon the earth and turned his eyes
About the world and said with no surprise—
"I am a god. I may not seem to be,
The other gods have disinherited me.

"This is the patrimony of a god,
Nature's instant obedience if he nod;
But in my poverty and disrepute
I will, and have no way to execute.

"The better part of godhead is design.
This is not theirs only, for I know mine,
And I project such worlds as need not yield
To this commanded April on the field.

10| *F*: kept and
18| *F*: For the
*SP*69a: For the green cycle
19| *F*: quivered—grass—the
22| *TGB*: the word #last word emended to# world #see Emendations#
24–29| *SP*69a: me. / "The better

"And it is ample. For it satisfies
My royal blood even thus to exercise
The ancestral arts of my theogony.
I am a god, though none attend to me."

And he watched, with large head resting in the sun,
The gods at play, and did not envy one.
He had the magic too, and knew his power,
But was too tired to work it at that hour.

Two in August (*SP*45)

Two that could not have lived their single lives
As can some husbands and wives
Did something strange: they tensed their vocal cords
And attacked each other with silences and words
Like catapulted stones and arrowed knives.

Dawn was not yet; night is for loving or sleeping,
Sweet dreams or safekeeping;
Yet he of the wide brows that were used to laurel
And she, the famed for gentleness, must quarrel,
Furious both of them, and scared, and weeping.

How sleepers groan, twitch, wake to such a mood
Is not well understood,
Nor why two entities grown almost one
Should rend and murder trying to get undone,
With individual tigers in their blood.

She in terror fled from the marriage chamber
Circuiting the dark rooms like a string of amber

36| *SP*69a: god though < > attends
40| *SP*69a: at this hour

9| *PE, SP*63, *SP*69: quarrel.
15–16| *TGB*, MS*SP*45: blood. // In spring's luxuriant weather had the bridal / Transpired, nor had the growing parts been idle, / Nor was it easily dissolved; / Therefore they tugged but were still intervolved, / With pain prodigious. The exploit was suicidal. // She
17| *TGB*: room
MS*SP*45: dark room #last word crossed out and replaced above by word illegibly crossed out and replaced by# rooms

Round and round and back,
And would not light one lamp against the black,
And heard the clock that clanged: Remember, Remember.

And he must tread barefooted the dim lawn,
Soon he was up and gone;
High in the trees the night-mastered birds were crying
With fear upon their tongues, no singing nor flying
Which are their lovely attitudes by dawn.

Whether those bird-cries were of heaven or hell
There is no way to tell;
In the long ditch of darkness the man walked
Under the hackberry trees where the birds talked
With words too sad and strange to syllable.

Somewhere Is Such a Kingdom

The famous kingdom of the birds
Has a sweet tongue and liquid words—
The red-birds polish their notes
In their easy practiced throats—
Smooth as orators are the thrushes
Of the airy city of the bushes—
And God reward the fierce cock wrens
Who have such suavity with their hens.

To me this has its worth
As I sit upon the earth
Lacking my winter and quiet hearth.
For I go up into a nook
With a mind burdened, or a book,
And hear no strife or quarreling
As the birds and their wives sing.

2| MS*SP45*, *SP45*, *PE*, *SP63*, *SP69*: words,
4| MS*SP45*, *SP45*: throats,
PE, *SP63*, *SP69*: throats.
6| MS*SP45*, *SP45*, *PE*, *SP63*, *SP69*: bushes,
13| MS*SP45*, *SP45*, *PE*, *SP63*, *SP69*; burdened or
14| MS*SP45*, *SP45*, *PE*, *SP63*, *SP69*: strife nor quarreling

Or, so it has been today.
Yet I cannot therefore say
If the red-bird, wren, or thrush
Know when to speak and when to hush;
Though their manifest education
Be a right enunciation
And their chief excellence
A verbal elegance,
I cannot say if the wind never blows,
Nor how it sometimes goes.

This I know, that if they wrangle
Their words inevitably will jangle.
If they be hateful as men
They will be harsh as we have been.
When they go to pecking
You will soon hear shrieking,
And they who will have the law,
How those will jaw!
Girls that dream unlawful dreams
Will waken full of their own screams,
And boys that get too arrant
Will have rows with a parent—
And when friend falls out with friend,
All songs must have quick end.

Have they not claws like knives?
Have not these gentlemen wives?

But when they croak and fleer and swear,
My dull heart I must take elsewhere;
For I will see if God has made
Otherwhere another shade
Where the men or beasts or birds
Exchange few words and pleasant words.

21| MS*SP*45, *SP*45, *PE*, *SP*63, *SP*69: enunciation,
23| *PE*, *SP*63, *SP*69: elegance.
26| MS*SP*45, *SP*45, *PE*, *SP*63, *SP*69: wrangle,
34| MS*SP*45, *SP*45, *PE*, *SP*63, *SP*69: that have unlawful
38| MS*SP*45, *SP*45, *PE*, *SP*63, *SP*69: with friend

And dare I think it is absurd
If no such beast were, no such bird?

Persistent Explorer

The noise of water teased his literal ears
Which heard the distant drumming and thus scored:
Water is falling—it fell—therefore it roared.
But he cried, That is more than water I hear.

He went yet higher, and on the dizzy brink
His eyes confirmed with vision what he had heard:
This is but tumbling water. Again he demurred:
That was not only water flashing, I think.

But listen as he might, look fast or slow,
It was water, only water, tons of it
Dropping into the gorge, and every bit
Was water—the insipid chemical H_2O.

Its thunder smote him somewhat as the loud
Words of the god that rang around a man
Walking by the Mediterranean.
Its cloud of froth was whiter than the cloud

That clothed the goddess sliding down the air
Unto a mountain shepherd; white as she
That issued from the smoke refulgently.
The cloud was, but the goddess was not there.

1| *SP69*: ear
2| *SP69*: drumming, and so scored:
3| *SP69*: "Water
4| *PE, SP63*: However: That < > hear!
SP69: Yet something else is there: is it cheer or fear?"
5| *PE, SP63*: went still higher
SP69: He strode much faster, till on
6| *SP69*: eye < > he'd
7| *SP69*: "A simple physical water." Again
8| *SP69*: "More than a roaring flashing water, I think."
10| *SP69*: was common water, millions of tons
11| *SP69*: Gouging its gorge deeper, and
12| *SP69*: water, the
18| *PE, SP63, SP69*: shepherd, white

The sound was tremendous, but it was no voice
That spoke to him. The spectacle was grand
But still it spelled him nothing, nothing, and
Forbade him whether to cower or rejoice.

What would he have it spell? He scarcely knew;
Only that water and nothing but water filled
His eyes and ears, nothing but water that spilled;
And if the smoke and rattle of water drew

From the deep thickets of his mind the train,
The fierce fauns and the timid tenants there,
That burst their bonds and rushed upon the air,
Why, he must turn and beat them down again.

So be it. And no unreasonable outcry
The pilgrim made; only a rueful grin
Spread over his lips until he drew them in;
He did not sit upon a rock and die.

There were many ways of dying; witness, if he
Commit himself to the water, and descend
Wrapped in the water, turn water at the end
And flow with a great water out to sea.

But there were many ways of living too,
And let his enemies gibe, but let them say
That he would throw this continent away
And seek another country—as he would do.

21| *PE, SP63*: Tremendous the sound was but there was
SP69: Deafening was the sound, but never a voice
22| *PE, SP63*: him. Furious the spectacle
SP69: That talked with him; spacious the spectacle
23| *PE, SP63*: But it spelled nothing, there was not any spell
SP69: But it spelled nothing; there was not any spell
24| *PE, SP63*: Bidding him whether cower
SP69: Whether to bid him cower
27| *SP69*: ears; only water
30| *SP69*: there
36| *SP69*: He would not
37| *SP69*: Many are the ways
39| *SP69*: end,
40| *SP69*: Part of a water rolling to the sea.
41| *SP69*: living, too,

Morning

Jane awoke Ralph so gently on one morning
That first, before the true householder Learning
Came back to tenant in the haunted head,
He lay upon his back and let his stare
Penetrate dazedly into the blue air
That swam all round his bed,
And in the blessed silence nothing was said.

Then his eyes traveled through the window
And lit, enchantedly, on such a meadow
Of wings and light and clover,
He would propose to Jane then to go walking
Through the green waves, and to be singing not talking;
Such imps were pranking over
Him helpless lying in bed beneath a cover.

Suddenly he remembered about himself,
His manliness returned entire to Ralph;
The dutiful mills of the brain
Began to whir with their smooth-grinding wheels
And the sly visitors wriggled off like eels;
He rose and was himself again.
Simply another morning, and simply Jane.

Dog (*SP*45)

Cock-a-doodle-doo the brass-lined rooster says,
Brekekekex intones the fat Greek frog—
These fantasies do not terrify me as
The bow-wow-wow of dog.

I had a little doggie who used to sit and beg,
A pretty little creature with tears in his eyes

HM: #poem in italics#
18| *HM*: wheels,
20| *HM*: He was

1| *SP69*: rooster goes,
2| *SP69*: frog,
3| *SP69*: not worry me as does

And anomalous hand extended on his leg;
Housebroken was my Huendchen, and so wise.

Booms the voice of a big dog like a bell.
But Fido sits at dusk on Madam's lap
And, bored beyond his tongue's poor skill to tell,
Rehearses his pink paradigm, To yap.

However. Up the lane the tender bull
Proceeds unto his kine; he yearns for them,
Whose eyes adore him and are beautiful;
Love speeds him and no treason nor mayhem.

But, on arriving at the gap in the fence,
Behold! again the ubiquitous hairy dog,
Like a numerous army rattling the battlements
With shout, though it is but his monologue,
With a lion's courage and a bee's virulence
Though he is but one dog.

Shrill is the fury of the proud red bull,
His knees quiver, and the honeysuckle vine
Expires with anguish as his voice, terrible,
Cries, "What do you want of my twenty lady kine?"

Now the air trembles to the sorrowing Moo

7| *G*: on a leg—
TGB: on his leg—
SP69: on a leg.
9| *SP69*: Booms a big dog's voice like a fireman's bell.
10| *SP69*: Madame's
11| *G, TGB, SP69*: And bored < > tell
12| *TGB*: yap . . .
14| P*SP63*, *SP63*: he years for #although JCR corrected this error on the page proofs, writing *yearns* in the margin, the mistake persists in *SP63*#
15| *SP69*: beautiful,
16| *SP69*: him, and
17| *SP69*: But having come to the gateway in
18| *G, TGB*: dog—
SP69: Listen! again the hateful barking dog,
20| *G, TGB*: monologue—
21| *G, TGB*: virulence,
SP69: With lion's courage and sting-bees's virulence
23| *SP69*: the royal bull,
25| *SP69*: voice, dreadful,
26| *SP69*: my bonded lady
26–27| *G, TGB*: kine?" / Ah, nothing doubtless; yet his dog's-fang is keen, / His dog's-heart cannot suffer these marriage rites / Enacted in the dark if they are obscene, [# semi-colon in *TGB*#] / Misogynist, censorious of delights. / Now

Of twenty blameless ladies of the mead
Fearing their lord's precarious set-to.
It is the sunset and the heavens bleed.

The hooves of the red bull slither the claybank
And cut the green tendrils of the vine; his horn
Slices the young birch unto splinter and shank
But lunging leaves the bitch's boy untorn.

Across the red sky comes master, Hodge by name,
Upright, biped, tall-browed, and self-assured,
In his hand a cudgel, in his cold eye a flame:
"Have I beat my dog so sore and he is not cured?"

His stick and stone and curse rain on the brute
That pipped his bull of gentle pedigree
Till the leonine smarts with pain and disrepute
And the bovine weeps in the bosom of his family.

Old Hodge stays not his hand, but whips to kennel
The renegade. God's peace betide the souls
Of the pure in heart. But in the box that fennel
Grows round are two red eyes that stare like coals.

Jack's Letter

Do not consider that Jack and Rose apart
Can thrive much, for they cannot lie together

28| *G*: Of the twenty
29| *SP69*: Who fear their
31| *SP69*: the brave bull
32| *SP69*: vine; the horn
33| *SP69*: birch into splinter
35| *SP69*: the late sky
36| *SP69*: Upright, two-legged, tall-browed
37| *SP69*: his blue eye
38–43| *SP69*: cured?" // Old
44| MS*SP45*: betides #altered to# betide
45| *G, TGB*: Of the just! But < > box grown round with fennel
MS*SP45*: heart #exclamation mark crossed out and replaced by full stop# but #altered to# But
PE, SP63, SP69: heart! But
46| *G, TGB*: Two red eyes shine with chemistry of coals.
MS*SP45*: round two red eyes #last three words crossed out and replaced by four words# are two red eyes
PE, SP63: round, are
SP69: Blaze two red eyes as hot as cooking-coals.

1| *SP69*: not imagine that

Nor under the same roof nor in the same weather.
These are the moons of absence grieving the heart.

And if I knew the gods upon the hill
I'd ask the kindest: Wet your lips and bless
The little ones that die of separateness,
Absent and impotent and unspoken still.

Poor Jack has wits which he would put to use;
He would convey to Rose his pent-up love
And duly receive acknowledgment thereof;
A letter is his passionate excuse.

But cold and dry he finds the paper sheet
And atrabilious and sour is ink;
He'd set his matter forth but stops to think
His passion must in transit lose its heat;

So plants on four sides of the folio
Himself in bulbs of cunning charactry,
But Rose must guess the cipher! seeing she
Must water him with tears if he would grow.

The glade is not so green now, Jack says there;
The fish have all swum down the dwindled stream;
The birds have scattered and become a dream;
But he supposes this is everywhere.

Here then lies Jack beneath a penny seal.
The dainty lady of the superscription
If she have very delicate perception
With eyes may see and with sharp fingers feel.

3| *F*: weather;
SP69: Under < > roof or the
5| *SP69*: If I knew any gods < > hill,
6| *F*: lip
9| *F*: Now Jack, sore-hearted, puts his wits to
SP69: But Jack
10| *F*: He must convey
11| *F*: And then receive
SP69: thereof.
12| *SP69*: his proper and pure excuse.
13| *SP69*: Too cold < > sheet,
18| *SP69*: charactery,
19| *SP69*: cipher, seeing
22| *SP69*: all gone down < > dwindling
24| *F*: Eheu, eheu! he'd latinize despair.
SP69: Himself works with his flowers and goes nowhere.
28| *SP69*: and with nice fingers

The post is gone, and the event will tell.
If only she should lay it to her bosom,
Her parcel might soon thicken to a blossom
Which would be soft to hold and sweet to smell.

Antique Harvesters (*SP45*)

(*Scene: Of the Mississippi the bank sinister, and of the Ohio the bank sinister.*)

Tawny are the leaves turned but they still hold,
And it is harvest; what shall this land produce?
A meager hill of kernels, a runnel of juice;
Declension looks from our land, it is old.
Therefore let us assemble, dry, grey, spare,
And mild as yellow air.

"I hear the croak of a raven's funeral wing."
The young men would be joying in the song
Of passionate birds; their memories are not long.
What is it thus rehearsed in sable? "Nothing."
Trust not but the old endure, and shall be older
Than the scornful beholder.

We pluck the spindling ears and gather the corn.
One spot has special yield? "On this spot stood
Heroes and drenched it with their only blood."
And talk meets talk, as echoes from the horn
Of the hunter—echoes are the old men's arts,
Ample are the chambers of their hearts.

Here come the hunters, keepers of a rite;
The horn, the hounds, the lank mares coursing by
Straddled with archetypes of chivalry;
And the fox, lovely ritualist, in flight

29| *F*: gone and
30| *SP69*: she will hug it < > bosom
31| *SP69*: parcel soon will thicken
32| *SP69*: Which will be

1| *SwR*: turned, but < > hold.
2| *SwR*: It is
3| *SwR*: juice.
7| *SwR*: the creak of
19| *SwR*: rite.
21| *SwR*: Under quaint archetypes

Offering his unearthly ghost to quarry;
And the fields, themselves to harry.

Resume, harvesters. The treasure is full bronze
Which you will garner for the Lady, and the moon
Could tinge it no yellower than does this noon;
But grey will quench it shortly—the field, men, stones.
Pluck fast, dreamers; prove as you amble slowly
Not less than men, not wholly.

Bare the arm, dainty youths, bend the knees
Under bronze burdens. And by an autumn tone
As by a grey, as by a green, you will have known
Your famous Lady's image; for so have these;
And if one say that easily will your hands
More prosper in other lands,

Angry as wasp-music be your cry then:
"Forsake the Proud Lady, of the heart of fire,
The look of snow, to the praise of a dwindled choir,
Song of degenerate specters that were men?
The sons of the fathers shall keep her, worthy of
What these have done in love."

True, it is said of our Lady, she ageth.
But see, if you peep shrewdly, she hath not stooped;
Take no thought of her servitors that have drooped,
For we are nothing; and if one talk of death—
Why, the ribs of the earth subsist frail as a breath
If but God wearieth.

Man without Sense of Direction (*SP*45)

Tell this to ladies: how a hero man
Assail a thick and scandalous giant

28| *SwR*: But the grey < > fields
29| *SwR*: you rumble slowly
31| *SwR*: arm too, dainty
34| *SwR*: these.

43–48| *TGB*: #last stanza not included#

TGB: #the following stanza precedes the beginning of copy-text# Spaced round

Who casts true shadow in the sun,
And die, but play no truant.

This is more horrible: that the darling egg
Of the chosen people hatch a creature
Of noblest mind and powerful leg
Who cannot fathom nor perform his nature.

The larks' tongues are never stilled
Where the pale spread straw of sunlight lies.
Then what invidious gods have willed
Him to be seized so otherwise?

Birds of the field and beasts of the stable
Are swollen with rapture and make uncouth
Demonstration of joy, which is a babble
Offending the ear of the fervorless youth.

Love—is it the cause? the proud shamed spirit?
Love has slain some whom it possessed,
But his was requited beyond his merit
And won him in bridal the loveliest.

Yet scarcely he issues from the warm chamber,
Flushed with her passion, when cold as dead
Once more he walks where waves past number
Of sorrow buffet his curse-hung head.

Whether by street, or in field full of honey,
Attended by clouds of the creatures of air

---

with perfect Forms, / There is no moon of them that draws / His flood of being, but concentric storms / Heaving the seas, and quaking to their pause.

1| *TGB*: ladies: when a

3| *TGB*: That casts a true

4| P*SP63*: And die #last word crossed out and replaced by# dies, but play #last word crossed out and replaced by# plays

8–9| *TGB*: That cannot < > nature. #a row of nine dots between stanzas# / The

10| *TGB*: lies,
SP63: lies
SP69: lies;

12| MS*SP45*: seized to otherwise?

21| MS*SP45*: the warm #last word inserted above#

23| *TGB*: waves beyond number

25| *TGB*: in mead full

26| *TGB*: by a cloud
MS*SP45*: Attended by #last word inserted above#

Or shouldering the city's companioning many,
His doom is on him; and how can he care

For the shapes that would fiddle upon his senses,
Wings and faces and mists that move,
Words, sunlight, the blue air which rinses
The pure pale head which he must love?

And he writhes like an antique man of bronze
That is beaten by furies visible,
Yet he is punished not knowing his sins
And for his innocence walks in hell.

He flails his arms, he moves his lips:
"Rage have I none, cause, time, nor country—
Yet I have traveled land and ships
And knelt my seasons in the chantry."

So he stands muttering; and rushes
Back to the tender thing in his charge
With clamoring tongue and taste of ashes
And a small passion to feign large.

But let his cold lips be her omen,
She shall not kiss that harried one
To peace, as men are served by women
Who comfort them in darkness and in sun.

Survey of Literature (*SP*45)

In all the good Greek of Plato
I lack my roastbeef and potato.

A better man was Aristotle,
Pulling steady on the bottle.

28| *TGB*: is upon him
47| *TGB*: peace! As < > women,

2| *TGB*: roast beef

I dip my hat to Chaucer,
Swilling soup from his saucer,

And to Master Shakespeare
Who wrote big on small beer.

The abstemious Wordsworth
Subsisted on a curd's-worth,

But a slick one was Tennyson,
Putting gravy on his venison.

What these men had to eat and drink
Is what we say and what we think.

The influence of Milton
Came wry out of Stilton.

Sing a song for Percy Shelley,
Drowned in pale lemon jelly,

And for precious John Keats,
Dripping blood of pickled beets.

Then there was poor Willie Blake,
He foundered on sweet cake.

God have mercy on the sinner
Who must write with no dinner,

No gravy and no grub,
No pewter and no pub,

No belly and no bowels,
Only consonants and vowels.

5| *TGB*: to Chaucer
15| *TGB*: The flatulence of
16| *TGB*: Came out of wry Stilton.
22| *SP69*: on too sweet

Amphibious Crocodile

In due season the amphibious crocodile
Rose from the waves and clambered on the bank
And clothed himself, having cleansed his toes which stank
Of bayous of Florida and estuaries of Nile.

And if he had had not water on his brain,
Remember what joys were his. The complete landlubber
In a green mackintosh and overshoes of rubber—
Putting his umbrella up against the rain

For fear of the influenza—sleeking his curls—
Visiting the punchbowl to the verge of hiccups—
Prowling among the petticoats and the teacups—
Breaching his promises and playing with the girls.

At length in grey spats he must cross the ocean.
So this is Paris? Lafayette, we are here.
Bring us sweet wines but none of your French beer.
And he weeps on Notre Dame with proper emotion.

This is the Rive Gauche, this is the Hotel Crillon.
Where are the brave poilus? They are slain by his French.
And suddenly he cries, I want to see a trench!
Up in the North eventually he finds one

Which is all green slime and water; whereupon lewd
Nostalgic tremors assail him; with strangled oaths
He flees; he would be kicking off his clothes
And reverting to his pre-Christian mother's nude.

Next on the grand tour is Westminster, and Fleet Street.
His Embassy must present him to King George.

Title| *SP69*: Crocodile
9–12| *F, SP69*: curls— / Prowling < > teacups— / Visiting < > hiccups— / Breaching
15| *SP69*: beer!
17| *SP69*: is Rive Gauche, here's the
20| *SP69*: he sees one

Who is the gentleman whose teeth are so large?
That is Mr. Crocodile the renowned aesthete.

To know England really one must try the country
And the week-end parties; he is persuaded to straddle
A yellow beast in a red coat on a flat saddle.
Much too gymnastical are the English gentry.

Surely a Scotch and soda with the Balliol men.
But when old Crocodile rises to speak at the Union
He is too miserably conscious of his bunion
And toes too large for the aesthetic regimen.

It is too too possible he has wandered far
From the simple center of his rugged nature.
I wonder, says he, if I am the sort of creature
To live by travel, projects, affaires de coeur? . .

Soberly Crocodile sips of the Eucharist.
But as he mediates the obscene complexes
And infinite involutions of the sexes,
Crocodile sets up for a psychoanalyst.

Great is his learning. He learns to discuss
Pure being, both the Who's Who and the What's What,
Affirms that A is A, refutes that B is not.
This is a clean life without mud and muss.

But who would ever have thought it took such strength
To whittle the tree of being to a point
While the deep-sea urge cries Largo, and every joint

27| *SP69*: gentleman having teeth so

28| *SP69*: is Mr. Crocodile, our renowned

40–41| *F*: by projects, travel, affaires de coeur? // Crocodile ponders the marrying of a wife, / She has a ready-made fortune and ready-made family; / The lady is not a poem but she is a homily, / But he hates the rectangular charms of the virtuous life. // Soberly
SP69: by projects, travel, affaires du coeur? // Crocodile ponders the marrying of a wife / With a ready-made fortune and ready-made family; / The lady is not a poem; she is a homily, / And he hates the rectangular charms of the virtuous life. // Soberly

44–49| *SP69*: Crocodile could be a psychoanalyst. // But

50| *SP69*: to its points

51| *SP69*: and all the joints

Tingles with gross desire of lying at length?

Of all the elements mixed in Crocodile
Water is principal; but water flows
By paths of least resistance; and water goes
Down, down, down; which is too infantile.

The earth spins from its poles and is glared on
By the fierce incessant suns, but here is news
For a note in the fine-print of the Thursday Reviews:
Old Robert Crocodile is packed up and gone.

His dear friends cannot find him. The ladies write
As usual but their lavender notes are returned
By the U. S. Postmaster and secretively burned.
He has successfully got out of sight.

Crocodile hangs his pretty clothes on a limb
And lies with his fathers, and with his mothers too,
And his brothers and sisters as it seems right to do;
The family religion is good enough for him.

Full length he lies and goes as water goes,
He weeps for joy and welters in the flood,
Floating he lies extended many a rood,
And quite invisible but for the end of his nose.

Fresco

From *The Last Judgment*

To his angel company drowsing on their strings,
"Go call my trumpeter!" said the King of Kings.

52| *SP69*: Tingle
56| *SP69*: is proper and infantile.
57| *SP69*: poles, and
59| *F*: fine-print column of
SP69: fine-print column of Thursday
60| *SP69*: Old Robert Crocodile has packed
64| *F, SP69*: has mysteriously gone out
71| *SP69*: extended nearly a

Title| *F*: *The Last Judgment/(A Fresco)*

So Gabriel gat him up from the trumpeting station
And winged into court with testy deliberation.

"Let Him wait. For I and my trump who have waited are old,
Our wind is short, our joints are harsh and cold."

But Jahveh's front was darkening like nightfall:
"Blow on thy trump, man! But what has thou done therewithal?"

"'Tis boxed for keeping, Sire. So noble a pelf,
'Tis fast in lock, and reposeth high on the shelf."

"Recover thy trump, and sound through all the earth
An instant cease to the works of death and birth."

The ancient hasted to do his Lord's command,
On high his pinions creaking on either hand,

Unwrapped his trump, and beginning pale as the tomb
By littles he purpled his cheek on Crack-o'-Doom.

The frantical sinners heard it, and sinned right on,
They were not probationers now but damned and done;

They clutched at their gold, and merry whores, and gin,
And cursed this Day that sundered them from sweet sin.

Laborious others, hunched by squat machines,
Rose as by habit to doff their greasy jeans;

It was a good hour till whistle, and they were glad
To go out sooner than yesterday they had.

But a widow woman laughed at the shapes of Doom,
Brandished at Heaven's host her crazy broom:

5| *F*: "Let them wait. My trump and I who < > old;
6| *F*: short; our < > and old."
7| *F*: nightfall.
15| *F*: tomb,
16| *F*: little
17| *F*: it; and < > on.
18| *F*: now, they were damned < > done.
20–25| *F*: sin. // But

"Ye have tarried I think by the way. The war is done.
Your summons had been timelier seven years gone.

"My two sweet boys are naked dissolute bones
As a million other murdered mothers' sons.

"Search France and find them. I shall thank you well
When ye dispose us in official Hell."

But how they inveighed on the tedious courts of Heaven,
Those queens, ungrovelling at Omnipotence even!

With such a wrack their empires had been strewn,
They had not marvelled at Gabriel's quaint tune;

Had shot precipitate like inverted rain
By routes converging to the heavenly plain;

And if they quaked in the transit, and felt pain,
Quite soon were grounded safe on the firm plain.

Luisa unlocked her smile, the rose and flaxen
Who published a sleepy beauty that was Saxon;

For since she was chosen once of Bonaparte,
All other women's husbands pricked her heart.

But swarthy and blotched was simpering Jezebel,
So late with the worms, so soon to be bride of Hell.

Then Cleopatra enacted every wile
That had ensnared the antique world at Nile;

29| *F*: bones,
31| *F*: them; I
33| *F*: they accuse the < > Heaven.
34| *F*: even.
36| *F*: They hadn't started at < > tune!
37| *F*: They shot
38| *F*: plain,
39| *F*: They quaked < > full of their sin and pain,
40| *F*: But soon they were grounded firm on Heaven's plain.
48–49| *F*: at Nile. // Her Eastern arts had never been withstood / Till Anthony's last drop of Roman blood // Had leaped, and he burst < > asunder,

When Antony had burst her coil asunder
And clattered to the field with Roman thunder,

The queen had not endured for her honor's repute
To be of a single old lover destitute;

Nor had her mirror comforted her in rage,
Discovering the creeping cracks of age;

She got a little snake, too sweet to hiss,
And propped him up for his long voluptuous kiss;

His venom mixed with the woman's milk and honey;
No doctors then would hire for the kingdom's money;

He sucked her sweet breasts with all his little strength
Till Egypt was quit of its curse at no great length.

But now in Heaven her harlotries were renewed,
For she loosed the cerements wherewith she was gewed;

Her side was buckled, but she undid the clasp
And showed her small round bosom kissed by the asp.

The Equilibrists

Full of her long white arms and milky skin
He had a thousand times remembered sin.
Alone in the press of people traveled he,
Minding her jacinth and myrrh and ivory.

50| *F*: thunder.
51| *F*: But she endured not for
53| *F*: Nor did her mirror comfort her
56| *F*: kiss.
57| *F*: honey,
58| *F*: money.
59| *F*: strength,
61| *F*: in Heaven here harlotries
62: *F*: gewed.

Title| *F*: History of Two Simple Lovers
4| MS*SP*45: jacinth, and myrrh #comma inserted #, and
*SP*45, *PE*, *SP*63, *SP*69: jacinth, and myrrh, and

Mouth he remembered: the quaint orifice
From which came heat that flamed upon the kiss,
Till cold words came down spiral from the head,
Grey doves from the officious tower illsped.

Body: it was a white field ready for love.
On her body's field, with the gaunt tower above,
The lilies grew, beseeching him to take,
If he would pluck and wear them, bruise and break.

Eyes talking: Never mind the cruel words,
Embrace my flowers but not embrace the swords.
But what they said, the doves came straightway flying
And unsaid: Honor, Honor, they came crying.

Importunate her doves. Too pure, too wise,
Clambering on his shoulder, saying, Arise,
Leave me now, and never let us meet,
Eternal distance now command thy feet.

Predicament indeed, which thus discovers
Honor among thieves, Honor between lovers.
O such a little word is Honor, they feel!
But the grey word is between them cold as steel.

At length I saw these lovers fully were come
Into their torture of equilibrium:
Dreadfully had forsworn each other, and yet
They were bound each to each, and they did not forget.

And rigid as two painful stars, and twirled
About the clustered night their prison world,

6| *F, FA*: From whence came
7| *PE, SP63*: head.
9| *SP45, PE, SP63, SP69*: love,
14| MS*SP45, SP45, PE, SP63, SP69*: flowers, but
16| *F*: they kept crying
23| *F*: Of such
FA: Oh, such
26| MS*SP45 SP45, PE, SP63, SP69*: equilibrium;
28–29| *F*: forget. // The beauty of their bodies was the bond / Which these incarnate might not pass beyond; / Invincible proud Honor was the bar / Which made them not come closer but stay far. // And

They burned with fierce love always to come near,
But Honor beat them back and kept them clear.

Ah, the strict lovers, they are ruined now!
I cried in anger. But with puddled brow
Devising for those gibbeted and brave
Came I descanting: Man, what would you have?

For spin your period out, and draw your breath,
A kinder saeculum begins with Death.
Would you ascend to Heaven and bodiless dwell?
Or take your bodies honorless to Hell?

In Heaven you have heard no marriage is,
No white flesh tinder to your lecheries,
Your male and female tissue sweetly shaped
Sublimed away, and furious blood escaped.

Great lovers lie in Hell, the stubborn ones
Infatuate of the flesh upon the bones;
Stuprate, they rend each other when they kiss;
The pieces kiss again—no end to this.

But still I watched them spinning, orbited nice.
Their flames were not more radiant than their ice.
I dug in the quiet earth and wrought the tomb
And made these lines to memorize their doom:—

Equilibrists lie here; stranger, tread light;
Close, but untouching in each other's sight;
Mouldered the lips and ashy the tall skull,
Let them lie perilous and beautiful.

28| MS*SP*45: They would #last word crossed out#
33| *F*: Ah the
38| MS*SP*45: death #altered to# Death.
43| *F*: tissue, sweetly shaped,
44| *F*: escaped;
47| *F,* MS*SP*45, *SP*45, *PE, SP*63, *SP*69: kiss,
48| MS*SP*45, *SP*45, *PE, SP*63, *SP*69: again, no
50| *F*: were no more
52| *F*: memorize the doom:
52–53| MS*SP*45, *SP*45, *PE, SP*63, *SP*69: doom:—/EPITAPH/*Equilibrists*
53–56| *F*: #no italics#
55| *PE, SP*63, *SP*69: *skull.*

Two Gentlemen in Bonds

A Tale in Twenty Sonnets

The Characters:

Paul,
Abbott, } brothers, and partners in the estate.
Edith, a cousin.
The King.
The King's Chamberlain.
Sire to Paul and Abbott, a spirit dwelling in the tomb.
A gelding.
A peach.
A bishop.
A rat.
Soldiers, courtiers, officers, servants, wines, viands, a castle, and other accessories appertaining to those times.

Pink and Pale

Paul, pinked with dozing, stood from the chair wherein
Digestion was assisted after lunch—
Roast chine and gravies, pudding, swigs of punch,
His manhood being strong, and it no sin
To feed—Paul stretched and tucked his loose ends in
And singing till he had sung himself outside
He went to banter Abbott, or to ride;
Poor company Abbott kept his nearest of kin.

For everything that Paul was, Abbott was not.
His legs were two long straws, his face was chalk,
He would not ride, nor run, nor drowse, but walk

1| *SP69*: the couch wherein
3| *SP69*: chines
4| *APM, SP69*: strong and
5| *SP69*: feed—then stretched
7| *SP69*: ride.
8| *SP69*: his next of
9| *SP69*: not;
11| *SP69*: ride nor run nor

The field in thought more passionate than another's;
You hadn't believed that two such men were brothers;
Yet it was credited, the same sire begot.

Thinking, Drinking

A young girl cousined them, whose character was
A wise bright head and grey eyes beautifuller
To Paul than his brave manhood seemed to her,
Though he was Greek enough for Phidias,
And she could ride; but about this Michaelmas
She wouldn't run quick and green in riding habit
To canter with him and hollo to every rabbit
That bounced across to thicket or to grass.

She listened too much to Abbott's music of words,
Savage and strange. "How noble is man thinking!
But we, my cousin, are filled with eating and drinking.
Should we not read philosophy?" But Paul said,
"Edith, my brother's a fool, and out of his head,"
And saw her thoughts fly over him, like the birds.

In Air

But Abbott when he sought him was nowhere.
Paul said not all his eggs therefore were addled,
No much: "For let my gelding Trey be saddled."
And he flies like a young rich landlord god on air,
The earth his wealth, ethereal, yet aware
Of the tread of the dark wood mold and turfy rye,
Rich smell of horse in his nostril, wind in his eye,
And galloping through the autumn all his care.

12| *SP69*: The wood in
13| *SP69*: You wouldn't believe

2| *SP69*: head, and
5| *SP69*: ride. But
6| *SP69*: wouldn't go in her green riding
7| *APM*: him, and
9| *SP69*: Too much she listened to < > words:
10| *SP69*: "O the wild flood! How
13| *SP69*: fool and
14| *SP69*: him like

The country beauty flushed him up to the ears.
He put the gelding to the hurdles, and Trey
Must take them every one in Paul's own way,
For if his spirit failed him and he shrank,
Right back Paul drove him rowelling his flank,
But clicking the boards he gave his master fears.

Thought, Distraught

Abbott proceeded soberly, with rhyme.
He heard the lone birds' cries, and his own tongue
Made melancholy more than the birds had sung.
The man could talk in Latin, music, mime,
Or sonneteer with Petrarch in his prime,
He had a prince's powers, but what he willed
Was to go down to dust with the unfulfilled
Rather than stint himself with space and time.

He was a specter gibbering under trees
Which preened their yellow feathers, while he thought,
"Flutter, then, flutter, for you shall fly distraught!"
He waved his black sleeves like an evil prophet,
Death in his every verse or not far off it;
Far down he hung his own head, mortal as these.

Meeting in a Garden

"Garden of no fruit! Lichen on a stone!
And what is life but a barren laborious tree
Too streaked and scored with black mortality?"
Abbott said several dooms with firm intone,
And had more worlds to sentence, he had not done,
When *trot, trot, trot,* and squeezing under the wicket
Where one peach hung there came a fellow to pick it;
It was his heathen brother, famished and blown.

13| *APM*: flank;

10| *APM*: yellow foliage, while
11| *APM*: "Flutter then < > distraught."
14| *APM*: Quite down

Paul had a smile always in waiting. "Brother,
Can you have kept this only peach for me?
If you want half of it though, I will agree."
But Abbott wanted nothing, he never took pleasure,
And now he glared on Paul and took his measure.
There was a fool in the family, one or the other.

Epithalamion of a Peach

She was small, ripe, round, a maid not maculate
Saving her bright cheeks, but the rude bridegroom
Claims her, his heavy hand has led her home.
Nor did he pull her gently through his gate
As had a lover dainty and delicate:
The two-and-thirty cut-throats doing his will
Tore off her robe and stripped her bare until
Drunken with appetite, he devoured and ate.

A pleasant slaver drools from off his tongue
Where he has eaten the admirable peach
Who nested high, but could not foil his reach;
His sharp work is unloverly, bringing the wry
To squeamish Abbott's face; unnoticed by
The oblivious gelding stamping in his dung.

Swine, Wine

In that country it happening that the King
Came now that way victorious from battle,

13| *APM*: measure;

1| *SP69*: was round, full, ripe, a maid immaculate,
2| *SP69*: her cheeks. Now Paul the hot bridegroom
3| *SP69*: Acclaims his treasure, his hand < > home;
4| *SP69*: through the gate
5| *SP69*: As would a lover more dainty
7| *SP69*: robes < > her down until
8| *SP69*: He looked upon her bare. Then turned and
9| *SP69*: Shame on him, juice is drooling from his
10| *SP69*: has absorbed the
11| *SP69*: high but not beyond his reach!
12| *APM*: work was unloverly
SP69: It was unloverly work, and brought the
13| *SP69*: face; not noted by

Title| *SP69*: Bad News
1| *SP69*: It happening in that country that
2| *SP69*: victorious in battle

Where he had slain some folk and stolen their cattle,
His chamberlain told Sir Paul an excellent thing
To do: Make ready with feast and furnishing
To lodge the King three days; and it was good
If the King favored his bed and relished his food,
For service helps a man in the sight of the King.

Now purple and linen, heifers, poultry, swine,
Paul loved not for themselves, but he loved yet
As he hated his belly empty and his skin wet;
It would impoverish his great country house
If the State descended for a week's carouse;
No more he napped in innocence after wine.

L'état C'est Moi

Abbott previsioning the pestiferous swarm
Of royal locusts: "Expect now, Brother Paul,
A trifling inconvenience, that is all.
These levies and tributes keep you out of harm;
The thieves the King has slain cannot alarm
His people now, but you pay for this relief;
Strong governments must always eat much beef;
On n'a de beaux états qu'avec gendarmes.

"It doesn't matter that your King's a fraud,
A great pig's-bladder prickable as any,

3| *SP69*: and taken their
4| *SP69*: told Sir Paul a proper thing
5| *SP69*: For doing
6| *APM*: days, and
SP69: days; it would be good
7| *SP69*: and savored his
8| *SP69*: service improved a < > of his King.
9| *SP69*: linen, or poultry and beef and swine,
10| *APM*: yet,
SP69: He loved < > but must accept
11| *SP69*: For his belly's sake, for his body and bed well-kept;
12| *SP69*: his country
13| *SP69*: the Court descended < > carouse.

1| *SP69*: the pestilent swarm
3| *SP69*: inconvenience; that will be all.
4| *APM*: and taxes keep
SP69: harm,
5| *SP69*: slain cause no alarm,
6| *APM*: now; but
SP69: But you have to pay a price for
7| *SP69*: Strong Kingdoms always manage to get their beef,
8| *SP69*: *Le Roi lui-même,* by grace of *ces gendarmes.*
9| *SP69*: matter if your
10| *SP69*: A gross pig's-bladder

A man whose nose runs probably more than many,
Whose beard is soused with gravy. He is the King.
He is the State, you are his littlest thing,
His man, else excommunicate and outlawed."

Misanthropy

"But I am no King's-man, Paul; I am amazed
We sovereignties should let them rule and range.
In the mother-house I dwelt severe and strange,
With cries was torn from my quiet cavern, ill-pleased;
A Form whose fixity everywhere is teased
With change—am enamored yet of that dark womb,
Devise no analogue but one—the tomb,
Where Kings are put to sleep and kingdoms razed.

"My compliments to your King. Say I'm not in.
I'll to your topmost Northern tower, a misanthrope
Too firm to wheedle a fat King or lean Pope,
And all the Pope's prayers and all the King's power
Shall not seduce me out of my grim grey tower;
But you have delicate skin, so save your skin."

12| *APM*: the King,
SP69: beard shines with its gravy; he < > King,
13| *SP69*: The State; you are his man, his < > thing—
14| *SP69*: Or would you go in hiding and be outlawed?"

Title| *SP69*: Misanthrope
1| *SP69*: am not of the King's table; nor his stable.
2| *SP69*: Once we were sovereigns, but there's been interchange.
3| *SP69*: strange
4| *SP69*: Till they ripped me out by the heels and cut the cable,
5| *SP69*: fixity always turns to fable
6| *APM*: womb—
SP69: By the force of things; am < > that womb
7| *SP69*: Which yields no < > one, the
8| *SP69*: Where Kings may lie and hear their Kingdoms babble.
10| *SP69*: I'll move to the Northern tower; your misanthrope,
11| *SP69*: to be wheedled by fat
12| *SP69*: the papal prayers < > all King's
13| *SP69*: not convey me from my absolute tower.
14| *SP69*: have sensitive skin

Vain Protestations

"What sort of notion is this, Abbott, dear man?
It isn't as if one had to bring oneself
To kiss the royal bottom of the Guelph,
Can't you control your devils any better than
To sputter this obscene blab, you Caliban,
And hadn't you rather acknowledge a higher power
By simple gesture than mould in your ratty tower
In cold and loneliness and hate unchristian?"

"But no, Cousin Paul! You can't scare a man like him,
That isn't the way! Abbott, for your brother's sake,
For the tenants, the land, a father's good name, don't make
A breach in the etiquette of the royal visit—
But Paul! there's something splendid about this—or is it
Terrible, rather—or eerie—or what synonym?"

Tones and Caparisons

Well, the fool wilfully had *chosen* his spare
Entertainment—and rooks flapping in his face—
And rats whiskering at his toes and every place—
And a crust and a cold house are philosopher's fare—
So his patriot brother hastened to prepare
The King his welcome. Edith with little heart
Helped him, and thought on Abbott's nobler part,
Till listen! A silver music of fanfare.

Strange how she managed more color then, and less cold.
Kings *are* divine—it is declared by tones
The horn-blowers send through the skies—caparisons
Heaven-golden on the horses—plume and lance
Their blue-eyed angels at the morning dance;
For their divinity is manifold.

8–9| *TGB*: #no break between octave and sestet; emended to restore break; see Emendations#

10| *APM*: way. Abbot

Disappointment of a Thrall

To an innocent knight should this great luck befall
That his King visit him, lord of his life and breath,
Whose ministers post and cry, "Thus saith, thus saith—"
His paths prepared by a chamberlain master of all
Husbandry whispering, "Spare no expense, Sir Paul—"
Noised in the East with horn and hoof and drum,
Marching to West till his plumy host are come
And stand in the gate and hail the loving thrall:—

Why, the young heart bursts with shame if such a King,
Helped from his horse, his fox-face peaked with travel,
His bowels infirm, his water stopped with gravel,
Must to bed, with a pair of leeches at his bedside
And a Bishop pouring medicine for pride,
And no stomach to hear the speech of welcoming.

In Bed, Not Dead

"Did you ever dream he'd be like this?" Paul said.
And Edith tossed her bright cloud: "Abbott was right,
I cannot endure this creature in my sight."
But the old King was so much this side of dead,
One day they nursed him, then he sat up in bed,
Then they arranged his chair with cushions and things

Title| *SP69*: Kingdom Come
1| *SP69*: an honest knight if the lucky break befall
2| *SP69*: breath
3| *SP69*: saith, Thus saith,"
5| *SP69*: expense, Sir Paul,"
7| *SP69*: But weathering West
8| *SP69*: gate to hail < > thrall:
9| *APM*: heart cracks for shame
SP69: bursts for shame
12| *APM*: bedside,
SP69: leeches by bedside
13| *SP69*: And Bishop saying prayers against his pride.
14| *SP69*: He'll have no stomach for speech

Title| *SP69*: In Bed Not Dead
1| *SP69*: "We never dreamed he'd be so bad," said thrall,
2| *SP69*: cloud, "Abbott
4| *SP69*: But they got him in bed and he made no fuss at all,
5| *SP69*: he put on his shawl
6| *SP69*: And made them fashion a throne of cushions

And he held his court in the old manner of Kings,
His minions bowing so low they stood on head.

The fishy green of the King's eye was not fast,
It veered to a mottled wrath or a yellow smile
If the brain behind was busy after that style;
And this inconstant orb perused Sir Paul
And his fine calves, which would make a Seneschal,
If aught was above the shoulders, which were vast.

Primer of Science

The King, to a diligent scholar of great laws
Politico-biological: "Little brown birds
Skittering to a pleasing song without words
Keep constantly their thoughts upon their craws;
The fiercer beasts work ravin to glut their maws;
The serpent has fangs, and travels on his belly,
But—this was pointed out by Machiavelli—
The serpent has no ear for public applause,

And could not found a State. But a King can;
He feeds with no stint his huge appetite
By instructing the people in his own divine right
And with great pomp and honor despoiling them,
Tickled with royal love and ruled with stratagem;
Now give me heed, Sir Paul, and play the man."

7| *SP69*: Where he held his court in the strictest manner
8| *SP69*: Whose minions bowed till they almost got their fall.
9| *SP69*: fishy hue of
10| *SP69*: a negative green or < > smile,
11| *SP69*: But brain < > busy in whichever style;
12| *SP69*: Now the inconstant
13| *SP69*: his pretty calves; he would do for a
14| *SP69*: shoulders; those

Title| *SP69*: Primer for Statesmen
1| *SP69*: The King, to a backward scholar of common laws
3| *SP69*: Seem bent on pleasing us with songs < > words
4| *SP69*: But actually dwell forever upon
6| *SP69*: serpent travels in fact upon his
7| *SP69*: A hardy soul, but according to Machiavelli
8| *SP69*: This creature has < > applause.
9| *SP69*: "He never could found < > can,
10| *SP69*: By policies wholly according with appetite,
11| *SP69*: Teaching his subjects the law of Divine Right,
12| *SP69*: Then with a show of honor < > them.
13| *SP69*: He must tickle with love, and rule by stratagem.

Fait Accompli

He sent for Edith—it was Paul's desire—
And found her very young, coming with face flushed
And her grey films averted and the storm hushed
In which she had cried like Abbott by the fire
To a maid smoothing her tangles and attire
On these incredible Kings that took your peace,
That bent the body and soul—death would release,—
Now the King sees the wild one caught in his wire.

He's taken Edith's little hand, to lay
In Paul's capacious. Hope now for no recourse,
My girl! Paul the Possessor. For better for worse.
Does the strange girl smile? "I wish you many joys;
My kingdom will be greater by many boys
If Heaven reward this union as I pray."

Implacable Tower

But what from the tower? There was a man shut there,
Vainglorious he may have been, stiff-necked;
His stars conspired together to deject
Him from conspicuous glories; he lived on air
And would not taste earth's sweetness; great and spare

1| *SP69*: He summons Edith, which is Paul's own desire.
2| *SP69*: He finds her very fair, but the face is flushed
3| *SP69*: And the grey < > averted. That storm is hushed
4| *SP69*: like prophetess on fire
5| *SP69*: (While the maid smoothed < > attire)
6| *APM*: How these < > Kings destroyed your
SP69: Upon the impossible Kings who broke your
7| *APM*: They bent < > soul; death
SP69: And ruled you body < > soul beyond release.
8| *SP69*: He smiles on the timid doe now come to his lair.
9| *SP69*: little left hand
10| *SP69*: On Paul's overpowering right. There's no recourse
11| *SP69*: Except in Paul's recital: "For better, for worse."
12| *SP69*: On whom is she smiling? "I < > joys,
13| *SP69*: be better by
14| *SP69*: reward your union, which I

#See earlier alternate version in Additional Published Poems#

And pale, his ghost still haunted the slight girl
Who, husbanded now with her fair lord the churl,
Must run away to the gloom of the tower stair.

Paul took his wine and slept, and his thought swirled
From dream to dream through Christendom. But Paul's bride
Climbed up, with a great rat scampering at her side,
Reached the top step of Abbott's Northern tower
And listening at his door, at the very hour
Heard bitter doctrine descending on the world.

Features of Creatures

"Fool, Fool," was Abbott's word; he turned that name
Outward upon a world of pretty creatures
With rooks' pleasant voices and rats' sweet features,
Born of their mothers noble yet sunk in shame,
Mouthing and nosing, flapping and creeping to fame—
Inward upon himself if in their faithless ways
He'd sniffed at gold, love, glory in other days
Or anywise had forgot to honor his Dame.

But Fool had the world said too, because he dwelt
Lone in his tower, long after the occasion
Of minatory Authority's invasion;
The King had gone and Paul restored his right
Yet he clung to his cold and poverty and night
And leaned in the rain; the rain came down unfelt.

Rain

"Rain is a long susurrance; it is no loud
Clamor, yet mutes the terrible bugles; no night,
Yet darkens the insupportable sunlight
And flame-borrowing bush and feather; it is a cloud,

1| *APM*: "Fool, Fool," said Abbott again, and turned
6| *APM*: himself, if

1| *TM*: Rain
SP69: susurrance; makes no
2| *SP69*: night
4| *SP69*: feather; a cloud

And cool upon your heads, poor wrinkle-browed
Percipiences! Not true Styx, yet a river
Washing the wounded senses of their fever;
Or like a wall let down, or like a blessed shroud.

"Think of the happy dead men lying in ponds
Filled of rainwater—eyeballs rolling wide
In the comfort of that undusty unlit tide—
Ears flowered green and huge beyond the bawling
That shook the air of earth—tumbled, or crawling
On naked legs among the lily-fronds."

Wrong

The sire of Paul and Abbott had lain long
In his clammy lodgment of no sunlight nor noise,
With handsome revenues left upon his boys,
And over him having been said much sermon and song
And from sweet Christian chimes much Ding, Dee, Dong,
And having earned his decease he intended now
To keep it. So the insufferable pow-wow
In his sons' house did him most unfilial wrong.

It pricked him wide awake. He was aware
That his two sons, his own hope and the mother's,
Damaged his name and were notorious brothers,
Paul waxing great and thirsting for the power,
Abbott a death's-head gibing from a tower;
His spectral image writhed as in nightmare.

8| *SP69*: A barrier wall < > down; or a makeshift shroud.
9| *TM*: Think
SP69: "Yes, think < > dead who fall in the valleys
10| *SP69*: Of gentle rivers—eyeballs opening wide
11| *SP69*: To the < > that unlit undusty tide—
12| *SP69*: flowering
13| *SP69*: Of air—and a brief sweet season of tumbling, crawling,
14| *TM*: lily-fronds.
SP69: On legs and arms among the waterlilies."

8–9| *TGB*: #no break marking sonnet's division; emended to restore break; see Emendations#

Weep or Sleep

"Now I remember life; and out of me
Lawfully leaping, the twin seed of my loins,
Brethren, whom no split fatherhood disjoins;
But in the woman's-house how hatefully
They trod upon each other! till now I see
My manhood halved and squandered, two heads, two hearts,
Each partial son despising the other's parts;
And so it is, and so it always will be.

"Yet might it be precarious to weep
With eyes slack-fastened and shake these rusty joints;
I am a specter, even if at some points
A father, touched too tender by his issue;
So weak and dusty I perceive my tissue,
I must not crack it—I will turn and sleep."

Title| *SP69*: *Injured Sire*
3| *SP69*: disjoins.
4| *SP69*: woman-house
6| *SP69*: squandered, one head, one heart,
7| *SP69*: part.
8| *SP69*: But so < > is; so all their lives 'twill be.
9| *SP69*: "Yet would it < > precarious, wanting to weep
10| *SP69*: From eyes unfastened, or to shudder with brittle joints.
11| *SP69*: some sore points.
12| *SP69*: father in ill repute with his own issue.
13| *SP69*: O Lord defend my poor old fragile tissue!
14| *SP69*: But I'll not risk it. I

ADDITIONAL PUBLISHED POEMS

1. Sundry Poems

What the Old Leaf Said

You are sharp, my wind, you are sharp today!
Sharp have you sharpened your little spears,
A thousand of them at my ears
And sticking in my side, I know.
"Go down," the shrill spears say, "Go down,"
The time is come and you must go
And you must lie upon the ground.
Enough of shuddering now, away!
One dizzy moment on the air
And then, my shuddering leaf, you're there."
My wind, you need not bluster so;
I have been ready for this day,
This dawn I felt the spears and knew,
And told my heart what it should do,
Obey as now it shall obey.

Now I have loved to wave in the sun
And have a little place my own
Where I the king might wave alone.
I would not care to wave too long.
You've heard perhaps the poet's song
About some aged yellow leaf
Who begged the winds to let him stay
And was so sick with fear and grief
When they were taking him away,
But when was ever such a one?
And why insult the yellow leaves
Who want no pity nor reprieves?
For none would willingly outstay
Companions that have dropt away,
And no proud leaf has ever been—
No, not a leaf was ever green—
But after months of merry use
The blight came down on all green stuff,

And green was green for long enough;
And dry is that leaf's goodly juice,
Cold unto death is his old heart,
Weary the leaf of a leaf's proud part
As he waits for the winds to set him loose.

Now it was good at growing-time.
(Pardon an old leaf's memories
Reviewing the life that is led on trees.)
For there are smells on a good spring day,
They made a wonder of our air,
And there are games and games to play,
Before we knew it night was there.
One tingles at the rain in spring,
(Swishy, swishy, foolish drops,
You'll never stick on our tree-tops),
One jumps to hear it thundering.

And then came full-grown knowing-time
What is a leaf? He has his prime,
And it is to perch so strong and high
And laugh at rough winds sailing by
And say no wind shall put him down.
Never a face of prying moon
But I outstared it, sneaking round.
Never a withering sun of June
But tried me all the blazing day,
Thinking to wither me so soon,
And then went red with rage away;
For I would fold, for prudence' sake,
And sit and study half-awake;
I could have folded more and slept,
But for the big black man below
Who came from a garden that he kept
And flung himself down by his hoe
And lay in the shadow pleased with me.
But I was better pleased than he
At answering a black man's prayer.
I brooded over lovers too
For many a languid evening thru,

I blest the dalliers unawares
Who thought of only lovc's affairs.
I thought it good to sit so high
Between the creatures and the sky,
Practicing love and wisdom there.

Two thrushes used to come and swing,
A blackbird too, the blackest thing,
A while each day to stay and sing
At many a serenade for me.
And they were serenaders three!
They do not serenade me now,
They do not like my yellow face,
They do not stop on a barren bough,
They are off to another and greener place.
The old leaves rattle on the stem
And birds have no more tunes for them.
So this is the end of a leaf at last.
Now why are you chanting words of cheer,
Why do you whisper words of hope,
When time for hope and cheer is past?
Bright are the heavens you bring so near
To leaves that agonize and grope;
Pleasant your easy theories,
Comfort the finest that there is!
I thank each friendly comforter,
Let him not trouble much, I ask,
We are less frightened than we were,
And more indifferent to his task.
The old leaves hardly care at all
What happens next—they only fall.

If you would really know the end,
Why, thus I think it happens, friend:
The dizzy passage soon is done
And you may say the old leaf's gone.
But consolation even then,
Behold! I shall not go alone.
Whoever lives upon the tree
Shall know the same mortality

And bear me thoro [*sic*] company.
A million leaves shall go with me!
Attended thus, it matters less
That I am plucked from happiness;
Befriended thus, it matters not
That I address myself to rot.
Is such an unconcern amiss?
Then hear me make one pious prayer,
There is a heaven for which I'd care.
Will the black gardener grant me this:
Let him come with a shining rake,
Swing and swing till his black sides ache,
Roll us over, pile us deep
Into a single mangled heap,
Haul us to his garden spot,
Dump us on that ground to rot.
Down where the roots of life are spread
Let be the burial of the dead.
But when it smells of spring again
The garden will know its good black stain,
And blest shall that garden grow,
Greener every vine shall blow,
We rotted that it might be so.

Blow sharp, O wind, blow sharper still!
The old leaf offers up his will,
Then blow and blow, my wind, until—

The House

With such strong arms I shut my Love about,
She rested there; which was to me a token,
This was a house she could not walk without,
Securely bricked; and never to be broken.
Alas, the tight imprisonment was vain,
'Twas much too wide and physical for hearts;
When we had come most near, and scarce were twain,
We had not met; some soul and secret parts
Escaped the snare; and most unperjured lips

That bargained sweetly for our souls' exchange
Must lie, and love be blocked with this eclipse,
That she and I would live and still be strange.
    And as for Death, whose stroke dissevers men,
    What fool would make a firm possession then?

[Minerva Had No Pride]

Minerva had no pride of pedigree,
And so they shot her, bent of a broken leg,
Without a grief: then they looked butcheringly
On the unprovided babe she left to beg.

But who came coursing, like the tall corn slanting,
Beautiful, proud, and furious with anger?
It was the farmer's slender daughter, panting,
And pitiful to orphans in their danger.

You flew your ribbon from his yellow head,
Managed his bottle over many a meal,
Now he is big, and tramps the flower-bed,
And still nobody dares pronounce him veal.
    But I make little marvel of this calf,
    Being not the whole of history, not half.

Halted at the Altar

I. Obeisance

Roger the beautiful, that finished blade,
    Descended full of conquest on a city,
And what a furious racket Roger made!
    He sacked the town, and ruled it without pity.

He jilted the city maids. The city mothers
    Prayed heaven to thunder on that yellow pate,
Until at last, surpassing all the others,
    Appeared a maid equipped for Roger's mate.

And her he royally wooed; for she had beauty,
    Estate, and loved him with a lacking wit,
A noble alliance being Roger's duty.
    Behold the nuptials set, the license writ.

But wait! The lordly lover has smelled a fault.
The bidden guests may laugh, the wedding must halt.

II. Obesity

Roger contemned the obese of woman-kind:
    Himself he teetered like a poplar tree,
His love was like a willow in the wind
    Albeit her mother ambled heavily.

But monstrous grandam, coming many a league
    To see the bridegroom, weighed upon his joy;
And pictures, showering on him like the plague,
    Ancestresses of huge avoirdupois.

He knew his beauteous bride was doubly doomed
    By two heredities to increase and thicken:
This bride, he swore, had better not be groomed!
    He took another town. But she was stricken.

—And has she waxed amain, and does she grow
Unto his dread?—Ironically, No!

The Song of Roland

I.

Once when the drift was deep upon the fold,
    And snow was tossed upon the bitter gale,
Roland fared forth. And all his joints were cold,
    But with his heart he warmed a wondrous tale.

Brave recompense! They welcomed him right well
And friendliwise, as royal folk will do.
For this was a palace whereabout I tell,
And they were kings and queens, and a princess, too.

With winter-spray they decked the sober wall,
With goodly cheer belabored the mighty board,
In fearful play, on either side the hall.
The hearth-fires flashed with many a quick bright sword.

And then those royalties sat down and ate:
How was it, Roland, sitting in such state?

II.

The music sounded, soft as sliding brooks,
Burdened of love, and summer trees, and flowers,
Of pale impetuous knights who rode in books,
And eke of maids who lay in steep strong towers.

And at the glowing and oppressive dance
Did Roland clasp his princess in her white,
And venture hopes too fond for furtherance,
And whisper much, as any mortal might?

The good knight Roland hath his lady's love,
'Twas won betwixt two measures meetly taken.
'Twas barely whispered, not a breath above—
Or doth Rolando dream, and will awaken?

It is no dream, but verity. O strange,
She that is proud, and bred to royalty,
To love with a squire! But royallest love can change
When priggish tongues make prattle of degree.

'Twere better Roland had dreamed, and nothing other:
She broke her faith, heeding that hen, her mother.

Garden Sonnets

1. Sweet Will His Sonnet Set Out

With sweet green circumstance, and leafy clutch,
    Swelleth my young rose (spake the potent Earl);
Small baggage, yet thy hope doth please her much
    Who goes amid my flowers, the English girl.
Up now and blaze upon thy mid career,
    Thy rich young April promise keeping quite;
Spread in the wind thy bravest crimson gear,
    And turn thy scented page for her delight.
Alas! thy beauty at the peak arriving,
    The ill-bred worm comes too, that hates thy scene;
I cut thee off in thy great show of thriving
    Lest she may shrink at thee and cry, Unclean!
Not long had rose to tarry in the sun,
A fortnight was his term, that soon was done.

2. He Burns for Her

He's in a vase, his branch is sawn asunder,
His beauty marketed, his utmost sky
The roof and walls, his kingdom shrunken under,
And this pale beauty sits to see him die.
Beauty for beauty. Cunning hide-and-seek,
She spied the bud; "A great rose fatteneth."
The seventh day she praised his glowing cheek
And stooping plucked him with a tender breath.
She praises, but he trembles on the change.
His rotten beauty barely keeps the stem.
Soon his obscene cadaver will estrange
These eyes that knew his glory, frightening them.
Have you thought, Innocence, your garden roses
A quenchless flaming bush like that of Moses?

Sonnets of a Selfish Lover

I.

The little cousin is dead, and what subtraction!
A green bough from Virginia's aged tree.
Aghast are the country kin at the rude transaction,
And some of the world of outer dark, like me.

The elder men have strode by the box of death
To the wide flag porch, and muttering low send round
The bruit of the day: O friendly waste of breath!
Their hearts are hurt with a deep dynastic wound.

He was pale and little, the foolish neighbors say:
The first-fruits, saith the preacher, the Lord hath taken:
O no! 'Twas the old tree's late branch wrenched away,
Aggrieving the sapless limbs, all shorn and shaken.

Aggrieving the tender boughs. O tender maid,
I fear what drooping heart this hurt has made.

II.

He was not good nor beautiful nor clever,
A black cloud full of storms too hot for keeping,
A sword beneath his mother's heart; yet never
Has woman wept her child as she is weeping.

A pig with a pasty face, I long had said,
Squealing for cakes, and fixing a shameful reign
On a suffering house. But the little man quite dead,
I see much hint of his forebears' noble strain.

One he loved, you; obeyed and honored, nearly:
Descended someway, from his little throne.
For such small honor O pay not too dearly!
Look up and laugh, go not so much alone.

She much too slowly walks, too great a way,
Too slowly smiles when other girls are gay.

III.

With low-hung head I step, look left nor right,
And tread a four-leaved clover in the path.
I pluck. Is it not written that it might
Convert my plaintive hath-not into hath?

Good health to cats and calves and puny pets
Whose mortal misadventures touch too quickly
Her tender heart! Absolved of these small debts
She'll turn to an old lover breathing thickly.

And now no more of little cousins dying!
And let the Indifferent Guardians no more dare
To fade this loveliness with tears and sighing
On horrid tombs that hardly old dames bear.

Alas! Ye poor petitioners of clover,
How simple is an unattended lover!

Sonnets of a Pastoral Pair

I. They Take to the Fields

Once went two lovers out to take their pleasure;
They trod the country paths, and hardly stayed;
The sunny air was all their wine and treasure,
But it was golden, wherewithal they played.

And I remember how that once or twice
They could not answer from the upfilled throat,
As cognizant of some rare green device,
Some white wing speeding, or a lingered note.

Much day was chattered down, and it was late,
Their shadows played a somber pantomime,
Whereat a fear contracted their debate,
Since even the good sun overstepped his prime.

In this strange pair I, Master Mock, was one,
Thinking how noble a scheme to sport in the sun.

II. They Praise the Sun

How shall the golden day discreetly pass?
Take shoe and staff, and mount the windy hill,
And see if 'twixt high heaven and the grass
One cloud, one leaf, make any motion ill.

What shall the text and homiletics be?
The kindly sun, who would not fade too soon;
These twain, the well-perfected you and me;
This flame, that pulses hotter than his June.

Grieve not too much, if afterward of burning
He sink so ashily! There is an art,
To grudge not greedily; take hands and turning
Go speaking not; this is the happy heart.

Sun after sun is yet to paint the skies.
Dark spaces intervene, but new suns rise.

III. They Brave the Night

At nightfall loving hearts are put aback.
The gods in blue have all been whipped from heaven,
Well-spoken winds are dead, green trees are black,
White clouds march not and spin, nor small birds even.

Take ye no courage in the heathens' tents
Who would put night away, and thickly dance,
And loudly roar, and smear them with hot scents,
Squeezed in dishonor from dead flowers of France.

But hide ye close, the one in the other's grip;
Your talk be decent small; to keep you brave.
Put you to sleep, and let sad night go skip;
And look! tomorrow clambers from his cave.

And soon the proud sun rides upon his arc
So hot, so bold, it never has been dark.

IV. They Hail the Sunrise

They swore they found the dark exceeding bitter:
Death's arm and captain, whose obscene commands
Sent beauty marching, save for some stars' glitter:
They were afraid, and took each other's hands.

But hands hold much of heat in little storage;
And eyes are flickerless torches good as day;
The flame of each to the other's flame cried courage;
Soon heart to heart they sighed their grief away.

The sun of a sudden glowing through the brushes,
They woke and laughed, their eyes again were blue,
They ran to the fields, and apprehending thrushes,
Spoke not a word, but traveled in the dew.

Traveled or tarried, breathing deep or breathless,
Strong as the sun, and girded up, and deathless.

April Absence

My winter's leave was much too cold for smarting.
What bitter winds, and numbing snows and sorrows,
And wheezy pines like old men undeparting
To funeralize against all green young morrows!

That was like death. But springtime coming forth,
The southern airs, that twitched anew my wound,
Sent Father Robin safely singing North.
And Brother Reynard leaping on his round.

On earth they danced (I only trod no measure).
In air they dived and floated in the flood,
Each other beast prepared his brood and treasure:
Hot fumes of April mounted to my blood.

I rose and came. I could have cleft asunder
Ten worlds of circumstance that held me under.

Destitution Raiseth Her Voice (1922)

Ye fatted in your fortresses,
Behold! that fretful tribe the poor
Come crying thinly on your house
With "Open us your door!"
Your bricks are tight, your jowls are firm,
Ye sit aside and lock the shelf,
Yet may these urgent pilgrims be
Lord Jesus, poor himself.

King Croesus shut his golden gate
To let no muddy almsmen in.
"The King," old wizard Solon said,
"Unkings him by that sin."
And soon the proud man hanged was,
The golden king upon the tree,
Begging the poor to stop and wet
Him parching piteously.

Ye all I know are beggars born
And walk by favor on the earth.
Once in the strict and sightless womb
Ye cried to come to birth,
Then wept ye next for mother's milk,
Nor think ye now ye earn your bread,
If ever upon a Sabbath morn
Lord Jesus hungered.

Poets Have Chanted Mortality

It had better been hidden
But the Poets inform:
We are chattel and liege
Of an undying Worm.

Were you, Will, disheartened,
When all Stratford's gentry
Left their Queen and took service
In his low-lying country?

How many white cities
And grey fleets on the storm
Have proud-builded, hard-battled,
For this undying Worm?

Was a sweet chaste lady
Would none of her lover.
Nay, here comes the Lewd One,
Creeps under her cover!

Have ye said there's no deathless
Of face, fashion, form,
Forgetting to honor
The extent of the Worm?

O ye laughers and light-lipped,
Ye faithless, infirm,
I can tell you who's constant,
'Tis the Eminent Worm.

Ye shall trip on no limits,
Neither time ye your term,
In the realms of His Absolute
Highness the Worm.

Virga

I am virga, a rod—
I am commandment, lex—
My soul's the antic boy
I must keep in for duty;
But he is plagued with devils
(The chief among them sex)
And crying for the whiteness
Of the bosom of beauty.

Poor soul, I keep him one day
Whipt and wept in charge,
I preach him to repentance
For his glorious fault;
Tomorrow he repays me
Incontinence as large,
Restores again the savor
That's forbidden in the salt.

For the body of my lady
Is a terror to me—
I would run to my house,
Like a fox, harried hard—
But my young courageous rebel
Is compounded curiously,
Her honorable beauty
Is fire to his petard.

So I took him out of town,
And I walked him in the country,
I put my young scholar
Unto a quiet school:
I bade him watch the shrub folk,
The chaste garden gentry,
For leaf and twig are lovely
But the sap runs slow and cool.

For the green ones grew upward,
Or they folded, or they leant,
From the sun they got the light,
From the earth sufficient lease,
Though their furniture was naught
Yet they aged in content,
And without a passion in them
They could praise God without cease.

And I marked one duteous bird
That delivered him of a song:
His notes thin and heartless
Came chanting from the tree
Like words of spinster ladies
That have been loveless long,
And lately are perfected
In sweet gentility.

One foolish wind was loose
Upon the peace of air,
And soon he had distempered
A sea of wheated hill;
But it seemed the wheat was bowing
In a pharisaic prayer
For the sinful souls like mine,
Not so beautiful and still.

I will sanctify this soul.
I will make him harbor there
Till obedience has purged him
Of his bravery, of his stain;
For I will keep him growing
Like the green things in the air,
Till he is washed to purity
By wind and sun and rain.

Applied Eleatics

It is better to be a mortal pursuing a fantom
Than a swift god in love with a little mortal.
If you look to Olympus, and love one chosen at random,
Your gallant chase is forever; she is not a turtle.

But to ride on wings, or a dolphin, or a zephyr,
Or enter her housetop in a rain of stars—
Would you have her bound as a sacrificial heifer?
Then you have abridged your epical desires.

Strange was a certain goat-god's misadventure.
He whistled approaching the bathers; but the fairest
Had listened too well; showed him her half dropped ceinture;
And soon right shrilly he fled her through the forest.

Nostri in Memoriam Doctissimi

(Herbert Cushing Tolman, Distinguished Classical Scholar and Assyriologist, Died on November 24, 1923.)

This man reduced the Achaemenidae,
    Kings that had mightily ruled and left behind
    Names on a shard or a sheer rock blunting the wind,
Whereon was writ their story. For only he

Could read it—though he was a friend too loyal
    To keep the treasures from our weaker wit—
    And I must suppose he apprehended it
By the affinity of his own blood royal.

The simple kings: who towered up and builded
    And shook their scepters over the low plain,
    Sounding their abracadabras in disdain,
Thinking the meek earth theirs, for so it yielded.

But now were they perished, and this antiquary
    Possessed their lands, their laws, even their words.

Their kingdoms by a compulsion sharper than swords
Came under his power and were tributary.

Therefore, with exultation let us talk
Of his new estate, and with assurance turn us
Unto that grotto deep beneath Avernus
Where he and the fierce kings empty-handed walk.

Think not of a new abasement in his look,
For he eyes the wildered kings in his old fashion
As but desolate ghosts meet for his old compassion,
Direly in need of his bell, in need of his book—

And he gathers them, dutiful scholars, at his feet,
Instructing them truly what a kingdom is,
And preparing them by gentle homilies
To approach the dreaded Ruler on the Seat.

Autumn Love

(*English Sonnet of Italian Parts*)

Easter thaws no overwintered mind
With its pale burning. Centered in the cake
Of cold the heart fluttering can but ache
And wish the spring away. On an Easter wind
Came she, his lump of locked earth to unbind.
But too white shone the unseasoned lilies plucked
Which still the snows attainted, and no bees sucked,
And he refused her bosom, white and kind.

Great was summer; its fat boughs unshaken,
Its red and thirsting face, its frowzy plumes
That nodded, and its fervent rosy fumes.
She leaned like a rich flower to be taken.
But his cold Northern heart would not awaken
To her strong fire, and fevered with half-love
He trembled and went stealthy through the grove,
Leaving her gift ungathered and forsaken.

Vengeance struck with autumn; flapped its blear
And ragged banners; spilled the blossoms; grayed
The plumes and dusted with its cannonade.
Then warned of winter, of these disgraced and dear
Already wasting, and bright crowns grown sere,
He ran to seek her, and by the rushes found
Her sunken cold with treachery on the ground.
There they clung, in the ashes of the year.

Her tears filled up her eyes, and unconfessed
His tears lumpily thickening in the throat
Muffled his valiant pledges, every note.
By the sad yellow passage of the sun
They kissed in tears, and heard the fowler's gun
Bark at a few faint birds far from the nest.

The Feasting of Maionides and Stephen Daedalus

For the credit's sake of a blind cook,
Folded, buttered, and meek they lie,
Flat as the pages in a book,
Four-and-twenty blackbirds to the pie.
A nameless fowler of Phoenicia slew them;
The Greek Maionides can bake and do them.

He that sat smiling at the board
A king was, and the world was young.
That king's company were of strong
Digestion, and they loved their lord,
And counted each an excellent thing,
To fight furiously, and hear birds sing.
A dainty dish now sat before the king.

They courteously by ranks reclined
And praised the pie's devout expansion.
With bright checks delicately wined
They waited. By the vertical dimension
The pie was opened. Oh, the magical birds,
They were alive, they had wings, they had words!

The sea-green air with flashing jet
They jeweled, and with instant whir
That made its sleeping thunder stir.
But soon they perched on each high fret
Transmuting the roofed cavern to a choir
From which the song came flaming like a fire.

Majestical was the music heard
By king and company that dined.
They praised Maionides the blind
For every marvelous god-bird
Of whom he caught and fettered the bird-wind.

For hearing how the world was bodied
Of myrtle grove and rocky plain
Where gods and demigods and men
Dallied and fought; of streams unmuddied
Where many ships with purple sails could go;
Of heaven bright above and Hades dark below;

Even of trouble taking noble joy;
Achilles, the blond sulking boy,
And many another wide in fame
Falling most hollowly, playing out their Troy—
The feasters went out better than they came,
Saying of life and death, they equal bore good name.

Maionides is gone. And Daedalus
Prepares the feast of the immortal birds.
Alas, it seems to us
They jangle sibilants and surds
Harsh, obscene, opprobrious.
Is this your mocking art, O Stephen?
The fiends requite you then, and make it even.

Pale banqueters though we be, and bilious,
Praying those proper kings' deserts
Impassion our enfeebled hearts,
Shall we let Stephen willy-nilly us

To hear a song dispirited as thought,
And no bird singing clearly as he ought?

But ah! suppose the birds that sing
Have tired of flying from a string,
Wearied of immortal song
Which shall not swell again to strong,
And sunken into whimpering
And the despair of a tired tongue?

Down sit we, small of appetite;
The pie is opened; out the creatures rush
And flutter pitiful in the cold light;
They sing a little, but had better hush;
For all the gods have vanished in the cold,
And Troy is fallen, and the world is old;
A bitter tale, and better far untold.

2. New Poems in the *Selected Poems* Volumes

What Ducks Require (*SP*45)

Ducks require no ship and sail
Bellied on the foamy skies,
Who scud north. Male and female
Make a slight nest to arise
Where they overtake the spring,
Which clogs with muddy going.

This zone is temperate. The pond,
Eye of a bleak Cyclops visage, catches
Such glints of hyacinth and bland
As bloom in aquarelles of ditches
On a cold spring ground, and render
A space supportable and a time tender.

The half-householders for estate
Beam their floor with ribs of grass,
Disdain your mortises and slate
And Lar who invalided lies,
Planting dangerous at the earth-heart
Where warm and cold precisely start.

Furled, then, the quadrate wing
From the lewd eye and fowler's gun
Till in that wet sequestering,

7| *PE, SP*63, *SP*69: The zone unready. But the
11| *NR*: ground and
MS*SP*45: ground, #comma inserted# and
*PE, SP*63, *SP*69: ground, a freak,
12| *NR, FA*: supportable, and
MS*SP*45: supportable, #comma crossed out# and
*PE, SP*63, *SP*69: A weathering chance even in the wrack #*PE* has no full stop following *wrack*#
14| P*SP*45: grass #comma inserted#
17| *FA*: dangerous by the
*PE, SP*63, *SP*69: The marsh quakes dangerous, the port
18| *PE, SP*63, *SP*69: Where wet and dry precisely
19| *NR*: wing,
20| *NR*: And, O lewd fox and fowler's ear,
FA: From the lewd fox and fowler's eye
MS*SP*45: eye of the fowler's
21| *NR*: The epithalamion unsung:—
FA: Till, in that dim sequestering,

Webtoed, the progeny is done,
Cold-hatched, and from the blink of birth
Is native to the rhythmed earth.

Prodigious in his wide degrees
Who, as the winds and waters blow,
On raveling banks of fissured seas
In reeds nestles, or will rise and go
Where Capricornus dips his hooves
In the blue chasm of no wharves.

Prelude to an Evening (*SP*45)

Do not enforce the tired wolf
Dragging his infected wound homeward
To sit tonight with the warm children
Naming the pretty kings of France.

The images of the invaded mind
Being as monster in the dreams
Of your most brief enchanted headful,
Suppose a miracle of confusion:

That dreamed and undreamt become each other
And mix the night and day of your mind;
And it does not matter your twice crying
From mouth unbreautied against the pillow

22| *NR*: Web-toes of progeny appear,
FA: Webtoed the lustrous progeny
23| *FA*: Is coldhatched
*PE, SP*63, *SP*69: Cold-hatched, the infant progeny tries
24–25| *NR*: Suckle the sweet cold breast of earth. // The prodigious duck makes melodies
FA: Suckles the sweet cold breast of earth. // Ridiculously born he is / Unto prodigious melodies
MS*SP*45: How loves and scorns #last word crossed out and replaced above by# spurns its base of earth. // The prodigious duck has melodies
P*SP*45: In #second letter crossed out and replaced by *s* to make# Is
*PE, SP*63, *SP*69: To preen his feathers for the skies. // Prodigious
26| *NR, FA*, MS*P*S45: You have not learned, pale scholars: low
*PE, SP*63, *SP*69: Who where the < > blow
28| *NR*: nestles or

#Notation for *SP*63 refers to the first of the two versions of the poem in that volume#
6| *AR, NV*: as the monsters

To avert the gun of the swarthy soldier,
For cry, cock-crow, or the iron bell
Can crack the sleep-sense of outrage,
Annihilate phantoms who were nothing.

But now, by our perverse supposal,
There is a drift of fog on your mornings;
You in your peignoir, dainty at your orange-cup,
Feel poising round the sunny room

Invisible evil, deprived and bold.
All day the clock will metronome
Your gallant fear; the needles clicking,
The heels detonating the stair's cavern.

Freshening the water in the blue bowls
For the buckberries with not all your love,
You shall be listening for the low wind,
The warning sibilance of pines.

You like a waning moon, and I accusing
Our too banded Eumenides,
You shall make Noes but wanderingly,
Smoothing the heads of the hungry children.

Of Margaret (*SP*45)

With the fall of the first leaf that winds rend
She and the boughs trembled, and she would mourn
The wafer body as an own first born,
But with louder destruction sang the wind.

13| *AR, NV*: of the same old soldier;
19| MS*SP*45: your orange,
21| *PE, SP*63: deprived, and
26| *AR*: buckberries, with
NV: buck berries, with
31| *AR, NV*: While you pronounce Noes wonderingly
MS*SP*45: make #next word, illegible, blotted out# < > wandering #altered to# wonderingly, #comma inserted#
32| *AR, NV*: And smooth the

Title| *SatR: Autumn Grief of Margaret*
1| *SatR*: At the fall < > wind rends
*SP*69b: Frost, and a leaf has quit the tulip tree
2| *SatR*: bough tremble < > she will mourn
*SP*69b: Wafting on brightest airs with twist and turn;
3| *SP*69b: body is Margaret's first-born.
4| *SatR*: destruction the wind sounds.
*SP*69b: A day of dark shall be her Calvary.

Soon must they all descend, there where they hung
In gelid air, and the blind land be filled
With dead, and a mere windiness unchild
Her of the sons of all her mothering.

No mother sorrow is but follows birth
And, beyond that, conception; hers was large,
And so immoderate love must be a scourge,
Needing the whole ecstasy of substant earth.

But no evil shall spot this, Margaret's page,
For her generations were of the head,
The eyes, the tender fingers, not the blood,
And the issue was all flowers and foliage.

Virgin, whose image bent to the small grass
I keep against this tide of wayfaring,
O hear the maiden pageant ever sing
Of that far away time of gentleness.

Painted Head (*SP*45)

By dark severance the apparition head
Smiles from the air a capital on no

5| *SatR*: Soon these all will decline who heavy hang
*PE, SP*63: So must the others drop, there
*SP*69b: Then shall the leaves be stained with weathering,
6| *PE, SP*63: Quaking and cold, and
*SP*69b: And the green sward of a sudden be defiled
7| *SatR*: and but a windless
*PE, SP*63: dead, till one least and last wind unchild
*SP*69b: With surfeit, till one soft wind of grace unchild
9| *SP*69a,b: birth,
10| *SatR*: And, behind that
13| *SatR, SP*69b: page.
14| *SatR*: All her
*SP*69b: The generations born of her loving mood
15| *SatR*: eyes begot but not the wishful blood
*SP*69b: Were modes of yellow greenery, not of blood,
16| *SatR*: was but flowers
*SP*69b: And the faithful issue was blossom and
17| *SatR*: image tall in the green grass
*SP*69b: whose bravest image in the grass
18| *SatR*: keep, you are acquit of statute wrong;
19| *SatR*: And let the
20| *SatR*: Of this far

Column or a Platonic perhaps head
On a canvas sky depending from nothing;

Stirs up an old illusion of grandeur
By tickling the instinct of heads to be
Absolute and to try decapitation
And to play truant from the body bush;

But too happy and beautiful for those sorts
Of head (homekeeping heads are happiest)
Discovers maybe thirty unwidowed years
Of not dishonoring the faithful stem;

Is nameless and has authored for the evil
Historian headhunters neither book
Nor state and is therefore distinct from tart
Heads with crowns and guilty gallery heads;

So that the extravagant device of art
Unhousing by abstraction this once head
Was capital irony by a loving hand
That knew the no treason of a head like this;

Makes repentance in an unlovely head
For having vinegarly traduced the flesh
Till, the hurt flesh recusing, the hard egg
Is shrunken to its own deathlike surface;

And an image thus. The body bears the head
(So hardly one they terribly are two)
Feeds and obeys and unto please what end?
Not to the glory of tyrant head but to

The increase of body. Beauty is of body.
The flesh contouring shallowly on a head
Is a rock-garden needing body's love
And best bodiness to colorify

17| *SP63*, *SP69*: Wherefore the
22| *NR*: For vinegar disparagement of flesh
25| *NR*: thus: the
29| *SP63*: The being of
SP69: The estate of

The big blue birds sitting and sea-shell flats
And caves, and on the iron acropolis
To spread the hyacinthine hair and rear
The olive garden for the nightingales.

Address to the Scholars of New England (*SP*45)

(*Harvard Phi Beta Kappa poem, June 23, 1939*)

When Sarah Pierrepont let her spirit rage
Her love and scorn refused the bauble earth
(Which took bloom even here, under the Bear)
And groped for the Essence sitting in himself,
Subtle, I think, for a girl's unseasoned rage.

The late and sudden extravagance of soul
By which they all were swollen exalted her
At seventeen years to Edwards' canopy,
A match pleasing to any Heaven, had not
The twelve mortal labors harassed her soul.

Thrifty and too proud were the sea-borne fathers
Who fetched the Pure Idea in a bound box
And fastened him in a steeple, to have his court
Shabby with an unkingly establishment
And Sabbath levees for the minion fathers.

The majesty of Heaven has a great house,
And even if the Indian kingdom or the fox
Ran barking mad in a wide forest place,
They had his threshold, and you had the dream
Of property in him by a steepled house.

34| *NR*: caves and

Title| *SP*69: To the Scholars of Harvard
Subtitle| *KR, PE, SP*63: #in italics#
*SP*69: Phi Beta Kappa Poem June 23, 1939 #in italics and without parentheses#

1| *KR*: rage,
4| MS*SP*45: essence #altered to# Essence
*SP*69: the Essence, sitting
8| MS*SP*45: Edward's #altered to# Edwards'
13| *SP*69: And put him < > steeple to
20| *SP*69: Of preference in

If once the entail shall come on raffish sons,
Knife-wit scholar and merchant sharp in thumb,
With positive steel they'll pry into the steeple,
And blinking through the cracked ribs at the void
A judgment laughter rakes the cynic sons.

But like prevailing wind New England's honor
Carried, and teased small Southern boys in school,
Whose heads the temperate birds fleeing your winter
Construed for, but the stiff heroes abashed
With their frozen fingers and unearthly honor.

Scared by the holy megrims of those Pilgrims,
I thought the unhumbled and outcast and cold
Were the rich Heirs traveling incognito,
Bred too fine for the country's sweet produce
And but affecting that dog's life of pilgrims.

There used to be debate of soul and body,
The soul storming incontinent with shrew's tongue
Against what natural brilliance body had loved,
Even the green phases though deciduous
Of earth's zodiac homage to the body.

Plato, before Plotinus gentled him,
Spoke the soul's part, and though its vice is known
We're in his shadow still, and it appears
Your founders most of all the nations held
By his scandal-mongering, and established him.

Perfect was the witch foundering in water,
The blasphemer that spraddled in the stocks,
The woman branded with her sin, the whales

21| *SP69*: entail should fall on
22| *SP69*: sharp of thumb,
23| *SP69*: they'd
25| *SP69*: laughter would rake
26| *SP69*: Yet like
27| *SP69*: boys at school
29| MS*SP45*: Construed form #altered to# for
32| *SP69*: We thought
36| *SP69*: There must have been debate
40–46| *SP69*: body. / Perfect the witch was, foundering
44| MS*SP45*: nations known# last word crossed out and replaced by# held

Of ocean taken with a psalmer's sword,
The British tea infusing the bay's water.

But they reared heads into the always clouds
And stooped to the event of war or bread,
The secular perforces and short speech
Being labors surlily done with the left hand,
The chief strength giddying with transcendent clouds.

The tangent Heavens mocked the fathers' strength,
And how the young sons know it, and study now
To take fresh conquest of the conquered earth,
But they're too strong for that, you've seen them whip
The laggard will to deeds of lunatic strength.

To incline the powerful living unto peace
With Heaven is easier now, with Earth is hard,
Yet a rare metaphysic makes them one,
A gentle Majesty, whose myrtle and rain
Enforce the fathers' gravestones unto peace.

I saw the youngling bachelors of Harvard
Lit like torches, and scrambling to disperse
Like aimless firebrands pitiful to slake,
And if there's passion enough for half their flame,
Your wisdom has done this, sages of Harvard.

Old Man Pondered (*SP*63)

Three times he crossed our way where with me went
One who is fair and gentle, and it was strange,

54| *KR*: done by the
*SP*69: Being surly labors done
55| *SP*69: The main strength
56| *KR*, MS*SP*45: strength
*SP*69: tangent Heavens teased the
58| *SP*69: To make fresh
63| MS*SP*45: metaphysics #altered to# metaphysic
70| *SP*69: has been valiant, sages

Title| *SR*: *Four Threesomes; or Three Foursomes?*
SoR: *The Eye Can Tell*
SatR: #subtitle# (*English Sonnet of Italian Parts*)
1| *SR, SoR*: he passed our park where
2| *SR, SoR*: Sweet Hope, the fair

But not once glancing did his vision range
Wayward on me, or my most innocent,
But strictly watched his own predicament.
How are old spirits so dead? His eye seemed true
As mine, he walked by it, it was as blue,
How came it monstered in its fixed intent?

But I will venture how. In his long years
Close-watched and dangerous, many a bright-barbed hate
Burning had smote against the optic gate
To enter and destroy. But the quick gears
Blinked shut the aperture. Else those grim leers
Had won to the inner chamber where sat Hope
To spin and pray, and made her misanthrope,
And bled her courage with a thousand spears.

Thus hate and scorn. And he must guard as well
Against alluring love, whose mild engine
Was perilous too for the lone sitter-in,
So hard consented to her little cell;
The tenderest looks vainly upon him fell,
Of dearest company, lest one light arrow
Be sharpened with a most immortal sorrow.
So had he kept his mansion shut of hell.

Firm and upright he walked for one so old,
Thrice-pondered; and I dare not prophesy

3| *SR, SoR*: That not
4| *SR, SoR*: me and my dear innocent,
5| *SR, SoR*: strictly nursed his
6| *SR, SoR*: Dying before his death? His eyes [#*SoR* has *eye*#]
7| *SR, SoR*: As ours, he walked with it
8| *SR, SoR*: Yet could be monstrous < > intent.
9| *SR, SoR*: And I'm for telling how
12| *SR, SoR*: destroy; but
13| *SR, SoR*: apertures
14| *SR*: inner house, where sat my Hope
SoR: won the inner house, where sat my Hope
15| *SR*: Who fancied him. He made < > misanthrope
SoR: Who fancied him. He made
16| *SR, SoR*: But bled < > with his softer spears.
17| *SR, SoR*: He's given to scorn. For he
18| *SR, SoR*: whose brave engine
19| *SR*: for lone sitter-in,
SoR: for long sitter-in
20| *SR, SoR*: consented with her
21| *SR, SoR*: Her tender
22| *SR, SoR*: He would not answer them, lest
23| *SR, SoR*: sorrow;
24| *SR, SoR*: his ticket shut
25| *SR, SoR*: Nearly upright he walks

What age must bring me; for I look round bold
And seek my enemies out; and leave untold
The sideway watery dog's-glances I
Send fawning on you, thinking you will not scold.

27| *SR, SoR*: me. But I
28| *SR, SoR*: To seek < > out, and
29| *SR*: side-ways watery dog's
SoR: side-ways waterydog's
30| *SR, SoR*: Keep fawning on her; Hope will never scold.

3. Alternate Versions of Poems (Early or Later Versions)

Sonnet of a Sure Heart (1920)

The way seemed full of her, but these came nigh,
Fluting like birds, and calicoed bright and clean,
And beautiful their bosoms poutering by!
"But ye are a cloud," I said, "too much between."
Beauties have called to me from the woody grot,
The quick brown fox, and the red-tail tanager,
And the balsam tree; and how ye prospered not!
Ye were but scene, but frame, for circling her.
Up once I rose, in a fury of heard-of things,
To travel the splendid sphere and see its fame;
But the wars and ships and towns and the roaring kings
But flashed with the image of her! And back I came.
Since when I stay; I let the wide world spin:
She brings me all the other wonders in.

Winter Remembered (1922)

Two evils, monstrous either one apart,
Possessed me, and were long and loath at going:
A cry of Absence, Absence, in the heart,
And in the wood the furious winter blowing.

Think not, when fire was bright upon my bricks
And past the tight boards hardly a wind could enter,
I glowed like them, the simple burning sticks,
Far from my cause, my proper heat, my center.

Better to walk forth in the murderous air
And wash my wound in the snows; that would be healing,
Because my heart would throb less painful there,
Being caked with cold, and past the smart of feeling.

Which would you choose, and for what boot in gold,
The absence, or the absence and the cold?

The Handmaidens (1922)

There is reason for scandal now, said we in France:
Was it ever other in war than a devils' dance?
Now the Force felt half-discredited in this light,
That women were working, and we still asleep in the night.
We crept out of billets and answered to roll with sneezing,
But the women were deep in their duty with fingers freezing;
We limbered the cannon and rattled to Fontevrault,
Shapes darker than darkness flitted and let us go;
And the Saumur wives went burdened, and heavily leant:
Could Heaven not darkly see? Yet on they went.
And plainer than seeing, and out of all season, the sound:
The clack of their sabots smiting the frosty ground.
But strange! having one observed how crimes are done,
I can find them here, as otherwhere under the sun,
And I am ashamed how I carried my head so high:
"Of God's own country I am a citizen, I!"
God suffers abuses here and suffered them there:
Is there too much business, think you, under his care
So quick is my pity, I never can keep it down,
Beset by the provocations thick in this town,
Where saints and sinners have juxtaposition so odd,
They ill consort with the fame of the only God.
I am plagued with pity, yet scared of giving it scope;
My powerless kind affords but a little hope;
For the world and its fine reformers are soon estranged,
The war's well over, and look! there is nothing changed.
But God on his throne, I fancy, one of these days,
Will smell of the hideous brew in hot amaze;
He will summon all Heaven, and sooner than day has broken,
His angels will stand on the carpet and hear it spoken:

"Are your eyes gone blind? For ye look not very low,
If you see not the woman, how meek and poorly they go.
It is not yet day, and our tale of the stars not told,

But the handmaidens bear their burdens and tremble of cold.
Do ye heed not her, ye stony and reconciled,
One gathering sticks for a fire and heavy with child?
And many are heavy with sleep, and they watched not but slept;
Now it neareth dawn, and up they have started, and wept.
We are high on an absolute heaven, and nothing dependeth,
Still it twitcheth our heart when weeping of women ascendeth.
Say not, 'But a small sound of weeping, not much tears:'
Doth the Lord God need the thunder to tickle his ears?
We appointeth the strength in flesh and the pith in bones,
Endurance we measured them straitly, the little ones:
The vigils are early, the burdens uneasy to heave:
The thin bones verily ache, the flesh doth grieve.
We descried not the issue, devising the distant and soon,
Commending our young creation that first Sabbath noon,
For the woman we fashioned delicate, fairer, slight,
With intent of warmth for her day and sleep by night.
And season she still hath to go by the sun as of old,
But she falleth, poor wretch, to the devils of dark and cold.

"Now man, doth he up and constrain her, bone of his bone?
When he stretcheth his hand in sleep, the woman is gone.
It is writ he shall toil, he shall fight, he shall weep: and he can:
But ye have not to hear at this hearing the pity of man;
Say not that his road runneth steeply assuming the sin,
For we stomach it hard how he swelleth up in his skin.
Abject from the Garden ye heard him howl at the portal,
But the curse sitteth easy now on the stubborn mortal.
He braggeth and gameth, and brawleth the best of the time,
Nor faileth to gird at us with a villain rhyme,
He marshalleth kingdoms like ant-packs, holloweth ships,
He seeketh the bear in the ice and cometh to grips.
Not lions, deities, dead men shall catch him afeared!
A valiant tune doth he sing to his red little beard.
He picketh up fire and putteth it under a seat,
Whereon he shall ride, nor blister himself with heat,
Through the earth, through the air, for he thinketh it little ado,
And he findeth our hidden things, and whistleth 'Pooh!'
So he deemeth him king, yet cometh at length to complain
Of the dearth in his belly, and home to his pots again.

And the foolish woman is glad—O ye dubious queens!
She hath rubbed on the pot till it shone, then hath put in the beans;
While he was impounding his pleasures, pursuing his brawl,
She swept out his litter and knocked off the flies from the wall;
She hath put out a pickle, a pudding, a book, and a chair,
And his house hath order, if very small looks to spare.
His house is a squat thing, twenty by some eighteen,
But it keepeth him dry, and the woman keepeth him clean.
We impute to the hutch which his hares inhabit the pattern,
Such a box did he build for himself and the woman his slattern.
She hath gathered a poppy to stick in the blue of the crock,
But he tweaketh the blossom and maketh a sour 'Poppycock!'
Our intent was to chasten them, scuttling from Eden forth
To the taste of our scourge: but what was the lesson worth?
They are ripe for our hand, such twain, such an unkempt case,
He supping his sup by the sweat of the woman's face!

"Ye seraphim, elder, and more in our service rehearsed,
Ye remember the lady Eve as she walked at first;
Ye others may witness not to the lily Eve,
Yet of certain her daughters ye've gathered scope to believe.
A little beauty was vaunted after we smote,
For Delilah her bosom, for Sheba her tawny throat:
Madam Helen, a heathen, was not of a favor uncouth,
And ye know how her rumor ran and upseated the youth;
Much men and ships drew after her into battle,
They had seen no beauty before, they were witless cattle.
But fair as the moon was Eve, and clear as the sun,
Like terrible bannered armies in Lebanon;
Her breasts like the delicate Heshbon roes twin-born,
Her teeth were Hermon's sheep that are even shorn;
And the Rose of Sharon dwelt in Adam's court,
And Adam delighted, and published our good report.
But they sinned! And we stiffened our back and exceedingly sware
The curse of the broken commandment upon the pair.
The life we remitted, on pain of the toil and tilth,
Which meaneth, to handle the spade and the pot and the filth:
She must grabble and worry and tug, her face must sweat:
And we damned her bones to the bending, so bend they yet.
Ye have read that the lily need toil not, neither spin,

And the lily remaineth lily and knoweth no sin;
And the one is fair as the other, and either ye pluck
Is complected a lily, and taketh no smell from the muck.
But the daughters of Eve drop out of her favor clean,
They are used too badly, ill-favored, shrewish, and lean;
And one is snaggled of tooth, and one hath a wen,
And this is a fishface, and this one a peckish hen;
Nor to borrow of names from the flowers bettereth those,
The blear-eyed Dahlia, Viola, or Lily, or Rose.
What availeth the fame of our firmament keeping the way,
If the flesh of the women is troubled before the day?
Or spectacular stars as they race to encircuit the deep,
If our littlest people is driven and needeth sleep?
True it hardly beseemeth the Lord to forgive them the sin,
For the word went out, and we suck not the old words in;
We are ancient of days and travel an old way slowly,
We pity the woman's case but mend it not wholly:
There is labor appointed, we know not if it shall cease:
But at least by night shall the handmaidens lie in peace.
So arrange ye again how the people's task be done;
There shall no woman toil till they see our sign of the sun:
There shall none go creeping and cold till appeareth this token!
Remember and heed that the will be done! We have spoken."

Blue Girls (1924)

If I were younger, traveling the bright sward
Under the towers of your seminary,
I should get a look, and a thought, or even a word;
But I am old, and of aspect too contrary
For you who are less weary.

For why do you bind white fillets about your tresses
And weave such stately rhythms where you go?
Why do you whirl so lovingly your blue dresses,
Like haughty bluebirds chattering in the snow
Of what they cannot know?

Practice your beauty, blue girls, if you will;
The lean preceptress, she of history,
Showed you the manifold of good and ill,
And all you saw was princes crooking the knee
To beauteous majesty.

Do you think there are thrones enough, one for each queen?
Some thrones are chairs, some three-legged milking stools,
Or you even sit in ashes where thrones should have been;
And it is for this, God help us all for fools,
You practice in the schools.

Practice your beauty, blue girls, nevertheless;
Once the preceptress, learned bitter one,
Printed the sward in a flounce of purple dress
And was a princess pacing as to her throne;
But now you see she is none.

Implacable Tower (1925)

What from the tower? "Fool, Fool, I say to the man
That mightily scares his dog and horse and churl
But stumbles mortally on one big-eyed girl,
A flowing vine, uncaptured though well he can
Inscribe her ghost-white buds in his hand-span,
Killing him with cool innocence and able to deject
The vainglorious captain that had stood stiff-necked
Even to a King at court; Fool, Fool, to the man."

Paul took his wine and slept, and his thought swirled
From dream to dream through Christendom. But Paul's bride
Climbed up, with a great rat scampering at her side,
Reached the top step of Abbott's Northern tower
And listening at his door, at the very hour
Heard bitter doctrine descending on the world.

The Vanity of the Bright Young Men (*SP*63)

[Based on "Tom, Tom, the Piper's Son"]

You think in my tight black coat I'm like a beetle.
I never mind my looks,
I'm removed, a boy reported not liking people,
My familiars mostly are books.

I go alone to assembly, but I'd go pushing
Even to say my prayers,
Glaring with cold grey eyes at whom I am brushing,
Who would if they could with theirs.

But afternoons I walk in the primal creation,
In a spell, in a possible glory,
Counting on Nature to give me an intimation
Of my unlikely story.

One time I went, by the luck of my chances and choices,
Past certain Druid trees
Whose leaves were ears and tongues translating the voices
Hid in the muffling breeze.

Against me the counsels of spirits were not then darkened
Though out of my vision or reach,
As I set my boots to the path beneath and hearkened
Unto phrases of English speech.

#The page-proof revisions might represent an interim stage, for only some of the revisions are incorporated into *SP*63. Other revisions on this document accord with "The Vanity of the Bright Boys" in *SP*69. It seems likely that JCR made some of these revisions at one time and others at a later time. Some of the revisions are not reflected in any published version of either poem#

1| P*SP*63: You think #last two words crossed out and replaced by # Though #last word crossed out and replaced by# Grim in < > coat I'm #last word crossed out# like a #last word crossed out and replaced by two words# the sleazy

2| P*SP*63: I never mind #first three words crossed out and replaced by three words# But never minding

4| P*SP*63: Whose #first word crossed out and replaced by# My familiars mostly #last word crossed out# are #next two words inserted below# the great books

9| P*SP*63: the primal #last word crossed out and replaced by next three words# great green forest #*creation,* which *forest* would replace, is not crossed out#

10| P*SP*63: In a #last word crossed out and replaced by next word# the spell, in #last word crossed out#

One said, "This worm of the dust—he is strangely other
Than he and they suppose"—
But one, "Yet sired by his father and dammed by his mother?
Has he not acknowledged those?"

Again, "But wait—this man is a changeling but knows not—
I tell you this is a Prince"—
"From a far great kingdom and should return but goes not?"
"Fifteen long winters since"—

But like a King I was bound to a King's condition.
I steadied and marched right on,
Not testing by eavesdrop the wonder of my suspicion,
And quick that talk was gone.

And prompt I showed, as the tower's last throb appointed,
In the loud and litten room,
Nor was hailed by the love that leaps to the Heir Anointed:
"Hush, O hush, he is come."

Master's in the Garden Again (*SP63*)

(*To the memory of Thomas Hardy*)
[Based upon "Conrad in Twilight"]

i

Evening comes early, and soon discovers
Exchange between these conjugate lovers.

"Conrad! dear man, surprise! aren't you bold
To be sitting so late in your sodden garden?"

33| P*SP63*: Promptly I
35| P*SP63*: Not #first word crossed out and replaced by two words# Nor was
36–| P*SP63*: #the following additional stanza is crossed out# Remember, you're not to reveal a word I've said, / I'll be sorry if you do. / If I'm a case, I'll be just your Prince of Fools, / And I never will hurt you.

Dedication| VMS: (to the memory of Thomas Hardy)
KR: to the memory of Thomas Hardy
*SP69*b: #no Dedication; Roman numerals indicating sections are capitalized and centered throughout#

"Woman! intrusion! does this promise well?
I'm nursing my knees, they are not very cold.
Have you known the fall of the year when it fell?
Indeed it's a garden, but if you will pardon,
The health of a garden is reason's burden."

"Conrad! your feet are dripping in muck,
The neuralgia will settle in your own neck,
And whose health is it that catches an asthma?
Come in from foul weather for pity's sake!"

"No," says the thinker. "Concede. I am here,
Keeping guard of my garden and minding miasma.
You're lonely, my loony? Your house is up there.
Go and wait. If you won't, I'll go jump in the lake."

ii

And the master's back has not uncurved
Nor the autumn's blow for an instant swerved.

Autumn days in our section
Are the most used-up thing on earth
(Or in the waters under the earth)
Having no more color nor predilection
Than cornstalks too wet for the fire
And black leaves pitched onto the byre.

The show is of death. There is no defection.

iii

He will play out his mood before he takes food.

8| *SP69*b: pardon
9| *SP69*b: is somebody's burden."
14| *SP69*b: He is gentle but firm. "Concede, my dear,
15| *SP69*b: I'm warden of garden, and mind its miasma.
16| *SP69*b: If my loony is lonely her house < > there,
17| *SP69*b: wait! If < > won't I'll
23–24| *SP69*b: predilection / Than a man's face as weathered as straw / By summer's flare and autumn's flaw, / Or cornstalks < > fire,
25| *SP69*b: Or rain of leaves that writhe in the mire.
26–28| *SP69*b: The leaves are all dead. There < > // III / By the breath of

By the bob of the Power the dark skies lower,
By the bite of Its frost the children were lost
Who hurt no one where they shone in the sun,
But the valiant heart knows a better part
Than to do with an "O did It lay them low,
But we're a poor sinner just going to dinner."

See the tell-tale art of the champion heart.

Here's temple and brow, which frown like the law.
If the arm lies low, yet the rage looks high.
The accusing eye? that's a fierce round O.
The offense was raw, says the fix in the jaw.
We'll raise a rare row! we'll heave a brave blow!

A pantomime blow, if it damns him to do,
A yell mumming too. But it's gay garden now,
Play sweeter than pray, that the darkened be gay.

Prelude to an Evening (*SP63*)

(*A poem revised and explicated: the soliloquy of a man returning home to his wife*)

Do not enforce the tired wolf
Dragging his infected wound homeward
To sit tonight with the warm children
Saying the pretty Kings of France.

29–31| VMS, *KR*: lost, / But
35–42| VMS, *KR*: #like lines in Old English verse, these have two hemistichs with spaced caesuras#
35| *SP69*b: brow which < > law,
36| *SP69*b: low yet < > high,
37| VMS, *KR*: eye? it's a
*SP69*b: eye is a < > O!
38| *SP69*b: the stubborn jaw,
39–40| *SP69*b: a big row and heave a hard blow, / And let's do it now! // A < > damned
41| VMS: mumming, too
42| *SP69*b: gay. / #the following two lines were added# Here is a man who has done what he can, / Now he will defer to the house and to her.

Title and subtitle| *KR*: Prelude < > Evening: A POEM REVISED AND EXPLICATED
P*SP63*: *(A Poem Revised and Explicated)* #last five words and parentheses crossed out and replaced above by fourteen words and parentheses# (Soliloquy of a man going home to his wife; a poem revised and explicated)
*SP69*a,b: #no subtitle#

You are my scholar. Then languish, expire
With each day's terror and next week's doom
Till we're twice espoused, in love and ruin.
And grave but smiling though the heavens fall.

The images of the invaded mind
Were monstrous only in the dreams
Of your most brief enchanted headful.
Suppose a miracle of confusion:—

That dreamed and undreamt become each other
And mix the night and day of your soul.
For it never mattered your twice crying
From mouth unbeautied against the pillow

To avert the gun of the same old soldier,
If quickly cry, cock-crow or bell
Breaking the improbable black spell
Annihilated the poor phantom.

And now? To confirm our strange supposal,
Apparitions wait upon sunny mornings;
You in your peignoir commend the heaped oranges
Gold on the platter for cheeky children

But freeze at the turbulence under the floor
Where unclean spirits yawn and thrash;
The day-long clock will strike your fears;
The heels detonating the stair's cavern.

4–9| *KR*, P*SP*63: France. / The images
5| *SP*69b: expire,
6| *SP*69b: doom,
7| *SP*69b: ruin,
8| *SP*69b: smiling as the
10| *KR*, P*SP*63: Are monstrous
*SP*69a: Being as monsters in
12| P*SP*63: confusion:
18| *KR*, P*SP*63: If surely cry
19| *SP*69b: the dark improbable spell
21| *KR*, P*SP*63: But now, by our confirmed supposal,
22| *KR*, P*SP*63: Apparition waits
23| *KR*, P*SP*63: peignoir dividing the oranges;
*SP*69b: peignoir put marvels of oranges
24| *KR*, P*SP*63: But gathering its strength in the shadowed places
25–27| *KR*, P*SP*63: Invisible evil, deprived and bold. / The day-long clock will metronome / Your gallant fear; the needles clicking;

Freshening the water in the blue bowls
For the buckberries with not all your love
You listen for a low lost wind to awaken
The warning sibilance of pines.

Finally evening. Hear me denouncing
Our equal and conniving Furies;
You making Noes but they lack conviction;
Smoothing the heads of the hungry children.

I would have us magnificent at my coming;
Two souls tight-clasped; and a swamp of horrors.
O you shall be handsome and brave at fearing.
Now my step quickens; and meets a huge No!

Whose No was it? like the hoarse policeman's,
Clopping onstage in the Name of the Law.
That was Me; forbidding tricks at homecoming;
At the moment of coming to its white threshold.

I went to the nations of disorder
To be freed of the memory of good and evil;
There even your image was disfigured;
Then the boulevards rocked; they said, Go back.

I am here; and to balk my ruffian I bite
The tongue devising all that treason;
Then creep in my wounds to the sovereign flare
Of the room where you shine on the good children.

31| *KR*, P*SP*63: You shall be listening for a low wind,
*SP*69b: for another wind to waken
32| *SP*69b: The sibilant warning of sentinel pines.
37| *SP69b*: coming,
38| *SP*69b: tight-clasped, in a < > horrors,
39| *SP*69b: But you
40| *SP*69b: quickens—and
42| *SP*69b: on stage < > Law?
43| P*SP*63: That #crossed out and replaced by # It
*SP*69b: me, forbidding < > homecoming
44| *SP*69b: Just as I'm nearing the white
45| *SP*69b: I have gone to
46| *SP*69b: be quit of
47| *SP*69b: disfigured,
48| *SP*69b: But the
50| *SP*69b: tongue rehearsing all
51| *SP*69b: Then stride in

April Treason (*SP69*)

So he took her as anointed
In the part he had appointed,
She was lips for smiling faintly,
Eyes to look and level quaintly,
Length of limb and splendors of the bust
Which he honored as he must.

Queen of women playing model,
Pure of brow but brain not idle,
Sitting in her silence meetly,
Let her adjective be stately;
So he thought his art would manage right
In the honest Northern light.

But he fashioned it too coldly,
April broke-and-entered boldly,
Thinking how to suit the season's
Odor, savor, heats and treasons:
Painter! Do not stoop and play the host
Lest the man come uppermost.

Yet he knew that he was altered
When the perfect woman faltered,
Languish in her softly speaking,
Anguish, even, in her looking:
All the art had fled his fingertips
So he bent and kissed her lips.

He and Venus took their pleasure,
Then he turned upon his treasure,
Took and trampled it with loathing,
Flung it over cliffs to nothing;
Glittering in the sunlight while it fell
Like a lovely shattered shell.

Strict the silence that came onward
As they trod the foothill downward,
One more mocking noon of April,

Mischief always is in April;
Still she touched his fingers cold as ice
And recited, "It was nice."

Nocturne (*SP69*)

Where now has our young Adam
Gone from his sultry Eden,
And where it that Goat-footed
Chasing his willing maiden?
Our man shall cut few capers
In his dark seersucker coat,
With gravest eye subduing
The outrageous tie at his throat;
Wondering if he should carry
His dutiful flesh to the ball,
Or open books that are symbols
And rules and manual.

The intellect bore so hard
Upon the tortured blood,
It dried to a quaint quintessence
The dignities of manhood;
The rivers have passed the bridges
And riding far and free,
Have pitched his boats of passion
Into the sportive sea;
No storm is in this dusk,
But there's a distant flash
That signals brine and foam
And booming floods that thrash.

But still the plum-tree blooms
Despite the rocks at root,
Despite that everyone knows
Its wizened and little fruit;
And the white moon plunges wildly
Like an ubiquitous ghost,
Seeking her own old people

Who are a long time lost;
Till he is almost persuaded
And might yet go to the ball,
If head would concede to heart
A trip to the bacchanal.

Two Gentlemen Scholars (*SP69*)

(*a pastoral*)
[Based on "Overtures"]

The scene is a private study,
in late evening.

FRIEND
Tell the whole history which I crave
And I'll go, secret as the grave.

HUSBAND
Neighbors, in woodland half-begirt
With ribbon of silver, mine and hers,
We walked like knowing foresters
Till I spoke rime, and she looked hurt.

Soon she was bride beneath my roof.
We walked like pilgrims by the stream,
The whiles I sang she took to dream,
My younger songster, still aloof.

Now we have spent sweet moon together,
But Lord! even we must disagree.
Shall not bold mariner rule the sea
Though sailing in the worst of weather?

On one page of my poet's book
She wrote a little hateful screed.
I could have shook her like a reed
But I did bleed her with a look,

And thanked her for her kind opinion,
That from a girl who wore my ring!

I said that some day she might sing
But John Donne kept his sure dominion.

She flung my ring upon the floor,
Exchanging scorns, and went her way.
But I have tarried day by day
A cast-off lover by my own door,

Until this morning early; when
A midnight thought had augured well.
Now will you hazard what befell,
Brother to women and to men?

FRIEND
Perhaps a virtuous gentleman
Accomplished it, who saw her bleed?
Or did she send if you would read
A riddling verse if you could scan?

Well then, she crept to you and cried
And took upon her all the blame.

HUSBAND
O no, do proud girls cry for shame?

FRIEND
The rainstorm sent her to your side.

HUSBAND
Never. My kingly moment came.
I'd find her by the siren stream
And careless how she'd fight or fume
I'd clutch her tight and take her home.

FRIEND
And call a truce?

HUSBAND
                Just say that I
Meandering in the rainy wood

Beheld her dropping by the flood.
She's resting now. I ask you why
Kingdom may not go twice awry?
I have repaired one widowhood.

FRIEND
I peer into your fearful mind.
Be you a king, and do you anoint
Her as a queen, two sovereigns joint.
O, never again be you unkind,
Nor even tutorial. Let her find
Her own words, up to the breaking point.

Her voice is modern, and we know those
Young bards who listen to the birds
And sing with insufficient words.
Yes! Fate, uneasy, may propose
A second reckoning with her woes
Whose lute is tuned to such discords.

HUSBAND
You've fed my fears. She'll fly again
To the hurtling wave, and before I come
She's jumped! and how shall I get her home?
May the Lord deliver us from that pain.

FRIEND
I love you well, and I'll not tell.

Agitato ma non troppo (*SP*69)

This is what the man said,
Insisting, standing on his head.

Yes, I have come to grief,
It was not furtive like a thief,
And must not be blown up beyond belief.

4| *NYR*: That was

They know I have no bittern by the lake
To cry it up and down the brake,
And nothing since has been like Dante's fury
For Beatrice who was not his to bury,
Except, if the young heart faltered, they may know
How Shelley's throbbing reed sang tremolo.

They say, "He puts a fix upon his mind,
And hears at beside or in the moaning wind
The rumor of Death; yet he can't mount one tear
But stalks with holy calm beside the terrible bier."

Lest we wreck upon a reef,
I go according to another brief,
Against their killing blasts of grief.

My head, outposted promontoried chief,
Frowned, and elected me to the common grief,
By whose poor pities I'm shaken, but not as a leaf.

The Vanity of the Bright Boys (*SP69*)

[Based on "The Vanity of the Bright Young Men"]

Absurd in his tight black coat like a sleazy beetle
He wasn't minding his looks,
He looked inside, as the boy bereaved of his title
Minding his dreams and books.

To assembly he walked alone, but forever pushing
Even to say his prayers,
Glaring with coldest eyes at whom he was brushing
Who could, if they would, with theirs.

In late afternoons he walked in a green fable
And wasted for his miracle,
Should a yellow beak intone from a throat of sable
One syllable of his Oracle.

21| *NYR*: Shaken by their poor pities but not

Even walking he dreamed; and partial in his choices
He called on the Druid trees,
Dark gods whose leaves translated the judgment voices
Stitched in the wind's wheeze;

He shortened stride at a shrubbery where two together
Parleyed, and question rose:

One saying, "The boy who tugs at tether may be other
Than he and they suppose."
But one, "Yet sired and dammed by a father and mother
And you have record of those?"

"That sweet babe royal, if he was changed unknowing
Though still he plays the Prince—"
"A King to be? With his sword and crest not showing?"
"Fifteen long winters since—"

He awoke, ashamed, absolved of brain-washed ambition
And tired royal blood;

Of malingering Prince, from whose vegetary operation
He sprang to his ravening stride—

Stopping eavesdropping for wavering name and nation
From wrangling ghosts and wide—

To see if he throve where the tower's last throb expired
And was dumb in the unlistening room
And the babble of boys. O if they'd stared and adored
Crying "Look, hush, he has come!"

No; but they waved a welcome to bright boy returning
As blest for having him there,
Who laughed and sat; with only an instant's mourning
For castles in the air.

The evening's orator rose to his height of speaking
And wantoned with Heaven and Doom;

The boy indifferent; all that long Night of Waking
Addressing his blessings at home.

L'Envoi

Dawn, you've purpled a politic Prince,
He's done no running and peeking since,
Thrones are trash, and Kings are dumb,
Say, would he rather his kingdom come?

Birthday of an Aging Seer (*SP*69)

(*b. June 24, 1865*)
[Based on "Semi-Centennial"]

When the green army drove the black one North,
An overwintered seer came smiling forth
From hearth whereof the stain of ash and spittle
Compounded with his thought, which was not little.

Outdoors he hopped stiff-legged on his stave
To quiz the spring and see if it would grave
Fresh images on a screen so brightly starred
It scarcely took the print of his backyard.

That sexagenarian head we worship almost,
For so much it had kept, and so much lost,
It could not loud applaud the laboring earth
For hatching another salad brood to birth.

Business better than that had been enacted,
Year in and out, within the curled compacted
Grey hemispheres; love dreams, and histories
Brisker even than springtime novelties.

If the wide wave of thought for once was stilled
For his annual cycle a sixtieth time fulfilled,
It was bird-feather that quivered, grass, the bee,
The foal, the darling yellow bloom, not he.

He leaned upon the earth, he lifted eyes
Unto the heavens, and said with no surprise:

"I am a god transcending things that be,
And the proper gods have disinherited me.

"Such is the parsimony of proper god,
Illiterate nature minds, if he but nod;
But with my power, and thriving on disrepute,
I speak, and pure souls hear and execute.

"The better part of godhood is design.
If other gods have theirs, then leave me mine,
For I compose such worlds as do not yield
To that commanded pageant of the field.

"My worlds are Irish, and it satisfies
The Irish folk that I should exercise
The ancestral arts of their theogony.
I am their god, and they depend on me."

UNPUBLISHED POEMS

Hallowe'en Poem

There was once an old witch on a broom
Riding holes through the wall of my room,
'Til I said to her, Moddam,
I don't scare worth a goddam, [*sic*]
So begone or I'll switch you, by goom.

Guarded Protest (1922)

I'll break no lances over the flower-pot!
But she espied a sisterhood of three,
And one the eldest; went, and blanching not
Plucked her forever from the mortal tree.

And when she struck again, and even thrice,
My ravaged ladies tugged at fealty:
I had some fury—small and imprecise;
I said she murdered—in a far degree.

God's wounds be ope if this be not a pity!
How shall that Empery of Beauty be
Whose citizens run killing through the city,
Whereof each beautiful snares other three?

Quarrel (1922)

We found a quarrel, and disputed hard
Whether a poppy or a rose was fairer.
They both were beautiful in your regard,
And any flower advantages the bearer.

Roses are queens, whose subjects throne them well
In gardens full of lesser lovely things,
Dressing their cheeks too artfully to tell
Till they are gathered by the proper kings.

Poppies are gipsy girls exposed to weather,
Their rich complexions never catch a prince,
They have no use of pretty odors either,
Yet lovers withered in their spell long since.

And which were you? You did not ask to know.
Nothing in red: a white thing, frail as snow.

Mr. Hopper (1922)

At the ball, at the ball,
Who was this exceeding all,
Shaven as a shark's coat,
Unrelenting asymptote
For chivalry afoot?

Mr. Hopper carried through,
Squiring maid and madam too,
Hopper weighed three hundred though;
Floors cracked, walls started,
Hopper was not heavy-hearted,
Conquered and departed.

Atlas manful bare his load
In a wild excess of good.
Hopper carries holy freight
Of flesh and wife, church and state.

Funerals, christenings,
Mr. Hopper speaks and sings,
Mr. Hopper anythings;
Take a hundred pounds away,
Spirit shaking off its clay,
What would Hopper be today?

Mr. Hopper on his knees
Was heard imploring Heaven please
To shape him agile, unobese.
Neighbors, interpose a word,

Afflicted all ye may afford:
Deliver us, O Lord!

Address to the Importunate Deacons (1922)

Ye spectacled elders, who stubbornly conjure
Ye are creatures of Vast Design, weary yet sure,
Whose world is an intricate Engine strung and taut,
A miracled Order beyond my petulant ought:

Ye have said that your humbled God on earth did little;
Some blind perhaps were smeared with a lucky spittle,
But still we are sick and blind, and say as ye please,
There is no pure Perfect but suffers of deep disease.

I approve the aim and equity of your Plan,
But it turns too mortal and quick where it touches man;
And your virtuous souls will rot, and your temple rust,
Seeing nothing is strong that builds of delicate dust.

Oh, I know in a girl's young body is wondrous merit
Of myriad fleshy cells concerting with Spirit;
There is naught your Gods more perfectly can compose
Than a young girl's beauty that blooms before it goes;

But quicker than all it travels to its defeat,
(Ashes are fruit of fire, bitter of sweet),
So I take no profit further into my ear,
I must run to pluck at the beauty, and quake with fear.

Annotations

Poems About God

COMPOSITION AND PUBLICATION

In early May of 1917, Ransom sent from US Army Officers' Training Camp near Chattanooga, Tennessee, a manuscript of twenty-nine poems (the basis for *Poems About God*) to his friend and fellow Rhodes Scholar Christopher Morley, and also appointed him as his literary executor. Ransom had already sent the collection of poems to Doubleday, Page, and they were to have given him a decision by the end of the first week in June (JCR to Morley, 4 June [1917] [HRC]). When Doubleday declined, Morley sent the poems to Henry Holt and then to Harcourt. The Holt reader had not declined outright but apparently wanted revisions, giving "a rather post-poning answer." Ransom responded to the Harcourt reader's criticisms: "At first I was inclined to accept Harcourt's and his reader's criticisms, but I am more rebellious as I think of it. No doubt half of my efforts are weaker than the other half. But as for the sentiments of the weary half, I can't take 'incredible stupidity,' 'banalities,' 'priggish moralizing,' and 'commonplace' as adverse criticisms. They would be if I wrote in one systematic character, but I don't. I want a lot of attitudes in these, including the conventional. I don't want it all to be 'caustic satire.'" Ransom asked Morley to return the manuscript so that he could undertake the "dirty work" of revision: "Several of the poems need stern revision," he wrote on 4 July—and then: "I have several new ones up my sleeve. I also have Sundays completely off, and I fully expect to get 2 or 3 weeks off after this camp is over before I enter upon the hypothetical state of lieutenantship. So I plan a thorough revision of the whole thing, and then a whack at Macmillan's." He did not want to "wait till after the war before making another effort to publish. Maybe Fritz will nail me before that." On 2 December, Ransom sent two handwritten poems ("Roses" and "The Resurrection") to Morley, but then his duties in the army put a quietus on further work on poetry, he wrote the day after Christmas 1917 (JCR to Morley, 4 July [1917], 2 December, [1917], HRC; *SL*, 96).

On 13 March 1918, Ransom wrote to Morley that he believed he had a manuscript that might "engage Holt's attention. Since his destructive criticisms I've taken out half a dozen, revised half a dozen more, and added a dozen new ones" (HRC). On 13 May 1918, Ransom sent the poems to Morley together with a rather extensive introduction (*SL,* 100). After trying Macmillan, which declined the book, Morley succeeded in getting the book of now thirty-three poems reconsidered by Henry Holt. In fact, Robert Frost was the firm's reader of poetry manuscripts at the time; he found that the young poet "had the art and . . . the tune" and recommended the collection for publication (Young, 103).

Poems About God was published in the spring of 1919. Although Ransom had written to Morley more than a year earlier that he would "like dearly to read proof and make a few vital corrections," the war intervened: mail was at its best "frightfully irregular," eight thousand bags of American Expeditionary Forces mail being lost, in the autumn of 1918, and Ransom thought it likely that "my book was in one of the bags." As an alternative to reading the proofs if they indeed did not show up in France, Ransom sent a list of revisions to Morley so that he could enter them on the proof-sheets (letters of 30 September 1917 [Haverford]; 12 November 1918, SL, 103–4). Ransom could count on Morley to attend to these requests assiduously and not to make any revisions in the poems that Ransom had not authorized. On 30 November, Ransom wrote again that the proofs had not arrived, and he sent additional revisions that he wanted Morley to introduce (HRC). Ransom did not see the poems again until he held his first published book in hand.

Nevertheless, this first edition is the best text for these early poems. Nine of the poems from *Poems About God* were published by the Hogarth Press, arranged for by Robert Graves, in 1924 in *Grace After Meat,* but this is not a reliable text because Ransom, deferring to the more experienced poet, granted Graves permission to re-title and revise any of the poems. Graves did this, even changing the original title of the collection, "Philomela," to *Grace After Meat.* Textual variants from *Grace After Meat,* therefore, will not be recorded (see "A Note on *Grace After Meat,*" above).

Three of the poems from *Poems About God* were previously published in the *Independent* and one in *Contemporary Verse*; the notes will record the variants belonging to these earlier versions of the poems. Apparently some of these poems would have appeared in a short-lived little magazine called the *Seven Arts,* which sent Ransom a check for fifty dollars, but the magazine, which operated from November 1916 to October 1917, closed before Ransom's poems could be published (JCR to Morley, 4 June [1917], HRC). Ransom apparently erred in saying that some of the poems in *Poems About God* had been published in the *Evening Public Ledger* (Philadelphia) and the *Liberator.* His friend Christopher Morley had begun his association with the *Ledger* in March 1918, and he did arrange for the publication of two of Ransom's poems at about the time of the publication of *Poems About God,* but these poems were not in *Poems About God* and were never published in any other volume. Ransom never had any poems in the *Liberator* (see Variants).

RECEPTION

Although by the time Ransom finished writing and revising *Poems About God,* he felt he had moved on in his development, his early efforts seeming "a bit artificial" to him, he nonetheless had a keen interest in having those early poems published; and he could not have been altogether displeased by the critical attention that some significant publications gave his first effort.

The *New York Sun* announced that these poems "by Lieut. John Crowe Ransom of Tennessee, are baffling. We first endure (or possibly reject with violence), then pity, then embrace. Christopher Morley, to whom the book is dedicated, warns us against a too hasty judgment of it and makes a few remarks about its honesty, humility, simplicity and humor, which are even truer than they are polite" (*Sun,* 13 April 1919, 12).

The reviewer in the *Nation,* though troubled by "some trivialities" and some poems that only the author seems to understand, was prepared to "pardon many things little to [his] liking for the sake of the delightful 'Noonday Grace,' a country-life study full of character and flavor, touched with some ironic reflectiveness." This reviewer's judgment on the whole was mixed: "'Honesty' is one convenient word; 'blasphemy' another" (*Nation,* 26 July 1919, 116).

Maurice Francis Egan seemed to have had a firmer grasp of what Ransom was up to—"to discard the God of the Calvinist." "There is a robust sincerity about him," and he "has the good sense . . . not to attempt to shock readers for the sake of shocking them." Like the *Nation*'s reviewer, Egan gave special attention to "Noonday Grace," and there is nothing nuanced in his overall judgment of *Poems About God*: "This is a very honest book; it has a really poetic and original charm of its own" (*Bookman* 1:2 [October 1919], 222, 223).

Poetry, however, was not so readily impressed by Ransom's honesty. Its reviewer remarked that Ransom needed to abandon his "studied attitude" and write "with a real instead of a strained sincerity"; if he can do this, "greater possibilities" await him. *Poetry* judged "Sunset" and "The Ingrate" as the two poems that "exhibit [the poet's] skill at its best": in "these he captures the sense of a scene, his own scene, with no small degree of individuality; and one admires his terse phrasing, as well as his sensitive perception of the psychology of a mood" (*Poetry* 16:1 [April 1920], 52).

Louis Untermeyer, writing in *Dial,* took Ransom's book as a serious response to "purely decorative literature." Later becoming a champion of Ransom, here Untermeyer's praise is tentative and mixed with disapprobation: "The lines run from the surprisingly powerful to the incredibly banal, from epithets that are forceful to phrases that are both flatulent and flat." In *Poems About God,* this critic found "the promise of stronger things" (*Dial,* 31 May 1919, 562, 563).

COPY-TEXT

The copy-text is the first edition (1919), unless otherwise noted.

The Swimmer

1 *dog-days* The days associated with the rising of the Dog-star, "noted from ancient times as the hottest and most unwholesome period of the year" (*OED*).

22 *escheat* The lapsing of property to a superior.

31 *By the sweat . . . bread* Cf. Genesis 3:19.

32 *garden* Eden.

Noonday Grace

First published in *Inde* 97 (22 February 1919), 66. On 27 December 1918, JCR wrote to Christopher Morley, who had arranged for *PAG*'s publication by Holt: "By way of variety I've touched up one of my earliest efforts, *Noonday Grace*—my favorite, I think. I send it so touched up. . . . I'd like awfully well to get this in my book as revised. Will you please see about it?" (Haverford).

46 *Old Black Joe* A tender, melancholy song by Stephen Foster (1826–1864), published in 1853.

Sunset

First published in *Inde* 97 (28 June 1919), 261. The only free-verse poem Ransom published, it was the first poem JCR wrote (in May 1916). It is "concerned with the theme that was to prove central to Ransom's poetry: the haunting dualism in man's experience" (RPW Notes, 322).

One Who Rejected Christ

First published in *Inde* 95 (27 July 1918), 116.

Grace

Published also in *GAM*. The differences in the texts are few and insignificant.

4 *rivers of Babylon* The phrase is from Psalm 137:1. The rivers are the Tigris and Euphrates.

9 *sorrel* The color of a chestnut.

20 *"Down at the cross . . . died"* The words for this Pentecostal hymn were written in 1878 by Elisha A. Hoffman (1839–1929), the music by John Hart Stockton (1813–1877).

22 *"There did I bury . . . pride."* This is the hired man's response to the gospel song's refrain.

39 *John* John the Baptist.

46 *customers* Colloquial for things one has to deal with.

63–64 *corn . . . carnival* The figure represents dancing corn engaged in revelry.

70 *froward* Perverse.

103 *little lower than angels* Cf. Psalm 8:5: "For thou hast made him a little lower than the angels, and hast crowned him with glory and honor."

116 *He cawed . . . sigh* The awkwardness of this line "reflects the narrator's disordered feelings at the time of the original experience" (KQ, 20).

Moonlight

A very different, twelve-line version was published in *GAM*. The totally revised first stanza is given here (rather than in the textual notes—see Copy-Text); it was followed by the very same middle stanza from *PAG*, and then the final *PAG* stanza was omitted in *GAM*:

> When only moonbeams lit the dusk,
> The world was somewhat set to right,
> For all the piteous twisted things
> Had lost the crooked marks of spite
> Which seared the eyeballs to behold,
> As man to man, in broad daylight.

Darkness

A brief notice in the *Inde* 93 (28 June 1919), 498, which remarked on Ransom's "far from orthodox" poems about religion, "full of infinite suggestion," quoted this poem in full directly from *PAG*.

12 *wail and teeth . . . gnash* Cf. Matthew 8:12.

Geometry

A neighbor of Ransom's in Gambier, Ohio, George Lanning wrote: "At the rear is Mr. Ransom's garden—everything separated according to its nature, and lined up firmly and confined squarely. 'It's not what *I'd* call a garden,' a[nother] neighbor says every summer. 'I wish John would mix things up a little, and stop putting all his plants in rows.'" Ransom's interest in "geometric gardening" suggests that he might well have, like the narrator in this poem, felt a temptation to "improve on the ways of God" (George Lanning, "Ransom as Editor," in *John Crowe Ransom, Critical Essays*, ed. Thomas Daniel Young [Baton Rouge: Louisiana State University Press, 1968], 210–11; *KQ*, 22). JCR's gardening practices are alluded to in his granddaughter's novel *Fortunate Lives* when the character Dinah Howells is said to be "uneasy with the order her son had imposed on the little plot of land. He had planted not only the vegetables but the flowers, too, in militant rows according to species" (Robb Forman Dew, *Fortunate Lives* [Boston: Little Brown, 1992], 62).

The Lover

The copy-text for this poem is *FA* (see Variants). Published in *GAM* with a half-dozen variations in wording.

Overtures

Published in *SP69* as the first in "Sixteen Poems in Eight Pairings." The "revised" second poem, "Two Gentleman Scholars," appears in AP.

24 *riddling* enigmatic.

Under the Locusts

Ransom sent this poem to Christopher Morley on 31 October 1917, and on the same day Morley forwarded it to the *Inde.* Although the magazine did not accept the poem for publication (Morley to Ransom, 24 November 1917, [Haverford]), it made up for that rejection by quoting the poem in full in the course of a brief notice on *PAG* (*Inde* 98 [28 June 1919], 498). Copy-text is *FA*.

The poem was published in *GAM,* with the second stanza rearranged ("Locust trees are sweet in spring / For trees so old and tough; / Locust trees give sorry shade, / Hardly good enough"), and the final line ("And old men never tell") turned into a question: "And why should old men tell?"

12 *fiddle on* Play a trick on.

Worship

16 *Forgives . . . seven times* Cf. Matthew 18:21.

The Cloak Model

There is a typescript of "The Cloak Model" in the Ransom collection at Vanderbilt, but there is no indication that it is either compositional or printer's copy and therefore must be considered secondary material, and for this reason variants are not recorded. The difference between the typescript's and *PAG*'s final stanza is of interest, however. In the typescript, JCR wrote in the final stanza, "We think the moralists will thresh / . . . / Their gruesome joke, forever fresh: / They say that in the finest flesh / There isn't much of soul." In *PAG* "We think" is "I wish," and the joke is not attributed to the moralists but to God: it is "God's oldest joke." Finally, *PAG* concludes by insisting that in "the finest flesh / There isn't any soul," making the poem one representing intense disillusionment.

The poem was published in *GAM,* which has some significant variants. Lines 3–4 substitute "These mannequins are lovely as / The Trojan beldame ever was." Also, lines 18–19 were altered to "That perfect lips conveyed a cue, / And bosom's rhythm said it too," perhaps evidence of the polishing hand of Graves. The other noteworthy difference in texts is the substitution of "touched" for "immune" in line 10.

In 1973, the poem was published as a broadside by Pomegranate Press (Cambridge, MA); there were sixty-five numbered copies. The broadside's illustration is by Karyl Klopp (1941–). In the year before his death, JCR revised the poem for this printing; variants are in the textual notes.

7 *daffy* Fairly new slang for "daft."

12 *Titianesque . . . hair* Suggesting the manner of the Venetian Renaissance painter Titian. Ransom probably had in mind such full and long-haired depictions as Titian's *Vanity* or *Venus of Urbino.*

17 *sapphic youth* Period of erotic indulgence, alluding to the Greek lyric poet of Lesbos, Sappho.

By the Riverside

Published in *GAM* with minor differences in punctuation.

Roses

First published in *CV* 6 (December 1918), 86. From the Field Artillery Training Base in Saumur, France, on 2 December [1917], JCR sent a handwritten manuscript of this poem to Morley. Because this manuscript is secondary material, it will not be included in the variants. This early version has three lines significantly different from those published in *PAG.* Instead of the published lines 8–9 ("Who, where she turns her smiling face / Makes heavy earth a hopeful place"), the manuscript has "When men are made for her sweet face. / I waited by the door a space." *PAG*'s line 21, "And in their perfect date unfold," was in the early manuscript "Till all the fragrance may unfold." There were two other one-word differences between the versions (HRC). JCR had originally sent this poem to the *Yale Review*, *Inde*, and *AM*; all three rejected it (JCR to Morley, 13 February 1918 [Haverford]).

A typescript in the Heard Library, Vanderbilt University, is clearly the typescript for the *SP69* revision of this poem.

6 *celestial rose* An Alba rose with white to light pink flowers.

16 *brick-a-brac* Here meant to refer to a purely decorative artificial rose.

November

5 *traffics . . . goods* A woman of easy favors (Buffington 34).

22 *meeting* Originally a nonconformist worship service and by extension here an evangelical, in this case Baptist, service; see line 50.

36 *Grand Vizier* In the Ottoman Empire, the prime minister of the sultan and holder of his seal.

47 *sceptic* Ordinarily "skeptic."

51 *Accept the fables* Accept Bible stories as literally true, as Southern Baptists do.

52 *Jewish God* God of Justice.

Passion Play A dramatic representation of the trial, suffering, and death of Jesus, originating in the ritual of the Catholic Church.

54 *drabs* Prostitutes.

A Christmas Colloquy

14 *piece* Here referring to a girl (*OED*, sense II, 9b; see Thomas Hardy, *The Woodlanders* [London, 1974], 58).

32 *hark! . . . sings* A direct reference to the Christmas carol by Charles Wesley.

62 *Gethsemane* The garden at the foot of the Mount of Olives in Jerusalem, where Jesus prayed the night before he was crucified.

The Power of God

The basis for "The Handmaidens," *F* 1 (April 1922), 26–32.

On 30 November 1918, JCR wrote to Morley: "I've re-written *Power of God*. I think it's all right—am deeply anxious for it to go in [*PAG*]."

1 *turn* Change in course.

3 *In the fare . . . state* That is, in my fare state.

4 *to reprobate* In order to censure them (*OED*, sense 1).

6 *of my handmaidens* "Of" seems meant in the sense of "among"; "handmaidens" is an archaic term for female servants.

9 *reconciled* Probably in the sense of reconciled to present conditions.

13 *Previsal* Perhaps a pretentions form of "previse," to inform beforehand.

16 *Anon* Straightway. This obsolete form seems to signal the speaker's sudden adoption of archaic verb inflections like "cometh" and "avoideth." The resort to archaic forms might be an indication that, although the speaker is taking a turn at exercising God's power with the intention of being more kindly disposed to suffering humanity than the old God has usually been, he quickly falls into old ways. The absurdity of his failed effort is suggested by the laughable "twitcheth my heart" in line 22.

19 *encircuit* Not in any dictionary. "En" is a superfluous prefix to the word "circuit," to move over a circuit.

The Resurrection

On 2 December [1917], JCR sent this poem to Morley, saying that it was his first sonnet. This early holograph varies from the *PAG* text in only one line (6): originally, JCR had written, "Stopping our smooth white roads up till they lean"—which was revised for *PAG* as "Stopping the headlong highway till they lean," a line perhaps metrically superior. This manuscript being secondary material will not be included in the variants (HRC). This is one of only two sonnets in *PAG*. JCR originally submitted this poem, along with "Roses" to the *Yale Review*, *Inde*, and *AM* (see note on "Roses" above).

Published in *GAM* as "Resurrection." Here the original Shakespearean sonnet has become a hybrid of sorts: it has the Petrarchan rhyme-scheme, which continues into a third quatrain, and it keeps the couplet at the end. The *GAM* version follows:

> Long, long before men die I sometimes read
> On stoic backs as plain as graveyard stones,
> Which stand awry, being old and crooked bones,
> As epitaph of poor dead men indeed.
>
> Ridden far down with burden and with age,
> Deaf as the dead that all these years they've been,
> They stop the headlong highway till they lean
> Aside in honour of my equipage.
>
> "My old defeated traveller," I say,
> What pretty piece of hope then have you spun
> That keeps you marching on? For I have none
> That you will rise and righten any day;
>
> "I have looked often and I have not found
> Old men bowed low who ever rose up sound."

Men

Source This poem is based upon a passage in Shakespeare's *Tempest.* When Miranda, the daughter of Prospero, sees the men who had survived the shipwreck, she exclaims, "O wonder! / How many goodly creatures are there here! / How beauteous mankind is! O brave new world / That has such people in't!" (5.1.181–84).

Morning

2 *confute* Bring to naught (*OED,* sense 3).

April

Stanza 1 presents the poet's natural accord with seasonal change; stanza 2 represents God's perverse reasoning on a season's change.

8 *vengeant* Inclined to vengeance. *OED* cites only Hampole's *Psalter* (ca. 1340).

10 *temperature* The middle condition, a mean between opposites (*OED,* sense 3b—obsolete).

11 *Covenants . . . equinox* The spring and autumn equinoxes represent the natural changes in seasons, which have nothing to do with any covenants made with God.

14–18 *My agate . . . soft amend* God says that he must make amends for "the icy death" of winter by changing the season to spring—so that the "emaciate minstrals" (human beings) will sing His praises again.

16 *emaciate* = emaciated.

Wrestling

Published in *GAM.* The only significant variation from *PAG* is in the first line: "Came threshing-time, the height of all our seasons" replaced "At last came threshing-time, the manly season." It is tempting to imagine this as Graves's gesture to tone down Ransom.

Prayer

18–19 *As having . . . ought not, / And left undone . . . ought* Cf. Book of Common Prayer: "we confess that we have sinned against thee / in thought, word, and deed, by what we have done, / and by what we have left undone."

41 *To shrew* Obsolete term for "to curse" (*OED,* sense 1).

This is one of only two sonnets in *PAG.*

The School

Published in *GAM,* with only spelling and punctuation differences.

3–4 *Helen's unforgotten face . . . war* Wife of the Greek Menelaus, Helen was, because of her beauty, carried away to Troy by Paris, which act brought on the Trojan War, subject of Homer's *Iliad.* When Dr. Faustus sees the illusion of Helen, he exclaims, "Was this the face that launch'd a thousand ships / And burnt the topless towers of Ilium?" (Christopher Marlowe, *The Tragical History of Dr. Faustus,* 3.112–13).

5 *hecatombs* Sacrifices to the Gods (hecatomb = a hundred animals).

6 *Pericles* The Golden Age of Athenian culture occurred under the leadership of Pericles (495–429 B.C.); *fishes . . . purple* Perhaps a reference to the dolphin friezes in some ancient Greek houses.

8–9 *Athens . . . hill* The Acropolis, site of several buildings from Pericles's day, the most significant being the Parthenon.

38 *Apollo* Greek god of light, poetry, healing, and more.

Sickness

42 *comrades* There is no record of "comrade" as a transitive verb in *OED* or *New Int.*

48 *office* Obligation, more particularly, a reference to prayers for the dead.

Chills and Fever

COMPOSITION AND PUBLICATION

The earliest sign that *Chills and Fever* was to emerge as Ransom's second collection of poems was on the last day of 1922. On that date he wrote to Christopher Morley: "And poor Kit! I am about to deliver you a terrific thrust for New Year's. I am sending you under separate cover a manuscript which I entitle 'Chills and Fevers.'" Ransom then told Morley that the manuscript had already been turned down by Holt, the publisher of *Poems About God,* and by Harcourt. Though he said he had "highly revised" what he had submitted to these publishers, Ransom allowed that the poems might still be insufficiently worked over; he invited Morley to suggest further revisions—and "then turn over the MSS. to the most gullible publisher" (letter of 31 December [1922], HRC).

This early manuscript originally contained only twenty-eight poems, but then on 12 February of the next year Ransom wrote to Morley saying that he had "ground out" a few more poems since sending the manuscript for the prospective new book (HRC). These were "On the Road to Wockensutter," "*Agitato ma non troppo,*" "Lichas to Polydor," and "The Inland City," bringing the total to thirty-two poems. Only twenty-three of those were ultimately included among the fifty published in *Chills and Fever.* In addition to the four above, those included are "Winter Remembered," "Sonnets I. Yea, II. Nay," "Triumph," "Spring Posy," "To a Lady Celebrating Her Birthday," "Grandgousier," "Here Lies a Lady," "Conrad Sits in Twilight," "The Vagrant," "In Process of a Noble Alliance," "Youngest Daughter," "Fall of a Leaf," "Night Voices," "Adventure This Side of Pluralism," "Plea in Mitigation," "Philomela," "Armageddon," "Necrological," and "Epitaph." (Some of these underwent title changes; I have listed here the final titles.) Those otherwise unpublished of the original twenty-eight that were eliminated are included in the Unpublished Poems section. These four—"Guarded Protest," "Quarrel," "Mr. Hopper," and "Address to the Importunate Deacons"—are published for the first time in this edition.

This early manuscript containing thirty-two poems Ransom submitted to Macmillan at the urging of the company's traveling college-sales representative; quickly he received "a most courteous expression of regrets" (17 July [1923], HRC). Though the "vaguely worded" rejection suggested that the reader at Macmillan had not "got below the surface in a single poem," Ransom nonetheless concluded—this was five months after sending "Chills and Fevers" to Morley—that the original manuscript "needs to be completely superseded by a revised one," explaining to Morley: "Since you received it I have added about a dozen poems which seem pretty fair, and God has given me the courage to excise about half-dozen not so fair." He then told Morley that, unless he should counsel otherwise, he intended to "try the mettle of Knopf's with it" (letter of 17 July [1923]), even before he had completed all the revisions he had in mind to do. Morley apparently wrote to Knopf encouraging acceptance, and that finger on the scale apparently helped to secure a happy outcome for Ransom: in November, Ransom received acceptance of his manuscript, now with the "s" on "Fevers" removed. Ransom dashed off a quick note to Morley:

> Just a line at this moment to say A. Knopf has accepted and will bring me out in early autumn of 1924.
>
> Many grateful thanks!
>
> He says, "after very careful consideration we are extremely enthusiastic," etc. etc., implying that without the very careful c[onsideration], the second and third reading, etc., which your seasonable word doubtless inspired the result would have been different (letter of 13 November 1923, HRC).

His fertile imagination still in high gear, Ransom began to add to, revise, and rearrange the poems. Knopf was naturally nervous about losing control, and so the publisher worked out an agreement whereby Ransom could "freely make excisions, additions, and revisions against the date when the printer should want it. Such date would be middle of May." Knopf insisted, however, that Ransom "consult the literary taste of one Christopher Morley" for all such changes (letter of 27 February [1924], HRC).

Ultimately, Ransom redid the entire manuscript and sent it to Morley on 1 May 1924, saying to Morley: "Poor man, here are the poems. I have selected, revised, and arranged them just as carefully as I could. . . . I had others, but I couldn't like them sufficiently. Somehow I have set my head on a volume of fifty, and here they are. But I believe I am sending along two or three extras in case you would swing the axe on some that I have included. Maybe you can excise and still find fifty. If you can't, what difference does it make anyway?" (HRC). The fifty Ransom sent are the fifty poems making up his second collection.

As for the arrangement of those poems, Ransom explained his thinking as follows: "I have tried all sorts of arrangements and orders; they are a terribly mixed lot of pieces, and evade classification and sectioning. By chronological order, even, there's no sense in them; and I gave up that and all others in favor of the present order, where I am somewhat chronological, but where still more I progress from the more simple and romantic to the more philosophical, and wind up with my favorite "Philomela" (letter to Morley, 1 May [1924], HRC).

In his acknowledgments for this volume, Ransom allowed that some poems had appeared in "the *Literary Review*, the *Bowling Green* (New York *Evening Post*), the *Chaffing* [*sic*] *Dish* (Philadelphia *Evening Public Ledger*)," and several other publications. Morley had begun his association with the *Ledger* on 11 March 1918, and his valedictory column was on 31 January 1920 (p. 8). During this period, Morley arranged for the publication of two of Ransom's poems in the *Ledger*, but neither of these was included in *Chills and Fever*. When Morley left the *Ledger*, the quality of poetry published in its pages took a plunge; Ransom would not have enjoyed seeing his poems displayed alongside "Tell Mother I'll be there to answer her prayer," by Mrs. J. R. Gunson, or "The Cow" ("The friendly cow, all red and white"). In fact, Ransom's submissions went with Morley to the *Evening Post*, which had become serious about publishing good poetry. Four of Ransom's poems that eventually went into *Chills and Fever* were published in the *Post*, two in "The Bowling Green," Morley's new column, which first appeared in February 1920 (other contributors to "The Bowling Green" were Stephen Vincent Benet, Vachel Lindsay, and Edna St. Vincent Millay). Most of Ransom's poems published in Morley's column, however, did not appear in *Chills and Fever* or any subsequent volume. In 1921 Morley was assigned to the newly established literary supplement to the *Post*—the *Literary Review*, and "Miriam Tazewell" and "Here Lies a Lady" were published in it.

RECEPTION

The tentative critical acceptance of *Poems About God* gave way to a full-throated celebration of *Chills and Fever*. The "promise of stronger things" that Untermeyer saw in the early volume was fulfilled in Ransom's second book (*Dial*, 31 May 1919, 563). The *Bookman* declared the volume "a find to enrich any bookshelf," for its author "has more substance on any page he writes than some books contain in their entirety. He is daring of thought, dramatic, 'civilized,' . . . erudite, and . . . esoteric in places, requiring study and considerable time from his readers for the full appreciation of what he has to say. His lyrical sophistication, his whimsical agility in thought and words, give him the power to say the almost unsayable and to suggest accurately what cannot be said" (*Bookman* 60:3 [November 1924], 346). The *Bookman*'s reviewer concludes by urging that "anyone wanting to read what is new and original in American poetry might turn to Mr. Ransom's 'Triumph,' 'In Process of a Noble Alliance,' 'Here Lies a Lady,' 'Miriam Tazewell, 'Nocturne.'" He might read the book "slowly" (346).

Robert Graves, in the *Saturday Review of Literature* commentary devoted entirely to *Chills and Fever*, named some of its poems "as great poetry," citing "Winter Remembered" and "Adventure This Side of Pluralism" in particular. Graves proceeded to lay out the primary features of the diverse collection, whose subjects "range widely from AntiChrist to Rapunzel, from Nicodemus to a beautiful bantering description of a Southern mansion in decay." Those features that mark "his Ransomness" are, first, "a humorous turn of speech, including a sweetening skepticism; second, a muscular quality of both metre and thought, and third, the periodic detonation of most unlikely and effective phrases" (*SatR*, 27 December 1924, 412). Finally, Graves gave perspective on those poems of a fantastic quality—"Grandgousier," "Boris of Britain," "Captain Carpenter," and so on: "Written in a manner of a fantastic dream, they have no meaning to which immediate logical reference can be made; yet their powerful persistence in the memory suggests that they have a meaning all right but one which the mind has grasped in other than logical routes of thought" (412).

Another powerful force in modern poetry taking a serious interest in Ransom was Louis Untermeyer. In the *Yale Review* he held *Chills and Fever* to be "the best volume of American verse which has lately come to the reviewer's table. No book of the year—and not many of the last decade—has revealed a finer craftsman, a more sensitive musician, a richer personality. In short—if I may be allowed the uncommon extravagance of the capital—a Poet" (July 1925, 797).

Four years earlier, the *Poetry* reviewer of *Poems About God* had closed by saying, "A second book by Mr. Ransom will tip the balance one way or the other. Either he will repeat the present vein, which will hardly be worthwhile, or he will do something different, and better. Either he will not count, or he will count quite significantly" (16:1 [April 1920], 52). The reviews of *Chills and Fever* told that Ransom had fulfilled his promise.

COPY-TEXT

The copy-text for most of these poems is the 1924 first edition; those few poems for which the 1945 *Selected Poems* is copy-text will be identified with "*SP*45" in parenthesis following the title.

Agitato ma non troppo

First published in *F* 2 (April–May 1923), 56.

JCR wanted this poem first in the volume and italicized to emphasize it as "a sort of key-note speech" (JCR to Morley, 1 May [1924], HRC).

Title Agitated but not too much (Italian musical direction).

3 *bittern* A bitter substance.

5–6 *Dante's . . . bury* Dante Alighieri (1265–1321), Italian poet and author of *Vita nuova* and the *Divina Commedia,* which celebrate Beatrice, the girl he fell in love with early in his life. When Beatrice died, Dante was grief-stricken, but he had nothing to do with her burial. Ransom corrected this error in *SP*69 (see ll. 8–9).

8 *Percy Shelley's . . . tremolo* Shelley (1792–1822) often expresses grief in his poetry; for example, in "A Lament" he is "Trembling" (l. 3) with grief. These lines are probably not a specific reference but rather a general one to the special quality of Shelley's poetry. (*Tremolo* = in music, a trembling effect.)

9–12 "*If . . . bed?*" These lines in quotation marks refer to Shelley.

10 *his fair child* Shelley's "Lines Written Among the Eugenean Hills" expresses his grief over the loss of one of his children.

11 *white frost snowing on* JCR acknowledged that this phrase is "hardly logical" (*SP*69, 126).

Spectral Lovers (*SP*45)

First published in *F* 2 (June–July 1923), 68.

Title The lovers are "spectral" because they materialized out of the mist and because of "the restrictions which they impose upon the flesh, their ideal quality" (CB 410).

13–15 *batteries . . . yield* The artillery of nature assaulted the walls defending the woman's virginity.

19 *moon of Easter* The paschal full moon used to fix the date of Easter.

31 *They passed . . . April* CB points out that this line "pushes the whole scene back into the past," and the reader realizes that the poem has a speaker who has observed the lovers and imaginatively created the words spoken by them (412).

Bells for John Whiteside's Daughter (*SP* 45)

First published in *F* 3 (February 1924), 17.

Source The poem springs from two clichés—"Heavens won't that child ever be still, she is driving me distracted," and "She was such an active, healthy-looking child, who would've ever thought she would just up and die?"—and a famous statement in the burial service of the Book of Common Prayer: "In the midst of life we are in death" (Robert Penn Warren, "Pure and Impure Poetry," in *Selected Essays* [New York: Random House, 1989], 13; Ashby Bland Crowder, "The Book of Common Prayer in the Midst of Ransom's 'Bells for John Whitesides's Daughter,'" *Mississippi Quarterly* 66:2 [Spring 2013], 339–442).

3 *brown study* A serious reverie, thoughtful absent-mindedness, or a state of mental abstraction or musing. The term alludes to the erstwhile lively inner life of the girl as it ironically provides a picture of her stillness in death.

5 *bruited* Noised, reported.

19 *vexed* This word sums up the whole range of emotions experienced by the speaker: to be annoyed or irritated, to have one's peace and quiet interfered with, to be distressed deeply, and to be in a state of grief (*OED,* senses, 1, 3, and 4).

Winter Remembered

An early version as a sonnet was published in *SR* 30 (January 1922), 1. In *CF,* the poem was expanded into one with twenty lines. The poem was among those sent to Robert Graves, who published it in *GAM* with an additional stanza. While this edition is an unreliable text (see Note on *Grace After Meat*) and therefore not included in the variants, the additional stanza, which appeared between the first and second stanzas is here provided:

> My winter's leave was much too cold for smarting.
> What bitter winds, and numbing snows and sorrows,
> And wheezy pines, like old men undeparting,
> To funeralize against all green young morrows!

3 *A cry of Absence* Madison Jones took this phrase for the title of his novel published in 1971. The phrase was also appropriated in 1989 by Martin Marty and R. Scott Appleby for their *A Cry of Absence: Reflections for the Winter of the Heart.*

20 *frozen parsnips* This image perhaps owes something to John Donne's "ragged carrets" [*sic*] for fingers in "The Comparison," according to Joseph E. Duncan (*The Revival of Metaphysical Poetry* [Minneapolis, 1959], 186).

Triumph

First published in Morley's "The Bowling Green," *EP,* 5 April 1920, 8, under the title "On a Superior Woman." In that version it was a sonnet, but apparently Morley preferred the shorter version; JCR to Morley, 12 February 1923: "You are right about the proper version of 'Athens, —,'" referring to the poem by its first word (HRC). The original title was "On a Strange Woman"; when JCR mailed the manuscript to Morley on 6 March 1920, he said that the poem "is quite light weight, and might do, I thought, for the purpose of baiting the Philistines" (HRC).

Title In Rome a triumph was a victorious general's "celebratory procession" to the Temple of Jupiter Capitolinus (M. C. Howatson, *Oxford Companion to Classical Literature,* 2nd. ed. [Oxford, UK: Oxford University Press, 1989]).

1 *Athens . . . foam* Cf. "The School" (*PAG*), 8–9.

3–4 *unbred . . . Greek* Perhaps a reference to the Romans' imitation of—but failure to absorb—the true values of the Greeks.

Two Sonnets

These poems appeared in *GAM* with few differences of consequence; the most noteworthy was in line 9 of "Nay": *CF* begins with "Therefore I knew" and *GAM* with "My hope was sprung."

I. Yea

3 *fluttering it* Exciting it with pleasure.

6 *Gabriel* According to tradition, this angel sounds his trumpet to signal the Day of Doom.

8 *unconcessive* Unyielding.

Spring Posy

A sonnet version of this poem was published in *EP*, 18 February 1920, 8, and is included in the Alternate Versions of Poems; the title was "Sonnet of a Sure Heart." A sixteen-line version was published in *F* 1 (June 1922), 54, under the title "The Sure Heart," and a similar version, under the title "Heart Too Sure," was among those poems in the original manuscript of twenty-eight poems titled "Chills and Fevers" that JCR sent to Morley at the end of 1922, and this version, with the last quatrain lopped of, is essentially the poem appearing in *CF*. The typescript of another sixteen-line version of this poem, titled "As We Two Walked at Dusk," which is dedicated "(To R.R.R.)," referring to Robb Afton Reavill Ransom, whom JCR married on 22 December 1920, is in the Fugitive and Agrarian Collection, Special Collections, Heard Library, Vanderbilt University. This typescript version is as follows:

> As we two walked at dusk, came neighbors' daughters nigh.
> Fluting like birds they passed, and calicoed bright and clean,
> And beautiful else had been their bosoms poutering by,
> "But ye are a cloud," I said, "too much between."
>
> I was waylaid by beauty deep in the woody grot,
> The gentle fox in the fern, and the scarlet wing on the green,
> In her widow's weed the balsam: but how did ye prosper not!
> With thought of her did I fill your tedious scene.
>
> Up once I rose and hasted in fury of heard-of things
> To travel the splendid sphere that twirleth in its fame,
> But the wars and ships and towns, and the orgulous roaring kings,
> These all were mad, for they fought unknowing her name.
>
> Lovely the moons will rise, loudly the peoples will shout,
> But this is the house I have built, and my young love stayeth within.
> Ye kingdoms may fight and fall, ye stars as ye please go out,
> O world I have honored not, be off and spin!

In line 11, "*orgulous*" means haughty (*OED*, archaic).

The "Chills and Fevers" manuscript has three significant variants: instead of "the scarlet wing on the green" it has "a wing's blue sheen" (l. 6); instead of "the orgulous roaring kings," it has "the pestilent roaring kings" (l. 11); and instead of "These all were mad" it has "They angered me" (l. 12).

3 *poutering* Protruding, suggesting undisciplined sensuality.

5 *grot* Grotto.

7 *balsam* A healing, soothing agent.

To a Lady Celebrating Her Birthday

First published in *F* 1 (April 1922), 21–23. This version of the poem was among those in the early manuscript of "Chills and Fevers" (see Composition and Publication, above).

9 *ken* Range of vision.

14 *Perdure* Last on.

19 *clomb* Archaic past tense of "climb."

30 *Thing* Death.

32 *Babylon* A Christian figure of evil, the Whore of Babylon is "a woman . . . arrayed in purple and scarlet color, and decked with gold and precious stones and pearls, having a golden cup in her hand full of abominations and filthiness of her fornication" (Rev. 17:4).

37 *burghers* A burgher is a citizen; the term is mainly used in European towns and some English boroughs (*OED*).

44 *mortuary* Like death.

49 *grizzled polls* Grey heads.

Vaunting Oak (*SP* 45)

First published in *F* 2 (December 1923), 174–75, and included in *GAM*, which contains the two additional stanzas between lines 9 and 10 included in *CF* (see Textual Notes).

Title The oak represents permanence, but the image turns ironic.

3 *concumbent* Lying together (archaic).

7–8 *susceptive / Of* Affected by (*OED,* sense 2).

9 *captive* Literally "held," from the Latin *captivus,* though the usual sense of "captive" is retained: the leaves would leave if they were not held captive (CB 406).

10–11 *mortally / Linked* Married "till death do them part" (CB 406).

12 *eminent* Remarkable, but also (from the Latin *eminens*) "projecting, lofty" (CB 406).

13 *phantasy* Visionary notion, as opposed to *fantasy,* which suggests "caprice, whim, fanciful invention" (*OED*). The woman is "wrapped in a phantasy" as protection from the truth.

19 *And . . . fetch me* Here it becomes clear that the speaker in the poem is the "unbeliever of bitter blood" (l. 11); *fetch me* = attract me.

21 *populace* JCR follows Edward Young, *Night Thoughts* (1742), in this figurative application of the term to flowers: "Queen lilies! And ye painted populace! / Who dwell in fields and lead ambrosial lives" (3:124).

24 *purlieu* Outlying area, mean and squalid (*OED,* sense 4), here where the daisies and field flowers grow as opposed to the eminence of the vaunting oak.

35 *reverberance outsounded* These neologisms contribute to the onomatopoeic vibrations of "v"s and "n"s, which create the "singing of bees" (l. 36).

In Process of a Noble Alliance

First published in *F* 1 (December 1922), 126. *Bookman* 47:1 (March 1923) quotes the poem according to *F.* In *GAM* and in the table of contents (but not in the text) of *CF,* the poem is given the title "In Process of the Nuptials of the Duke." Most of the variants in *GAM* are in punctuation. In the MS that JCR brought to a Fugitive meeting, the poem has the title "Upon the Celebration of a Noble Alliance." JCR published a revised version, with the title "Grim Wedlock," in *MQR,* 10:3 (Winter 1971), 165. The last line of this version contains a nod to Sir Arthur Wing Pinero's comedy play *The Gay Lord Quex* (1899). An early MS for this revised version at Vanderbilt contains variants in the first two lines: "Liken the girl to a marble statue, / Array her < >."

Source The source of this poem seems to be Robert Browning's "The Statue and the Bust," wherein the woman fails to embrace love and eventually is represented by a marble bust.

8 *Ye* This usage is "intentional. 'Ye' is a vocative, going with 'Musicians'" (JCR to Robert Graves [*SL*, 124]); *springe* Snare, made by attaching a noose to a branch under tension.

Parting at Dawn

First published in *F* 3 (August 1924), 99.

Title The title refers to Robert Browning's "Parting at Morning." JCR's poem is a strong contrast to Browning's. Graves made the title "At Dawn" in *GAM*, which contains only minor variants.

1–2 *broken whispering . . . / . . . heart* The opening contrasts with "a voice less loud, thro' its joys and fears, / Than the two hearts beating each to each" in Browning's "Meeting at Night," the companion piece to "Parting at Morning."

4 *cold glitter . . . light* This image seems meant to contrast with Browning's "Parting at Morning": "the sun looked over the mountain's rim: / And straight was a path of gold for him" (ll. 2–3). Seamus Heaney was to use the phrase in "Limbo": "A cold glitter of souls" (*Poems, 1965–1975* [New York: Farrar, Straus and Giroux, 1980], 148).

8 *Cenobite* A member of a communal religious order.

12 *Lethe* In Greek myth, one of the rivers of Hades. When the dead taste the waters of Lethe, they forget everything about the life they had led.

Miriam Tazewell (*SP* 45)

First published in *LR* 4 (2 August 1924), 929.

2 *wrathy* Violent (*OED*, sense 2).

8 *empyrean* Visible heavens.

13 *transpired* "To escape from secrecy to notice" (Johnson's *Dictionary*). Perhaps the more literal sense, plants giving off watery vapor from the surface of leaves, is also in play (see *OED,* sense 1).

16 *bitten* Damaged.

Here Lies a Lady

First published in *LR* 3 (24 March 1923), 545, and quoted in full in *LD* 84 (7 February 1925), 34. It was under the title "Mary Monette" that this poem appeared on the original manuscript for "Chills and Fevers" in 1922.

2 *chills . . . chills* The reversed repetition of the phrase "chills and fever" alludes playfully to the lady's being a beauty of "high degree" (l. 1). Buffington suggests that Ransom might be implying that life is a sickness and that the lady's manner of dying might imply that life is an unreasonable war between spirit and body, between chilly reason and feverish emotion" (60). Fred H. Stocking says the line "playfully makes the illness sound like a jig" (*Explicator* 8 [October 1949], Item 1).

3 *delight* The grammar of the sentence allows "delight" to apply to the lady but also to the chills and fever that killed her.

4 *Medicos* This jocular slang for medical practitioners continues the oddly playful tone.

13 *toughly* In the sense of "bravely" or "strongly."
thole The ironic tone is enhanced by this archaic term meaning "struggle" and "endure."

The Tall Girl

This approximation of a sonnet was first published in *F* 3 (April 1924), 39, under the title "Ada Ruel."

1 *Queens . . . lissome necks* Cf. the Antichrist of "Armageddon" who plays a "lissome flute."

8 *tomorrow . . . again* The Queens tempt the girl with a false promise.

9 *Queen of Heaven* For the Greeks it was Hera; for Roman Catholics, the Virgin Mary.

13 *crisped* Sharpened.

Fall of a Leaf

First published in *F* 1 (October 1922), 94–95.

37 *Holy Rood* A fragment of the cross of Jesus's crucifixion.

38 *Saint Margaret's sisterhood* The Society of St. Margaret, an Anglican sisterhood, was founded in 1855. Margaret (ca. 1045–1093) was a Saxon princess who brought the Holy Rood with her when she fled to Scotland to marry Malcolm.

42 *Woodwife* A female spirit of the forest, often dressed in red, in Germanic myth.

49 *Saint Gregory's tomb* St. Gregory (ca. 540–604) was the first monk to become pope; he is credited with giving form to medieval Christianity. His tomb is in St. Peter's Basilica.

50 *strictest monks* The Trappists are the strictest monks, but they did not tend St. Gregory's tomb.

62 *Babes . . . Wood* The traditional children's tale *Babes in the Wood* was printed by Thomas Millington in Norwich in 1595. The two small children in the story die in the woods, and robins cover their bodies with leaves.

Rapunzel Has Submitted Herself to Fashion

First published in *F* 2 (October 1923), 151.

Title "Rapunzel" is one of the traditional German fairy tales assembled by the Brothers Grimm in 1812. There are several versions of the tale of a beautiful girl placed in a tower by a witch. She is visited by a prince who says, "Rapunzel, Rapunzel, let down your hair, so that I may climb the golden stair." Like William Morris ("Rapunzel" [1858]) before him, JCR draws upon the story only to turn the traditional happy ending into a grim disappointment.

13 *beldame* An ugly old woman.

The Vagrant

First published in *F* 1 (October 1922), 80.

25–27 *others . . . Eden's* The vagrant visits in his imagination Queen Guinevere, unfaithful to King Arthur in various medieval romances (for example, Thomas Malory's *Le Morte d'Arthur* [1485]); the women of Troy, among them Hecuba, Cassandra, and Andromache, are portrayed in Euripides's play *The Trojan Women;* and the two women of the Garden of Eden are Eve and Lilith.

Boris of Britain

First published in *F* 1 (October 1922), 74–75.

2 *chymist* The sixteenth-century form of "chemist." In Britain a chemist is a pharmacist.

8 *green powder* Paris green, an emerald-green, poisonous powder made from arsenic trioxide and copper acetate.

43 *mad . . . hare* To be as mad as a March hare is an English idiomatic phrase often applied to human beings who behave in a bizarre manner.

55 *bobby* A slang term for a British policeman.

63 *publican* The keeper of a public house or tavern.

April Treason

First published in *F* 2 (April–May 1923), 36–37. The version of this poem from *SP*69 appears in AP.

Source The poem is an instance of the theme of Thomas Mann's "Tonio Kroger" (1903): "An artist stops being an artist the instant he becomes human and starts feeling" (*Death in Venice and Other Tales,* trans. Joachim Neugroschel [New York: Penguin, 1999], 187). JCR's poem, especially the third stanza, seems suggested by a passage in "Tonio Kroger" in which a writer says that spring makes him too restless to write: "'God damn the spring!' says he in his aggressive style. 'It's always been the worst season of the year! Can you come up with a sensible idea, Kroger, can you calmly work on the tiniest climax or effect, if your blood is prickling indecently and you're harassed by a swarm of inappropriate sensations, and the moment you examine them, they turn out to be a lot of absolutely trivial and totally useless junk?'" (185). JCR makes the artist that is interfered with by spring a painter.

19–24 *he was changed . . . / . . . her lips* JCR's painter has failed to maintain a distance between himself and the object of his art, as in Mann's "Tonio Kroger": "If you care too much about what you have to say, if your heart beats for it too warmly, then you can look forward to a complete fiasco. You wax grandiloquent, you become sentimental—something gawky, awkwardly serious, uncontrolled, unironic, unspiced, boring, and banal emerges from your hands—and ultimately your audience feels nothing but indifference. . . . You have to be some kind of nonhuman and inhuman thing, you have to have a strangely distant and neutral relationship to the human, in order to be able, to be even tempted, to play it, to play with it, to depict it effectively and tastefully" (186–87).

First Travels of Max

First published in *F* 2 (June–July 1923), 86–87.

9 *Saint Michael's sword* St. Michael is usually depicted in art—Raphael's *St. Michael Vanquishing Satan* (1518) is an example—wearing armor and holding a sword with Satan under his feet.

25 *tarn* A small mountain lake; the term was originally confined to use in northern England.

27 *The Adversary* Cf. 1 Peter 5:8.

32 *casuistical* "[R]elated to the solving of cases of conscience" (*OED*).

36 *Prince of the Dark* Cf. Shakespeare, *King Lear* 3.4.147.

45–46 *Bashan's / . . . bellow* Psalm 22:12–13: "Many bulls have compassed me: strong bulls of Bashan have beset me round. / They gaped upon me with their mouths, as a ravening and a roaring lion." Bashan had the richest pasture in Palestine and thus produced the largest and strongest animals.

53 *innocency* Archaic form of "innocence."

Grandgousier

First published in *F* 2 (February–March 1923), 12–13.

Title Grandgousier is father of Gargantua in François Rabelais's story "La Vie trés horrificque du Grand Gargantua" (1534). He stands for living well and enjoying the pleasures of life.

17 *Bitters* Bitter is the English name for pale ale.

21 *freshet* A small stream of fresh water (*OED*, obsolete, poetic).

34 *beery* Abounding in beer.

39–43 *sponge . . . his day* A parody of the Roman soldiers' offering Jesus vinegar on a sponge to quench his thirst as he hung upon the cross (Luke 23:36).

Miss Euphemia

Published only in *CF.*

15 *frore* Cold, frost-like (*OED,* poetical).

32 *Till . . . Pentecost* The church season immediately following Easter and lasting till Advent.

Winter's Tale

Published only in *CF.*

1 *freight* Load.

22 *ingle* A hearth fire.

24 *Kilkenny* A county in the Southeast of Ireland.

34 *kit* Shortened form of "kitten."

37 *whither* Violent or impetuous movement.

Emily Hardcastle, Spinster

First published in *LR* 4 (3 November 1923), 201.

3 *stately ceremonial* Funeral (instead of a wedding).

7 *pepper-and-salt* A cloth made of dark- and light-colored wools woven together.

10 *Grizzled Baron* The personification of Death, a proper aristocratic mate for Emily.

12 *halidom* Sacred thing (*OED,* sense 3—archaic, obsolete).

Number Five

First published in *F* 2 (December 1923), 166.

14 *rummy* Odd.

26 *let* Hindrance (*OED*, archaic).

Good Ships (*SP*45)

First published in *F* 2 (October 1923), 131.

Title The "Good Ships" are a man and a woman.

1 *high seas* High society, according to the dominant metaphor of the sonnet.

4 *Mrs. Grundy's . . . teas* A spoken-of character that never appears in Thomas Morton's play *Speed the Plough* (1798), Mrs. Grundy has become the personification of the British idea of propriety. Thus the rare lovers met in the most conventional of occasions.

5 *baffle* Foil. JCR reverses the usual use of "baffle," which pertains to "the wind and weather defeating the efforts of a ship to advance" (*OED*, sense 8c).

8 *nautical technicalities* The small talk of society.

11 *could not sink* Fall in social standing.

13 *Beautiful timbers . . . storm and sport* These beautiful people were fit for difficulties and pleasures.

14 *miserly . . . converted* The man and woman, meant for authentic life, gave in to concerns about making money: "The good ships travel only the trade routes" (Buffington, 52).

Youngest Daughter

First published in *F* 1 (December 1922), 104.

7 *burgher* See "To a Lady Celebrating Her Birthday," l. 37n.

12 *rode . . . home* A double entendre, drawing upon *OED*, sense 3 of *ride*: "To mount the female."

18 *disport* Recreation, amusement (*OED*, archaic).

21 *carline* A disparaging term for an old woman, mainly Scottish (*OED*).

Necrological (*SP*45)

First published in *F* 1 (June 1922), 62–63.

Title The term from the Greek *nekros* (corpse), means "Death Notices."

1 *paternosters* Repetition of the Lord's Prayer as an act of worship, usually in Latin.

3 *riddling* Mental siftings in an attempt to sort out perplexities.

20 *foemen* Enemies in war (*OED*, archaic and poetic).

21 *ogive* A conture like that of an arch
firmament The arch or vault of heaven (*OED*, poetical).

23 *leman* A mistress (*OED*, sense 2—archaic).

27–28 *spilled . . . spilled* The word, especially in its repetition, conveys the frailty of life: "Brain and groin, the seats of life, are shown in all their fragility" (Parsons, 43).

30 *wight* A man, archaism of Old English origin. The term rubs ironically against the modifying Latinism "lugubrious."

32 *Carmelite* The Carmelites were originally an austere ascetic religious order, but by the thirteenth century their practice was less rigorous.

34 *riddling* See l. 3n above.

Armageddon (*SP*45)

First published as an octavo pamphlet in Charleston by the Poetry Society of South Carolina (1923). The poem won the Southern Prize for 1923 and a check for one hundred dollars. Then it appeared in *GAM* with the same additional stanza between lines 24 and 25 as *CF*, along with a good number of minor variations.

Title The place where the armies of good and evil battle at the end of times (Revelation 16:16).

1 *lissome flute* Antichrist's playing a limber flute associates him with the serpent (Buffington, 41).

4 *breviary* Book containing the "Divine Office" for each day (in the Roman Catholic Church).

5 *roundel* The small circular shield of the fourteenth century (Frederick Fairholt, *Costume in England* [1846], 592).
rose Perhaps engraved on the shield?
hall "Royal residence"? (*OED*, obsolete).

6 *monkery* A contemptuous term for a monastery (*OED*).

7 *cap-a-pie* From head to foot (*OED*).

9 *Barbary beast* A horse from the north coast of Africa.

10 *plume* An ornament symbolizing dignity or rank attached to a helmet.

11 *jennet* A small Spanish horse.

13 *they fingered chivalry's quaint page* Christ's and Antichrist's competition to renounce any advantage one has over the other points to the chivalric "Franklin's Tale" of Chaucer's, wherein the knight Arveragus and the squire Aurelius seem unable to outdo each other in courtesy, consideration, and magnanimity ("Thus can a squyer doon a gentil dede, / As well as can a knight, with-outen drede" [815–16]).

17 *Mahomet* An old popular rendering of Muhammad, founder of Islam. It appears that this name refers to Antichrist's warhorse, which Christ absurdly sits upon.

18 *Diomede* A military hero in Greek myth, who fought in the Trojan War.

19 *cynical* Dog-like (*OED*, sense 3)

21 *lordings* "A little lord, a petty lord, usually in a contemptuous sense" (*OED*—last citation is 1651).

25 *hierarchs* Those who have authority in holy things (*OED*).

26 *truce* Bring to an end by means of a truce (rare; last citation in *OED* is for 1706).

29 *rosemary* This herb is an emblem of love, loyalty, and remembrance.

31 *poll* Head.

34 *tiring-hall* Dressing room (*OED*, obsolete or archaic).

35 *finical* Affectedly fastidious.

36 *egregious* Renowned (used in a humorously pedantic manner) (*OED*, sense 2a).

dight Arrayed (*OED*, archaic).

39–40 *Water . . . wine* In the Eucharist, the priest adds water, representing baptism, to the wine.

41 *wassail* The salutation used in drinking the health of another (*OED*, sense 1—archaic).

43 *stave* A stanza of a song (*OED*, sense 5).

45 *Perruquiers* Variant of *perukier*, wig-makers (*New Int.*).

47 *chevelure* Head of hair.

48 *glozed* Caused to shine (*OED*, rare).

51 *paternoster* Cf. "Necrological," l. 1n.

52 *dithyramb* A Bacchanalian song.

53 *patriarch* In the primitive Church, a bishop.

64 *jennet* See l. 11n.

68 *Prince Beelzebub* Milton puts this demon next in rank to Satan (*Paradise Lost* 1:79–81).

69–72 *Christ . . . bloodshed* The characteristic roles of Christ and Antichrist are reversed: "while Christ and his followers thunder like bloodthirsty secularists," Antichrist and his armies only want to make peace (Parsons, 122).

myrmidons Soldiers who are faithful followers (*OED*, sense 2—obsolete).

73 *Adversary* Cf. "First Travels of Max," l. 27n.

Epitaph

First published in *F* 1 (June 1922), 35.

1 *Napoleon* Napoleon Bonaparte (1769–1821). After he was named first consul of France, he led a series of European conquests.

2 *Julius* Gaius Julius Caesar (102?–44 B.C.) was a great general, achieving 320 triumphs.

3 *Alexander* Alexander the Great (356–323 B.C.). This Macedonian king's conquered territory spanned from the Mediterranean to India. He died at thirty-two of malaria.

8 *Generalissiomo* Spanish term for the highest ranking military officer.

15 *fundaments* The foundation of a building (*OED,* sense 1—obsolete). As plural for a single building, *OED* cites only Caxton in 1481.

17 *Caesar's ghost* The poem does not allude to the famous appearance of Caesar's ghost to Brutus in Shakespeare's *Julius Caesar* (4.3.275–86).

Judith of Bethulia

First published in *F* 2 (October 1923), 140–41, and later in *GAM,* with minor variations.

Title The poem tells—with revisions—the story from the Book of Judith (Apocrypha). Bethulia was a small Samaritan town that stood in the way of the Assyrian army of Nebuchadnezzar on its way to Jerusalem and the temple. Holofernes was its general; Judith, a beautiful Israelite widow, beheaded him.

9 *emanations* Odors.

25 *fumiter weed* A plant of the genus *Fumaria,* a common European herb, sometimes used for medical purposes.

34 *chieftain's head* Holofernes's.

35 *epitaphy* The fourteenth-century form of *epitaph.*

Conrad Sits in Twilight

First published in *F* 2 (February–March 1922), 27, under the title "Conrad in Twilight." In the original manuscript for "Chills and Fevers" (1922) the title was "Conrad at Twilight."

Title JCR has said, "To the best of my knowledge I had chosen that name, in the early 1920s, because it had been the pen-name of a brooding and intellectual Pole who wrote novels [Joseph Conrad (1857–1924)], and I happened to have been born in a town called Pulaski, about sixty miles from where I wrote" (JCR, "Now the Grateful Author," in Anthony Ostroff, ed., *The Contemporary Poet as Critic and Artist* [Boston: Little Brown, 1964], 136).

5 *wraith* A spectral appearance.

Forest of Arden Shakespeare's *As You Like It* is set here. The playwright's mother was an Arden, the family name of prominent landowners in the real Forest of Arden in central England.

7 *miasma* Germs floating in the atmosphere.

21 *ribbon* "[A] wall or strip of wood" (*OED*, sense 8).

byre JCR has remarked, "I had taken the 'byre' to be the manure-pile by the stable: I have learned from my dictionary that it is the stable itself" ("Sixteen Poems in Eight Pairings," *SP*69, 119).

Nocturne

First published in *F* 2 (June–July 1923), 82.

Title A nocturne is a painting of a night scene (*OED*, sense 2).

1 *sultry . . . Aiden* Burns with passion in his Eden / Aiden.

2 *goat-footed* Allusion to Greek satyrs associated with sexual adventure.

3 *seersucker coat* In the 1920s "as characteristically Southern as mint julep and the 'Bonnie Blue Flag'" (RPW Notes, 333).

18 *bacchanal* An occasion of drunken revelry, originally in honor of the god of wine, Bacchus.

Blackberry Winter

Title Blackberry winter is a term common in the southern United States for a cold snap that occurs in late spring after the blackberries have bloomed. Robert Penn Warren has a short story with the same title.

First published in *F* 2 (August–September 1923), 107.

2 *steam* Fume given off by a substance when burned, an early sense (*OED*).

7 *pictures . . . dead* The golden and silver ages are gone, as well as "the goddesses who competed in beauty for the golden apple" (Buffington, 98).

9 *Daughter of Heaven* A name for the goddess of the dawn.

11 12 *Ficrccly . . . mould* Hcrc Romantic lovc givcs way to "barnyard naturalism" (Buffington, 98).

14 *convolve* Twist about (*OED*).

16 *wars . . . Troy fell* The Trojan War ended spectacularly, when the Greek warriors descended from the wooden horse that the Trojans had accepted as a gift and set the city on fire. All of its inhabitants were slain or carried into slavery, and the city was destroyed.

Lichas to Polydor

First published in *F* 2 (August–September 1923), 118.

Title Lichas was Heracles's servant who brought him a poisoned garment and was therefore thrown into the sea, whereupon he became a rock. Polydorus was the youngest son of Priam, king of Troy. There are several stories about him; in Euripides's *Hecuba,* he meets the same fate as Lichas: Polynester threw him into the sea in order so steal his gold (*CA*).

Subtitle Cytherea is another name for Aphrodite, the Greek goddess of love and beauty. The Graces (see below) were associated with her.

6 *Thalia, Charis* Two of the three Graces, according to Greek myth. Charis is also named Aglaia. "[T]he inspiration of the Graces was deemed as necessary to the plastic arts, as to music, poetry, science, eloquence, beauty, and enjoyment of life" (*CA*).

Melpomene The muse of tragedy. The Graces lived with the muses on Mount Olympus.

9 *bandy-legged* Hephaestus, husband of Cytherea.

Spiel of the Three Mountebanks

First published in *F* 2 (October 1923), 146–48.

Title A mountebank is an itinerant quack who appeals to his audience through stories and tricks.

44 *Prince . . . fardels ill* In his "To be, or not to be" soliloquy, Hamlet says, "who would fardels bear, / To grunt and sweat under a weary life, /

But that the dread of something after death / . . . puzzles the will, / And makes us . . . bear those ills we have" (*Hamlet*, 3.1.75–80).

fardels Burdens.

46 *incubus* "A feigned evil spirit or demon" (*OED*, sense 1).

58 *ounce* A feline beast resembling the leopard in markings, but it is smaller and has longer and thicker fur, sometimes called a mountain panther or snow-leopard (*OED*).

59 *gorge* The front of the animal's neck.

60 *Agnus* Lamb (Latin).

72 *Lay . . . lion's side* This common phrase comes from a combination of Isaiah 11:6 and 65:25. Cf. "No absolute is going to make the lion lie down with the lamb unless the lamb is inside" (D. H. Lawrence, *Twilight in Italy* [1916]).

82 *lion . . . bear* In Edward Hicks's *Peaceable Kingdom* (ca. 1849), the leopard lies down with the lamb, as the lion and bear stand nearby (there are sixty versions of this painting). See Isaiah 11:6–7.

Night Voices

First published in *F* 1 (April 1922), 10–11, and later in *GAM*, where the epigraph is "*And Nicodemus came by night.*"

5 *duologue* A dramatic piece spoken by two actors.

12 *darkling* In the dark. This word has a long literary history, used effectively by Shakespeare, Milton, Keats, Arnold, Hardy, and others. When the poem was published in *GAM*, Graves apparently disliked the literary "darkling" and changed it to "darkened."

13 *Nicodemus . . . sect* A Jewish religious leader of the Pharisees, Nicodemus visited Jesus in the night, and Jesus told him, "whosoever believeth in [the Son of Man] should not perish but have eternal life" (John 3:15).

14 *stiff-necked* Cf. Exodus 32:9 and Acts 7:51: "Ye stiff-necked and uncircumcised in heart and ears, ye do always resist the Holy Ghost: as your father did, so do ye."

22 *warty envelope* Body.

37 *sooth* Truth (a literary archaism).

39 *little carpenter* Jesus.

44 *cleft* Split.

Adventure This Side of Pluralism

First published in *F* 3 (June 1924), 83–86.

This poem, when it was included in the original manuscript of "Chills and Fevers" (1922), was titled "Adventure*s* This Side of Pluralism." Both the early manuscript and the published version consist of twenty-six four-line stanzas, and the poems are essentially the same in content, many stanzas being identical word for word. The earlier version, however, contains significant differences from *CF.* First of all, the 1922 poem is divided into five numbered and uneven sections, and then the order of the stanzas is significantly shuffled. The second stanza of the early manuscript ("Angered with a braggart kind . . .") became the first stanza of the published version, presumably so that the speaker can earlier and more clearly establish himself as the first-person narrator. The first stanza of the earlier manuscript then became the fifth stanza of the published version. Stanzas 6–8 of the published version were moved from a later position in the early manuscript to earlier-on establish a second speaker ("an ancient man withal, / Doctor of Genealogy") within the narration ("And lifted up his voice to me . . ."). This figure seems to be a tragic, impoverished wise man telling the story of a God before creation.

When this poem was published in *GAM,* an additional stanza appeared between lines 20 and 21: "If from one God's primal loins / All the creatures came to be, / It surpasseth creature brains / To find this family such tree." Most of the other differences in *GAM* are in punctuation and spelling, some exceptions being "The loosing of his Fiat" instead of "The whisper of the Fiat" (l. 48); "heart true centered" for "heart perfect centered" (l. 90); and "Swimming now in fratricide" instead of "Swimming deep in fratricide" (l. 99)—and "respective" in the place of "invective."

10 *springbok* "A species of antelope, . . . characterized by a habit of springing almost directly upwards when excited or disturbed" (*OED*).

12 *Shibboleth* A verbal formula adapted by a party or sect.

Fokmafok Apparently a made-up form meant to represent a magical incantation.

15 *cotillion* A variety of dance steps.

16 *Satyrs . . . swallowtail* Lustful woodland gods dressed in a "swallow-tailed coat" (*OED*, colloquial).

19 *Plato* Greek philosopher (427–348 B.C.).

Scythian A feared ancient equestrian warrior, Tamburlaine being the most famous—"that sturdy Scythian thief" who "Daily commits uncivil outrages" (Christopher Marlowe, *Tamburlaine: Part One* [1.1.36, 40]).

dog Despicable person.

wart Military slang for an officer of low rank.

20–21 *GAM* added four lines: "If from one God's primal loins / All the creatures came to be, / It surpasseth creature brains / To find this family such tree."

26 *wiven* Apparently a fanciful archaism for "married." "Wiven" is in fact a Middle Dutch form.

34 *Simplex* Having a single part.

37 *fief* In English feudal law, an estate held on condition of homage and service to a superior lord.

38 *Imperator* Emperor *Rex* King (Latin).

39 *Jahveh* An alternate spelling of "Yahweh," a name for God.

40 *Pontiff* Pope.

Mandarin Originally an official of the Chinese empire, only later the term for standard Chinese language.

Multiplex Made up of a combination of the preceding.

46 *Deathy* Deathly.

48 *Fiat* The "Fiat Lux" (let there be light). Cf. Genesis 1:3.

61 *obeisance* Obedience (*OED*, obsolete).

62 *Simplicissimus* Latin: the most simple one. The semantic range of the word also includes "the most ordinary," "the most straightforward," and "the most unelaborate." It is in the nature of JCR's humor to use a word for "most simple" or "most unelaborate" that does not sound simple or unelaborate at all.

64 *Hierarch* See "Armageddon," l. 25n.

68 *conveyed* "To transmit to posterity" (*OED,* sense 9b—obsolete).

72 *Aunt Piety* The bony woman who was the featured character in an amusing sketch called "A Specimen of Western Life," in the *New York Knickerbocker Magazine,* July 1850, 71–74: "I'm Aunt Piety, . . . and a dreadful pious creatur' I am" (74).

75 *Cicero's tongue* Marcus Tullius Cicero (106–43 B.C.) was the exemplar of classical Latin prose.

81 *Phoebe* In Roman myth, the moon, sister of Phoebus, the sun god.

89 *spied* Discovered, found out (*OED,* rare).

97 *pied* Meaning about the same as "motley," parti-colored.

101 *Dignities Respective* A phrase common in royal charters and acts of Parliament before and during the seventeenth century, as in "With all liberties, privileges, honours, jurisdictions, and dignities respective therein mentioned" ("Acta Parliamentorum Caroli Primi [1633], Act XXVIII," in *The Acts of the Parliaments of Scotland, 1424–1707* (1670; rpt. Ulan Press, 2012), vol. 5.

On the Road to Wockensutter

First published in *DD* 4 (November 1922), 233.

JCR wrote to Morley on 17 February [1923]: "On the Road to Wockensutter . . . [is] in some ways I think one of my best things, but withal rather brutal and . . . a little out of tone with my volume: bitter plus hard too" (HRC).

2 *Herodote* Greek historian (484–425 B. C.) known as "The Father of History."

3 *Sirocco* A Mediterranean wind, sometimes of hurricane force, that comes from the Sahara, reaching southern Europe. It was the unhealthy effects of sirocco that brought on the death of Gustav von Aschenbach in Thomas Mann's "Death in Venice" (1912).

4 *pulver* Dust (*OED,* obsolete).

14 *Principle of Venus* The principle of Venus is love.

17 *nit* Nothing. The first citation in the *OED* to this United States colloquial usage is to O. Henry, *Strictly Business* (1910).

19 *pert* Chirpy (*OED*, sense 6).
pewit The pewit flycatcher has yellow feathers on its underparts, after molting in the autumn. Pewit is the usual name in Scotland for the yellow-feathered Lapwing.

22 *emblistered* A neologism formed by introducing a prefix to "blistered."

24 *tablets . . . soul* The phrase apparently first appears in the anonymous *Casea Llanna: Love, Woman, Marriage* (1872), 393.

25 *choke* A choke-bore, which narrows towards the muzzle of a fowling gun in order to give the piece an increased range.

27 *Burd Helen* From Sir Walter Scott's *The Minstrelsy of the Scottish Border* (1802–3): "Curst be the heart, that thought the thought / And curst the hand, that fired the shot, / When in my arms burd Helen dropt, / And died to succour me!"

36 *obscene* Foul.

Prometheus in Straits

First published in *F* 3 (February 1924), 21.

Title Prometheus, who stole fire from heaven, is here punished by being hemmed in rather than by being chained by Zeus to Mount Caucasus so that an eagle could prey upon his liver.

2 *Bibbers* Tipplers.
Illicit potations Bootleg corn whiskey.

3 *acta* Latin feminine plural: acts.

9 *Westminster* The name of the abbey in London.

Plea in Mitigation

First published in *F* 1 (April 1922), 3–4, under the title "Ego." It was included in the early manuscript version of "Chills and Fevers" under the title "Appeal of an Egotist from an Adverse Judgment"; otherwise there is little difference between the manuscript and *CF.*

12 *bruited* Celebrated.

15 *tumuli* Hillocks.

28 *occipital* Bone at the back of the head.

36 *seven* A set of seven persons.

Tom, Tom, the Piper's Son

First published in *F* 3 (August 1924), 100–101.

Title From "Tom the Piper's Son," a nursery rhyme in *The Real Mother Goose* (1916).

19 *attent auricles* Attentive ears.

27 *dammed* Given birth, said of animals (*OED*, obsolete and rare).

29 *changeling* A changeling is a child switched for another in the cradle by fairies. There are many folk tales in which such a swap occurs.

38 *litten* Lighted.

Old Man Playing with Children

First published in *F* 2 (December 1923), 183.

11 *wrappers* Loose-fitting outer garments worn by women for indoor housework.

Captain Carpenter

First published in *F* 3 (February 1924), 18–20.

JCR said of this poem: "There's an old hero who dies with his boots on, so to speak, and I've been asked if he could not have represented the Old South. Or if he could not have stood for the old-time religion. But those ideas did not enter my mind when I was composing the little ballad" ("John Crowe Ransom Reads from His Own Works" [Buffington, 90]).

7 *main* Physical strength (*OED*, sense 1—obsolete).

8 *twined* Separated (*OED*, Scottish dialect).

16 *stick* Remain in place (*OED*, sense 6—colloquial).

Tub Cask or keg, sometimes applied to a corpulent person (*OED*, sense 1e,f).

47 *bust* Although this term usually refers to the bosom of a woman, I do not think JCR means to suggest that Captain Carpenter suffers from gynecomastia.

48 *alack* An exclamation indicating pity that it should be so (*OED*, archaic).

55 *enow* Enough (*OED*, archaic).

These Winters

14 *mows* Derisive grimaces (*OED*, sense 1).

Old Mansion (*SP*45)

First published in *F* 3 (April 1924), 40–41. Graves presents stanzas 1, 2, 3, 6, 8, 10, 11, and 12 in his introduction to *GAM*, renaming the poem "The Southern Mansion." This abbreviated version of the poem has "legend" for "annals" (l. 10); "their full store" instead of "their great store" (l. 32); and "my Russian weed" in the place of "my foreign weed" (l. 46). Though JCR had hoped the poem could be included in the body of *GAM*, it arrived too late to be included.

4 *weed* Tobacco, especially a cigar or cheroot (*OED*, colloquial).

6 *chateaux . . . Loire* Large country houses or castles in the Loire Valley of France, built during the fifteenth and sixteenth centuries.

31 *dole* Gratuitous bestowal.

38 *wrappered* Covered up.

42 *petted* Made much of.

46 *weed* See l. 4n above.

Inland City

First published in *F* 2 (April–May 1923), 53.

Philomela

First published in *F* 2 (February–March 1923), 8–9.

JCR wrote to Robert Graves, "The substance of it is that my fellow-countrymen seem to be without the faculty for song—the nightingale doesn't inhabit here" (letter of 11 July 1922, *SL*, 111).

Title Tereus, the husband of Procne, raped her sister Philomela and then cut out her tongue so that she could not tell (Greek myth). In *GAM*, Graves gave this poem the title "An American Addresses Philomela."

1 *Itylus* In a parallel Greek myth to that of Philomela and Procne, Amphion, by mistake, killed her son Itylus, whereupon Zeus changed her into a nightingale who sang melancholy songs.

3 *classic numbers of the nightingale* Philomela and Procne were turned into birds, the former a nightingale, the latter a swallow, so that they could escape Tereus. These women sing songs (numbers) from classical myth.

4 *our numbers* American songs, our poetry.

6 *ilix* Oak tree.

7 *Ovid* This eight-century (A.D.) Roman poet reproduced the Greek myth of Philomela and Procne in *The Metamorphoses* (Book 6).

8 *Teutons* Germans.

9 *Fontainebleau . . . gallicized* Fontainebleau is a satellite of Paris that contains a forest. There the nightingale's story underwent a French adaptation.

10 *Never . . . baptized* Never incorporated into Christian beliefs.

11 *To England . . . pain* The story of Philomela, "by the barbarous king / So rudely forced," makes its way into section 2 of T. S. Eliot's *The Waste Land* (1922): "Jug, Jug to dirty ears," the song persists.

12 *Fleeing the hawk . . . husband* See Ovid: "Changed to a bird, his crown spiked quills, his beak / A long spear pointed toward revenge, slow-winged / He was a red-eyed plover, armed for war" (*Metamorphoses*, Book 6).

16 *these shores* The shores of America.
Thrace Tereus was the king of Thrace.

17 *Attic* Greek.

21 *pernoctated . . . Oxford* Oxford University students were in the habit of engaging in all-night talks; "in order to discourage the practice the

dormitory proctor checked the beds of the students each morning. If the bed showed that it had not been slept in the student was called up and charged with pernoctating" (MW, 73).

22 *Cher* The River Cherwell, which joins the Thames at Oxford.

23 *Precociously . . . ajar* A reference to JCR's course of study at Oxford, *Literae Humaniores,* the name given to the undergraduate course devoted to the Classics—Ancient Greece, Ancient Rome, ancient Greek, Latin, and Greek and Roman philosophy. The course is colloquially called "Greats."

24 *hierophants* In ancient Greece the priests presiding at sacred mysteries or religious ceremonies (perhaps here representative of the Classics dons JCR studied under).

26 *Bagley Wood* An ancient wood in Oxfordshire, most of which is owned by St. John's College, Oxford.

28 *sepulchral owl* The European brown owl.

29 *unfulfil* This invented form does not mean the same as "not fulfil," "which implies no more than passivity, as if we were leaving things no worse, if no better, than we found them. 'Unfulfil' is an active verb. It is an undoing of what has not been done" (MW, 73). JCR's usage was probably inspired by the negative certainty of Thomas Hardy's "Waits in unhope" ("In Tenebris").

30 *diuturnity* Continuance, lastingness (*OED,* rare).

32 *fairy numbers* See l. 3n above.

37–38 *I am . . . swarthy* The most significant change that Graves appears responsible for in *GAM* is to make these lines more direct: "I have despaired of three and am unworthy, / My scene is prose, this people and I are earthy."

Two Gentlemen in Bonds

COMPOSITION AND PUBLICATION

Chills and Fever having been well received, Ransom did not have to undergo the ordeal of uncertainty that had been a feature of his previous publishing experience; neither did he require the intervention of his friend Christopher Morley. In the past, Ransom had depended upon Morley, who in 1924 had moved on to the *Saturday Review of Literature,* to put his poems before the public in advance of a new volume's publication, but the confident and well-regarded Ransom now placed his poems in national magazines like the *Atlantic Monthly, Harper's Magazine,* and the *New Republic,* though he still published poems that would be a part of *Two Gentlemen in Bonds* in the *Fugitive* and other literary journals, the *Southwest Review,* for example.

A feather in Ransom's cap was his being invited to join T. S. Eliot, Wallace Stevens, Elinor Wylie, and others in Louis Untermeyer's *American Poetry 1925: A Miscellany.* Each poet was given twenty pages on which to place his most recent unpublished poetry; Ransom selected the twenty sonnets that constitute the sequence that would conclude *Two Gentlemen in Bonds.* The point is that Ransom was advancing under his own power.

In 1926 Knopf accepted *Two Gentlemen in Bonds* outright, promising to publish the book in the next year. It was released in January. The fifty poems were divided into three sections: "The Innocent Doves" (14), "The Manliness of Men" (16), and "Two Gentlemen in Bonds" (20).

RECEPTION

The reviews of *Two Gentlemen in Bonds,* in their number and judgments, make it clear that Ransom's reputation as a strong new force in American poetry was secure. He got some reviews all his own (in the *Nation* and the *New Republic*), and when his book was grouped with those of other poets, the company he was put with was not uncomplimentary—Ezra Pound, Hart Crane, Langston Hughes, Ford Madox Ford, Robert Graves, and others. The comparisons made by the reviewers emphasized that he belonged in such rare company: "we read him with the same sort of pleasure that we derive from Miss Edith Sitwell or Mr. Wallace Stevens, to whom he is closely akin," said the reviewer for the *New Republic* (2 February 1927, 310). Babette Deutsch remarked that Ransom "has several of the qualities of Pound. Like his senior, he is erudite and sardonic, with a liking for the tart and a rare virtuosity of technique" (*Bookman,* 11 April 1927, 220).

Yet Deutsch allowed that Ransom possessed many qualities particular to himself: "His cadences are peculiarly his own, and his most commonplace subject matter gives out, under his touch, a fresh earthy odor" (220). The reality of Ransom's poetry is, in her view, his singular quality. Herbert Gorman came close to saying the same thing: it is his "realism of phraseology that suffuses his poetry with a flavor peculiar to him alone" (*New York Times Book Review,* 27 March 1927, 2). Ransom's fellow southerner Allen Tate identified another sort of reality that his friend's poetry captures: a pure "sense of the humane tradition, a tradition lying at the very core of the old Southern order, stiffens his poetry with an irony and lucidity, and a subtlety, which elevate it with a unique distinction in the present American scene. His rationalism is the evaluating instrument of the code of honor; it gives the code a profundity and edge . . ." (*Nation,* 30 March 1927, 346).

While Tate saw Ransom as reflecting tradition, others saw something new in *Two Gentlemen in Bonds.* Marie Luhrs, the reviewer for *Poetry,* for example, said, "There is a freshness in Mr. Ransom's style," and "he achieves sharp new rhymes as fantastic pictures" (30:3 [June 1927], 163). Speaking particularly of "Dead Boy," Gorman remarked on Ransom's "careful abnegation of the usual poetic phrasing" (2), and John Gould Fletcher remarked on "the quality of surprise" in Ransom's poems (*Monthly Criterion* 6 [July 1927], 169). Even Tate admitted that Ransom portrayed his traditional themes "in new and unpredictable images" (346).

Some of the reviewers gave special attention to the title series, "A Tale in Twenty Sonnets." The *New Republic* was not overly impressed: "Mr. John Crowe Ransom is a poet of much charm and a certain amount of originality. The narrative in sonnet sequence which gives its title to this new book does not represent him at his best: it is quite prettily done, but all in a vein of rather too mild, too quaint, too sweetly wise irony—an irony suggestive of Mr. E. A. Robinson, but without the fine and delicately cutting edge which that poet occasionally unleashes" (310). (All comparisons to contemporaries were not in Ransom's favor.) Yet Marie Luhrs saw this "tale in twenty sonnets [as] a series of melancholy and beautiful cartoons" (165).

Luhrs concluded with a glance forward: "In the future it will be interesting to watch Mr. Ransom to find out whether the extreme cut of his poetic clothes will make him or break him. His is a dangerous originality; he will be so often tempted to astound with a phrase rather than with a thought. In *Two Gentlemen in Bonds* he is beautiful and strange. We hope he will grow in beauty rather than in strangeness" (165). Ransom was not to wear another suit of poetry: *Two Gentlemen* was his last collection. He added a handful of poems, which he included in *Selected Poems.* Most of his poetic efforts, however, went to patching his old "poetic clothes," even when they did not require patching.

COPY-TEXT

The copy-text is the first edition of 1927 unless *SP*45 prevails, in which case "(*SP*45)" appears following the title.

THE INNOCENT DOVES

RPW says the poems in this section are "about the victims of the world, who suffer without knowledge, without philosophy, in the world" (340). The contrast between this and the following section, "The Manliness of Men," follows the pattern of William Blake's "The Songs of Innocence and the Songs of Experience."

Vision by Sweetwater

Vanderbilt has the typescript corrected for *TGB.*

Title Although one might assume that the title refers to the small town in Monroe County, Tennessee, JCR said that the Sweetwater of this poem is near his wife's home in Colorado, where he got the idea for the poem. Sweetwater is in western Eagle County, Colorado (Vanderbilt Literary Symposium, April 1960; Buffington 75).

6 *tinkled* Made speech similar to a small bell (*OED*).

7 *hens* The "etymology of hen takes us back to *canticle* or *chant,* which suggests the chorus of a Greek tragedy" (MW 63)

13 *strange quick tongue* This phrase "lets us know that the recognition, when it comes, will not be of anything local or even English" (MW 63).

15 *old . . . scream* "[S]uddenly the speaker knows that what has been haunting him is the sense of the tragic and specifically the tragic as the Greek mind understands it" (MW 63).

Eclogue (*SP*45)

First published in *F* 4 (March 1925), 22–24, and the first nine stanzas were published in *Literary Digest* 85 (11 April 1925), 34.

Title The Greek *eclogue* means "selection," but the term came to refer to any formal pastoral poem that follows the traditional technique employed by Theocritus in the *Idylls*.

30 *fructify* Become fruitful.

33 *usurious* Exorbitant, excessive.

42 *Love . . . kind* "Charity suffereth long, and is kind" (1 Corinthians 13:3).

43 *banded* Bound.

47 *Theogony* The branch of theology that treats the "origin and descent" of the gods (*New Int.*).
hell's broth Such as was made in Shakespeare's *Macbeth* (4.1).

49 *God wroth* Cf. Psalm 78:59.

50 *Fingering . . . scars* Perhaps a reference to Christ's wounds.

52 *firmament* See "Necrological" (*CF*), l. 21n.

53 *Third Day's error* Apparently an error in the creation of dry land, fruit trees, and seeds.

63 *filialities* The relationships among sons and daughters and their parents.

Piazza Piece

First published in *F* 4 (March 1925), 21.

Title "Piazza" means porch.

Source Perhaps Death as a suitor was suggested by Emily Dickinson's "Because I could not stop for Death."

1 *dustcoat* The British term for a loose lightweight coat worn in the early days of motor cars when drivers and passengers sat in the open. The American term is "duster."

11 *grey man* Death.

Moments of Minnie

First published in *F* 4 (December 1925), 120.

Title The inarticulate Minnie experiences two moments, one of pain and one of happiness. The original title, on the manuscript that JCR brought to the Fugitives meeting, was "Minnie's Way."

5 *thralled* Enthralled (*OED*, archaic).

7–8 *outleaning . . . lips* JCR might well have adopted this feature from Frau von Rinnlingen of Thomas Mann's "Little Herr Friedemann": "She fixed her strange quizzical eyes on him and pushed out her lower lip as usual" (*Death in Venice and Other Stories,* trans. Joachim Neucrosche [New York: Penguin, 1998], 40).

23–24 *Mirth . . . South* Cf. "sunburnt mirth! / Oh, for a beaker full of the warm South / . . . / With beaded bubbles winking at the brim, / And purple-stainéd mouth" (John Keats, "Ode to a Nightingale," ll. 14–18).

Husband Betrayed

First published *F* 4 (September 1925), 85. A revised version titled "Farmer Husband" was published in *MQR,* 10:3 (Winter 1971), 164.

17 *dudgeon* Resentment.

Miller's Daughter

First published in *F* 4 (June 1925), 55–56.

4 *stillwater* "A smooth place in a stream which is usually rough" (*Transactions of the Royal Society of Canada* 2.2 [1896]).

17 *hind* Fellow (*OED,* sense 4—obsolete).

18 *fabulous* Legendary.

21 *pudding . . . head* A pudding head is a stupid person.

28 *chrome* Yellow.

29 *Astronomied* A neologism apparently meaning "made astronomical." *Oes* Obscure form of "ooze" (*OED*).

34 *pardee* Surely (obsolete).

35 *cleaves* Cuts down.

Blue Girls

Vanderbilt University has the first-edition manuscript for this poem.

First published in *F* 3 (June 1924), 82.

1 *blue skirts* The girls wear uniforms.

2 *seminary* A seminary for young ladies was a common designation for a private college for girls, the term persisting into the 1960s (for example, Shenandoah Seminary in Dayton, Virginia).

10 *I* Although most readers will probably assume the speaker to be a mature man, William Osborne argues persuasively that the speaker is a woman, perhaps even a teacher at the seminary (*Explicator* 19 [May 1961], Item 53). The version of the poem published in *F* and appearing in AP and the still earlier version in Appendix C support Osborne's view, but Ransom seems to have revised to create ambiguity as to the sex of the speaker.

loud lips Perhaps also "loud" lipstick.

13–17 *For . . . you* If the speaker be a woman, this entire stanza has her talking about herself, even engaging in a little vanity.

Her Eyes

14 *flare* Apparently these eyes take in light from the wind!—because "flare" means "dazzling but irregular light" (*OED*).

20 *smart* Sharp pain.

Parting, Without a Sequel

First published in *AM* 138 (October 1926), 517.

6 *functioner* JCR's own substitute for "functionaire" or "functionary."

13 *vaunting oak* Cf. "Vaunting Oak" in *CF.*

20 *Ceasing . . . again* Cf. Matthew Arnold, "Dover Beach": "Begin, and cease, and then begin again" (l. 12).

Hilda

Title The second of the two sonnets was originally printed in *HM,* December 1926, 50, by itself under the title "Ghosts." JCR proposed these sonnets for *FA,* but Donald Davidson, the organizer of the volume, did not include them. The manuscript contains no variants from *TGB.*

I.

5 *tinkling* See "Vision by Sweetwater," l. 6n.

14 *earth* The allurements of earthly life, as distinguished from spiritual concerns (*New Int.,* sense 6c).

II.

5 *disbodied* Disembodied.

In Mr. Minnit's House

JCR submitted the manuscript of this poem for *FA,* but the poem was not one of those selected by the volume's organizer, Donald Davidson. That manuscript contains a good number of variants in punctuation. The most obvious differences between it and the copy-text are in lines 3–4: ("But now these are our pleasures / Among its famous treasures:") and lines 130–31 ("O terrible if the taint in the blood / Corrupt the third Mortimer's blood—"). Yet none of the textual variants represents a significant difference in quality.

116 *Haman* A Persian official who plotted to kill all the Jews in Persia and was hanged on the fifty-cubits-high gallows that he had prepared for Mordecai (Esther 7:9–10).

Janet Waking (*SP*45)

First published in *F* 4 (September 1925), 86.

The easy movement from the ridiculous ("transmogrifying bee" and the entire bee attack) to the sublime of the final two lines ("the forgetful kingdom of death") perhaps owes something to Andrew Marvell's similar shift in "To His Coy Mistress."

2 *deeply morning* Pun (deeply mourning).

13 *transmogrifying* Transforming utterly.

Little Boy Blue

First published in *NR,* 22 September 1926, 122.
Source The poem plays off of the nursery rhyme "Little Boy Blue, come blow your horn. / The sheep's in the meadow, the cow's in the corn. / Where is the boy that looks after the sheep? / "He's under the haycock, fast asleep." / Will you wake hum? "No, not I; / For if I do, he'll be sure to cry."

1 *wound* Past tense of "wend."

3 *imps* Wicked spirits.

4 *blowzy* Coarse.

7 *bellweather* The leading sheep of a flock, from whose neck hangs a bell.

Lady Lost

First published in *F* 4 (December 1925), 119.

13 *West End* A section of Nashville.

14 *Injured . . . way* An allusion to Philomela; see "Philomela," *Title* note and l. 3n.

THE MANLINESS OF MEN

RPW suggests that the title of this section means that a man must perceive the "schisms" of the world, as exhibited in the poems that follow (for example, the difference between "the view held by the family and that held by the observer in 'Dead Boy'"; between the husband and wife in "Two in August," and so on), so that he can deal with them and thereby fulfill his "manliness" (336, 337). See "Men" (*PAG*), l. 6.

Our Two Worthies (*SP*45)

First published in *F* 4 (September 1925), 83–84.

3 *Paraclete* Intercessor, comforter.

4 *Exegete* One who explains or interprets.

32 *But for . . . spiriting* This line "carries out the motif of a military commander handing on his authority to a trusted lieutenant." The word "spiriting" is rich in suggestion, referring to the captain's spiriting away from battle, Christ's "departure from a fleshly state," and His providing inspiration (Parsons, 118).

42 *Seraphim* The highest order of angels.

58 *Tarsus* Capital of the Roman province of Cilicia, birthplace of Paul (Acts 9:11).

Dead Boy (*SP*45)

First published in *EP*, 24 February 1920, 8.

1–3 *subtraction . . . transaction* At one level, these terms of business suggest that the boy's death "is not outside the realm of the day-to-day business of the world" (MW, 33). Although a long-obsolete sense of "subtraction" ("removal from a place" [*OED*, sense 1]) literally indicates what has happened to the boy, the root meaning of the word's Latin origin is "A drawing from under"—a contrast to "transaction," which, according to MW, "is a carrying across," bringing to mind the River Styx (34). These ancient origins of the modern words create a distance between the observing speaker and the event.

4 *world . . . dark* Beyond Virginia.

13 *strode* This term, meaning to walk with "long steps," suggests that the Virginia Patriarchs were tall, or perhaps that they hurried past the open coffin.

18 *first-fruits . . . hath taken* Appropriate to an agricultural society, "first-fruits" means the first crop that is cut at harvest. The phrase "the lord hath taken" is from Job 1:21.

Puncture (*SP*45)

1 *Grimes* The name of a dying soldier.

6 *dartled* Robert Browning in "My Star" (1855) was the first to use the verb "dartle": "To dart or shoot forth repeatedly" (*OED*).

34 *defunctive* Funeral (only citation in *OED* is to Shakespeare, “The Phoenix and the Turtle” (1601).

43 *phiz* A colloquial abbreviation of physiognomy: face.

Semi-Centennial

First published in *F* 4 (June 1925), 58–59.

Title The occasion of the poem was the semicentennial of Vanderbilt University, 18 October 1925.

2 *one old fugitive* Also a local allusion to the Fugitive Group of poets.

5 *stave* Wooden stick.

6 *grave* To fix indelibly (*OED,* sense 6b).

35 *theogony* An account of the genealogy of birth of the deities of ancient myth (*OED*).

Two in August (*SP* 45)

30 *syllable* Utter distinctly.

Somewhere Is Such a Kingdom

1 *kingdom of the birds* This phrase suggests that the poem might derive from Chaucer’s “The Parliament of Fowls” (“Of foules every kynde / That in this world han feathers and stature / Men mighten in that place assembled fynde” [ll. 365–67]).

42 *croak* To talk despondingly, foreboding evil (like a raven) (*OED,* sense 2).

fleer Jeer, sneer (*OED,* sense 4).

Persistent Explorer

2 *scored* Reckoned.

23 *spelled him nothing* Did not charm, bewitch, or bind by a spell. The same sense of “spell” applies in l. 25.

25–32 Cf. JCR, *God Without Thunder* (Hamden, CT: Shoe String Press,

1965): "dryads, oreads, and nymphs have gone nearly out of use. In our period things have suffered the extreme of humiliation, and come to be generally disesteemed as simply the objects for our sciences to possess and for ourselves to use. The demonic terms have largely disappeared. . . . The personal terms nevertheless persist unquestionably in our thinking. They are those personifications of things that have been condemned" (290–91).

Morning

First published in *HM* 154 (December 1926), 50. This poem has no connection with a poem titled "Morning" in *PAG*.

Dog

First published in *G* 1 (October 1925), 440–41.

8 *Huendchen* A small dog (German).

35 *Hodge* Abbreviation of Roger, a typical name for an agricultural worker, especially in England.

40 *pipped* Defeated (British).

41 *leonine* JCR turns the adjective meaning "lion-like" into a noun, in context meaning a lion-like dog; he does the same with "bovine" in the next line in reference to the bull.

43 *Hodge* See l. 35n.

46 *two red eyes . . . coals* This image makes clear why the bark of a dog terrifies the speaker.

Jack's Letter

First published in *F* 4 (June 1925), 57.

14 *atrabilious* Affected by black bile and thus melancholic and acrimonious.

18 *charactry* A rare spelling of "charactery," "expression of thought by symbols or characters" (*OED*). *SP*69 adopts the usual spelling of the word.

20 *water . . . tears* Cf. William Blake, "A Poison Tree": "my wrath did grow. / And I water'd it in fears / Night & Morning with my tears."

Antique Harvesters (*SP*45)

First published in SwR 10:3 (April 1925), 13–14. JCR said at a reading that this "is my Southern poem" (Buffington 93). According to "The Authors in This Issue" in *SwR*, the poem represents "the viewpoint of the local lean old veterans," who wearily appeal to the young men to rally around the cause of the Old South (125).

Vanderbilt University's library has a fair-copy typescript of this poem, and it is essentially consonant with the first-edition version, the substitution of "shall" for "will" in l. 33 being an exception. There is no indication, however, that this manuscript was meant for printer's copy.

This poem was not included in the manuscript sent to the printer for *SP*45; apparently it was a last-minute addition.

Tagline "Sinister" = on the left. These two rivers mark the boundaries of the Old South, excepting Texas.

3 *meager . . . runnel* In these words, says F. O. Matthiessen, we hear the "old-fashioned expression, the Elizabethan or seventeenth-century usage that was brought to this country by the first settlers and that has disappeared now except for remote rural and mountain areas, especially in the South" (RPW Notes, 335).

4 *Declension* Declining from proper condition.

6 *yellow air* Suggesting the yellow autumn time of year.

43–48 *ageth . . . hath . . . wearieth* These archaic forms undermine the conviction that the old soldiers might wish to promote.

Man without Sense of Direction

40 *chantry* Chapel.

Survey of Literature (*SP*45)

Title An early manuscript title was "Roll-call of Eminent Poets and How They Subsisted."

Paul Schwartz of the Kenyon College Music Department set this poem to music (published by Broude Brothers, 1973). It was performed by the Kenyon College Community Choir at the dedication of James P. Storer Hall in October 1999 (http://bulletin.kenyon.edu/x1471.html).

1 *Plato* Athenian philosopher (c.427–348 B. C.).

3 *Aristotle* Greek philosopher from Stageira (384–322 B.C.).

5 *Chaucer* Geoffrey Chaucer (ca. 1345–1400), author of *Canterbury Tales.*

7–8 *Shakespeare . . . beer* Cf. "Doth it not show vilely in me to desire small beer?" (William Shakespeare, *Henry IV, Part 2* [1.2.7]).

9 *Wordsworth* William Wordsworth (1770–1850), Romantic poet.

11 *Tennyson* Alfred, Lord Tennyson (1809–1892), author of *In Memoriam* (1850).

15 *Milton* John Milton (1608–1674), author of *Paradise Lost* (1667).

16 *Stilton* An English cheese of strong taste and smell.

17–18 *Shelley . . . Drowned* Percy Bysshe Shelley (1792–1822), Romantic poet, drowned while sailing.

19–20 *Keats . . . Dripping blood* When this Romantic poet (1795–1821) coughed up blood in February 1820, he recognized the event as his death warrant. He died of consumption.

21 *Blake* William Blake (1757–1827), Romantic poet and engraver.

28 *consonants and vowels* While most of the poem suggests that literature is made of what writers "'had to eat and drink' (out of the raw experience of life)," the poem ends with another view: it is also made of language (RPW Notes, 336).

Amphibious Crocodile

First published in *F* 4 (December 1925), 121–23.

4 *estuaries of Nile* The Nile estuary in Egypt is also known as the Nile delta.

7 *mackintosh* British for raincoat.

13 *spats* Coverings for the instep and ankle worn mainly by men, fashionable in the late nineteenth and early twentieth centuries.

14 *Lafayette* Marquis de Lafayette (1757–1834), a Frenchman who fought for the Americans in the Revolutionary War.

16 *Notre Dame* Cathédrale Notre Dame de Paris, begun in 1163.

17 *Rive Gauche* La Rive Gauche is the "Left Bank," the side of the River Seine where lived artists and writers in the early twentieth century.
Hotel Crillon This hotel, located at the foot of the Champs-Elysées in Paris, opened in 1909 in a palace built in 1758 for King Louis XV.

18 *poilus* A poilu is a French soldier, especially one on the front line in World War I.

19 *trench* In World War I both sides constructed elaborate trenches.

21 *green slime and water* Sanitary conditions were poor in the trenches, resulting in widespread disease.

25 *Westminster* The area in central London on the north side of the Thames. Sometimes the term "Westminster" is used for the Houses of Parliament.
Fleet Street Headquarters of London newspapers.

26 *King George* George V was king of England, 1910–36.

33 *Balliol* The most distinguished Oxford college, founded in 1263.

34 *the Union* The Oxford Union debating society, founded in 1823, whose membership is mainly from Oxford University.

40 *affaires de coeur* Love affairs (French).

51 *Largo* Key Largo in Florida.

70 *welters* Rolls about (*OED*, sense 1b—obsolete).

Fresco

Title and tagline The idea of the poem is based upon Michelangelo's *The Last Judgment* (1536–41), which covers the wall behind the altar in the Sistine Chapel.

3 *Gabriel* The angel that is God's messenger. He appeared to Mary with the message that she was to give birth to the Messiah. Though he is often assumed to be the one who will blow the trumpet announcing Christ's second coming (Doomsday), the Bible does not so designate him.

7 *Jahveh* See "Adventure This Side of Pluralism," l. 39n.

9 *pelf* Possession (usually plural) (*OED,* sense 2—obsolete).

13 *ancient* Archaic title indicative of dignity (*OED,* sense 6).
hasted This old term is chiefly literary, the ordinary form being *hastened.*

16 *By littles* This appears to be a reduction of the obsolete "by little and little," meaning "gradually" (see *OED,* sense 7).
Crack-o'-Doom Cf. "What will the line stretch out to the crack of doom?" (Shakespeare, *Macbeth,* 4.1.113).

17 *frantical* Instead of "frantic," unique to JCR.

29 *dissolute* Disconnected (*OED,* sense 1—obsolete).

32 *dispose* Deliver authoritatively (*OED,* sense 3—obsolete).

36 *Gabriel* See l. 3n above.

41 *Luisa* Maria Ludovica Leopoldina Josepha Lucia (1791–1847), Austrian archduchess who was Napoleon Bonaparte's second wife (see l. 43n).

42 *Saxon* Belonging to Old Saxony.

43 *Bonaparte* Napoleon Bonaparte (1769–1821), emperor of France.

45 *Jezebel* A bold woman of loose morals (from Queen Jezebel, wife of Ahab).

47–48 *Cleopatra . . . Nile* The last Macedonian ruler (ca. 70–30 B.C.), whose powers of seduction were exercised upon Julius Caesar and the Roman General Mark Antony (l. 49). See "Amphibious Crocodile," l. 4n above.

55–57 *She got . . . honey* After Antony's suicide, Cleopatra took her own life by allowing a poisonous snake to bite her.

62 *cerements* Burial clothes.
gewed Wedded (obsolete).

The Equilibrists

Title and publication The original title was "History of Two Simple Lovers" when the poem was published in *F* 4 (September 1925), 87–88.

4 *jacinth* Perhaps a blue or purple fabric (*OED,* sense 1c—obsolete), though the word could also refer to a blue stone.

5 *Mouth . . . quaint orifice* "There is a startling repulsion-attraction between the Anglo-Saxon 'mouth' and the Latin 'orifice,' two words in one way identical and in another opposite and set against one another at opposite ends of the line" (MW, 22). *Quaint* probably means attractive and agreeable (*OED,* sense 8), and it should not be overlooked that "orifice" can refer to the opening of another bodily organ: the "quaint," which term in the sixteenth century was a common alternative to "cunt."

7 *spiral* In a circular manner, not directly.

8 *officious tower illsped* "Officious," meaning "efficacious" (*OED,* sense 2b—obsolete), runs against "illsped," which suggests a "malevolent action" (*OED,* sense 2 of "ill"). MW suggests that with the word "tower" JCR "begins to build a medieval scene" (22).

11 *beseeching . . . take* That is, to deflower her.

21 At this point the focus of the poem moves from the story of the lovers to what the speaker in the poem thinks about their plight. As Potter Woodbery says, "he struggles to comprehend their curious predicament" ("The Sword Between Them: Love and Death in Ransom's 'The Equilibrists,'" *Southern Literary Journal* 9:2 [Spring 1977], 57).

24 *grey word . . . steel* The "sword of chastity that divided the exiled lovers [Tristan and Iseult] in their forest bed becomes in the poem 'Honor,' the 'grey' word of prohibition that separates the lovers" (Woodbery, 56).

34 *puddle* Confused, muddled.

35 *gibbeted* Held up "to infamy or public contempt" (*OED,* sense 3).

37 *spin . . . out* A reference to the Fates of Greek and Roman myth, spinning the destinies of men.

38 *saeculum* World (Latin).

41 *In Heaven . . . marriage is* Cf. Matthew 22:30 and Luke 20:35.

43 *tissue* This term associated with biology works against "white flesh" of the previous line, helping to promote the tension that is the theme of the poem.

47 *Stuprate* Violate (*OED,* obsolete).

TWO GENTLEMEN IN BONDS

This sonnet sequence was first published in *Miscellany of American Poetry* (New York: Harcourt, Brace, 1925), 145–64. "Rain" is the only sonnet published earlier (see note for that poem).

Pink and Pale

1 *pinked* Looking with half-closed eyes or winking in a sleepy manner (*OED,* sense 1).

3 *chine* A "joint" of beef, mutton, or pork, including the animal's back.
swigs Drinks of liquor (*OED,* obsolete), though still colloq. in America.

Thinking, Drinking

4 *Phidias* The Greek architect, sculptor, and painter who erected the buildings on the Acropolis at Athens, under the administration of Pericles.

5 *Michaelmas* 29 September.

6 *green* Youthful (*OED,* obsolete).

In Air

2 *addled* Spoiled. Cf. Rudyard Kipling, "The Conundrum of the Workshops": "We have learned to bottle our parents twain in the yoke of an addled egg."

13 *rowelling* Digging spurs into (*OED,* sense 2).

Thought, Distraught

5 *Petrarch* Francesco Petrarca (1304–1374), Italian poet who wrote a series of sonnets to a woman named Laura.

Meeting in a Garden

8 *blown* Out of breath.

Epithalamion of a Peach

Title An epithalamion is a song written in celebration of a wedding.

1 *maculate* Defiled.

L'état C'est Moi

Title "The state is I," said by Louis XIV of France.

1 *pestiferous* Pestilential.

8 *On n'a . . . gendarmes* We only have good states when there are gendarmes (French).

Misanthropy

12–13 *And all . . . grey tower* Cf. Mother Goose: "All the king's horses, / And all the king's men, / Couldn't put Humpty Dumpty together again."

Vain Protestations

3 *Guelph* A member of the political group in medieval Italy supporting the sovereignty of the papacy against the German emperors.

5 *Caliban* The speaker in Robert Browning's "Caliban Upon Setebos" (1864). The savage Caliban acknowledges Setebos as his god. Browning took the name Caliban from Shakespeare's *The Tempest* (1611), wherein Caliban is the "savage and deformed slave" of Prospero.

Tones and Caparisons

Title A caparison is a kind of defensive armor for a horse (*OED,* sense 1b—obsolete).

6 *King his* Renaissance English grammarians mistakenly argued that the possessive form "King's" was a shortening of "King his."

8 *silver* Soft-toned, melodious (*OED,* sense 13).

Disappointment of a Thrall

Title A thrall is one in bondage to a lord.

4 *chamberlain* An officer of a king who manages his affairs.

6 *Noised* Reported.

10 *peaked* Pointed, but with a pun on "piqued" (offended).

11 *gravel* Stones in the urinary track causing difficulty in passing urine.

12 *leeches* Doctors.

14 *stomach* Disposition (*OED*, sense 7—obsolete). Last citation in *OED* is 1610.

In Bed, Not Dead

9 *fast* Permanent.

10 *yellow* Suggesting age or disease.

13 *Seneschal* In the Middle Ages, the official in charge of the administration of servants.

Primer of Science

5 *ravin* The devouring of prey.

7 *Machiavelli* Niccolò Machiavelli (1469–1527), Florentine political theorist, author of *The Prince* (1513).

Fait Accompli

Title Fact accomplished (French): a thing done and no longer worth arguing against.

3 *films* Growths in the eyes.

8 *wire* Fence (*OED*, sense 1e).

Implacable Tower

2 *stiff-necked* See "Night Voices" (*CF*), l. 14n.

3–4 *His stars . . . glories* The belief that the arrangement of celestial bodies at one's nativity determine one's prospects in life.

Features of Creatures

11 *minatory* Threatening.

Rain

First published in *TM* 52 (June 1925), 11, under the title "Proud Heart Rained Upon." When JCR brought the poem to a Fugitive meeting, it had the title "Dead Men."

1 *susurrance* Properly, susurrence—a low soft sound (*OED*).

6 *Percipiences* Perceptions.
Styx The river of Hades, over which the shades of the dead were ferried by Charon.

Wrong

13 *gibing* Taunting.

Additional Published Poems

Published poems other than those included in *Poems About God, Chills and Fever,* and *Two Gentlemen in Bonds* appear in this section. They are divided into three groups: (1) sundry poems, usually appearing only in a magazine, newspaper, or journal and not included in any collection; (2) poems published in book form for the first time in one of the volumes of *Selected Poems;* (3) alternate versions of poems, either earlier or later versions. It is sometimes difficult to determine if a poem should be considered a distinct poem. I have generally taken a conservative view in making these determinations. It is not enough for nearly every line to exhibit a difference from the standard version, for if the line of argument is followed on a line-by-line basis, then I do not think the revision is a new poem; but if a poem is revised and taken in new directions, if significant parts have been added or subtracted, if it is developed or reduced to such an extent that one poem becomes another poem, then textual variants are dispensed with in favor of the poem's being recognized as a separate work, or if it is given a new form, then it is reproduced as a distinct poem. If a poem, "Prometheus in Straits," for example, is extensively revised yet adheres to each line's original function, then it will be considered merely heavily revised, and the revisions will be recorded in the textual notes. The only time I might have stretched this principle is in the designation of the very heavily revised "Birthday of an Aging Seer" as an alternate version.

In *Selected Poems* 1969 there is a section at the end of the volume designated "Sixteen Poems in Eight Pairings *(with original and final versions studied comparatively)*." The original versions are designated "A," and the new versions, which Ransom's commentary argues, mostly unpersuasively, represent improved versions, are identified as "B." Some of these revised poems retain the original title; in the textual notes, these poems will be cited as *SP*69a and *SP*69b. The "original" versions are not always identical to the actual originals; variants will be noted.

1. SUNDRY POEMS

The newspaper, magazine, or journal in which the poems appear will be copy-text unless otherwise indicated in the note to the poem.

What the Old Leaf Said

Published only in the *Inde,* 27 October 1917, 180, the author's name being given as "John Crowe." In his letter of 31 October 1917 to Ransom, then in the United States Army during World War I, Christopher Morley enclosed a cutting of this poem, saying that he will insist that "in any future pieces they print they use your full name and military designation" (Haverford). Morley was charged with placing his friend's poems in magazines and newspapers.

The House

On 19 May 1918, JCR wrote to Christopher Morley: "today I was seized with a Shakespearean sonnet, which I have set down on the other page. If you care for it, put it just after 'The Resurrection' in the volume" (Haverford). Morley, charged with finding a publisher for *PAG,* did not see fit to include "The House" in that manuscript. The poem was first published in Young, 111. Copy-text is JCR's manuscript (Haverford) sent to Morley.

1 *shut* Closed.

[Minerva Had No Pride]

On 17 March 1919, JCR wrote to Morley: "I've been sonneteering a good deal of late. I've got a whole book in my head—a lot of sonnets in a lot of sequences with the same characters and history. But I am absolutely destitute of critics. That's why I don't know whether I'm well-advised. Here's one of a lighter tinkle I submit" (Haverford). This sonnet was first published in *SL,* 105. The Haverford manuscript is used as copy-text.

Halted at the Altar

Only publication is in the *Evening Public Ledger* (Philadelphia), on 26 May 1919, 10. The poem appears in Christopher Morley's column entitled "The Chafing Dish." In an editorial note between the title and the text, Morley writes, "The waggish humor of our friend Lieutenant John Ransom has not been tarnished by his military service. From his present post in the school detachment, Nancy, France, A.P.O. [Army Post

Office] 915, A.E.F. [American Expeditionary Forces], John sends us the following. And by the way, those who are inclined toward high-tension literature will do well to have a look at John's book, 'Poems About God,' some portions of which first saw the light in this department." The Library of Congress Index gives "Halted at the Altar" as the first of Ransom's poems to appear in the *Ledger.*

I. Obeisance

This term represents the character Roger's submission to the beautiful woman. Playing on the similar initial sounds of the subtitle headings for each sonnet, JCR portrays Roger's *Obeisance* as being undermined by his fear that her beauty will give way to *Obesity.*

1 *blade* "A gallant, a free-and-easy fellow" (*OED,* sense 11).

II. Obesity

1 *contemned* Despised.

8 *avoirdupois* More fully *avoirdupois weight,* the standard system of weights used in Great Britain.

11 *not . . . groomed* Punning, that she should not be spruced up and that she should not be provided a groom.

13 *amain* Greatly (*OED,* sense 3).

The Song of Roland

Published only in the *Evening Public Ledger* (Philadelphia), on 27 May 1919, 10. It appears in a feature called "The Tuning Fork." Following his signature, JCR's address was given: "A.P.O. 915, A.E.F."

Title Roland was the most famous of Charlemagne's knights, whose legend has been handed down in various forms, one of the better known of which is the medieval French poem *Chanson de Roland.*

1 *fold* The surface of the earth (*OED,* 1a—obsolete).

18 *eke* Middle English for "also."

24 *two measures* The Lady's and Roland's estimates of each other.

26 *Rolando* JCR combines "Roland" with "Orlando," the Italian form of the name in Ariosto's poem *Orlando Furioso* (1516).

Garden Sonnets

Published only in *EP*, in Christopher Morley's "The Bowling Green," the first of the two Shakespearian sonnets on 13 February 1920, 10, and the second on 16 February 1920, 8. The sonnets are printed just as they appeared in the newspaper, the first with alternate indented lines, except for the couplet, and the second with all lines flush left.

1. Sweet Will His Sonnet Set Out

Subtitle JCR employs the mistaken Renaissance notion that the possessive apostrophe in "Will's" is an abbreviation of "Will his," considered at the time the more proper form of the possessive case. One would think that the title refers to Will Shakespeare; indeed, Shakespeare, making a play on his name in Sonnet 134 (written to his Dark Lady), refers to "thy sweet will" (l. 4). But the speaker in JCR's sonnet, we are told in l. 2, is an earl; perhaps, then, "Will" refers to "desire," even sexual desire, which are plays on the word in Shakespeare's sonnet.

1 *circumstance* Surroundings (*OED,* sense 1—obsolete).

2 *spake* Archaic past tense of *speak.*

7 *gear* An old term for the "organs of generation" (*OED,* sense 5b).

8 *turn . . . page* The rose is asked to open up.

10 *ill-bred worm comes* Cf. William Blake, "The Sick Rose": "The invisible worm . . . / Has found out thy bed."

2. He Burns for Her

Subtitle While the rose is a means of courting the "English girl" of sonnet 1, here the man who pursued the girl has become the snipped rose stuck in a vase. Though he "burned" with passion, he now "suffers decay in such a manner as to present the appearance of being scorched"—the result of rapid oxidation.

14 *flaming . . . Moses* Cf. Exodus 3:2: "the bush burned with fire, and the bush was not consumed."

Sonnets of a Selfish Lover

These three sonnets were published on separate days in the *EP,* I on 24 February 1920, 8; II on 1 March 1920, 8; and III on 6 March 1920, 10.

"Dead Boy" (*TGB*) was condensed from this sequence. The first sonnet here contains all but the second stanza of "Dead Boy" and then adds the couplet.

I.

1–3 *subtraction . . . transaction* See "Dead Boy," ll. 1–3n.

4 *outer dark* See "Dead Boy," l. 4n.

5 *strode* See "Dead Boy," l. 4n.

10 *first-fruits . . . hath taken* See "Dead Boy," l. 18n.

Sonnets of a Pastoral Pair

This sequence was published in *EP*, each of the four sonnets on separate days—I on 12 March 1920, 10; II on 18 March 1920, 8; III on 20 March 1920, 10; and IV on 25 March 1920, 8.

I. They Take to the Fields

2 *stayed* Ceased going forward (*OED*, sense 1—obsolete).

13 *Master Mock* Personification of Death.

II. They Praise the Sun

Morley placed this sonnet in his anthology *The Bowling Green: An Anthology of Verse* (New York: Doubleday, Page, 1924), 126. The editor's preface says that the anthology, drawing from poems in his column from 9 February 1920 to 31 December 1923, offers "the most permanent" of the thousand poems printed in his column over nearly four years.

IV. They Hail the Sunrise

Published also in Morley's *The Bowling Green*, 127.

April Absence

This Shakespearian sonnet published only in *EP*, 24 April 1920, 10.

8 *Brother Reynard* "Reynard" is commonly used as a synonym for fox.

Destitution Raiseth Her Voice

Published only in *F* 1:2 ([June] 1922), 48, under the pseudonym Roger Prim.

7–8 *Yet may . . . himself* Cf. Matthew 25:40: "Inasmuch as ye have done it [that is, given a hungry stranger meat] unto one of the least of these my brethren, ye have done it unto me."

9 *King Croesus* The king of Lydia from 560 to 547 B.C., whose name became proverbial for a wealthy man.

11 *Solon* Croesus did not heed the advice offered by the Athenian poet Solon, born in 638 B.C.

Poets Have Chanted Mortality

Published only in *F* 1:3 (October 1922), 86. It was included in the original manuscript of "Chills and Fevers" sent to Morley on 31 December 1922 but was withdrawn when JCR revised his manuscript for the proposed collection.

3 *liege* Loyal subject of a king (this poem's last two lines refer to the Worm as "His Absolute / Highness").

5 *Will* William Shakespeare (1564–1616).

6 *Stratford's gentry* The privileged people of Stratford-upon-Avon, Shakespeare's birthplace.

7 *Queen* Elizabeth I, queen of England (1558–1603).

13–14 *chaste lady . . . lover* See Andrew Marvell, "To His Coy Mistress" (1681).

15–16 *Lewd One . . . cover* In "To His Coy Mistress," Marvell has the lover say to his chaste lady: "worms shall try / That long-preserved virginity" (ll. 27–28).

Virga

Published only in *F* 3:5–6 (December 1924), 151–52.

Title "Virga" is a "branch, rod, streak in the sky suggesting rain" (*New Int.*).

2 *lex* Law (Latin)

24 *petard* A firework that explodes with a loud report (*New Int.*).

54 *pharisaic* Resembling the Pharisees in making a big show of being religious and exhibiting self-righteousness.

Applied Eleatics

Published only in *Palms* 2:2 (1924–25), 53.

Title An ancient Greek school of philosophy founded by Parmenides in the fifth century B.C. in Elea, a Greek colony in present-day Italy, the Eleatics held that thought alone can take one beyond false appearances.

1 *fantom* An obsolete form of "phantom."

3 *Olympus* The mountain in Thessaly that ancient Greeks believed to be the abode of the higher gods.

5 *ride on wings, or a dolphin* Daedalus made wings of wax to escape the labyrinth at Knossos; see "The Feasting of Maionides and Stephen Daedalus [*sic*]," l. 42n. (James Joyce's character's name is spelled "Stephen Dedalus.") Poseidon is often depicted riding the back of a dolphin.
zephyr A light west wind.

6 *enter . . . rain of stars* When Danae, a princess of Argos, was shut in a tower, Zeus came down to her as a shower of golden stars. She is often depicted in art as naked and receptive.

9 *goat-god* Pan, who had the beard, horns, and feet of a goat, was an Arcadian god of hills and woods and was the deity that protected flocks, herdsmen, and hunters. He made goats and ewes multiply, bringing a phallic aspect to his divinity (*CA*; Felix Guirand, *Greek Mythology*, trans. Delano Ames [London: Paul Hamlyn, 1963], 119).

10 *He whistled* Pan played a syrinx, which he formed from the reed into which a nymph named Syrinx was changed; fearing Pan's pursuit, she prayed to her father to change her into a reed (Guirand, 119).

11 *ceinture* A girdle or belt worn in ancient Greece.

12 *he fled* Though Pan's practice was to pursue nymphs on a regular basis, he suffers an ironic reversal when he encounters a forward bather who then pursues him. This is his misadventure mentioned in l. 9.

Nostri in Memoriam Doctissimi

Published only in *In Memoriam: Herbert Cushing Tolman* (Nashville: Alpha of Tennessee, Vanderbilt Chapter of Phi Beta Kappa, 1926).

Title In memory of our learned one (Latin).

Tagline Tolman (1865–1923), a Yale PhD, was a professor of Greek—and later academic dean—at Vanderbilt University and one of JCR's professors during his undergraduate years. An Assyriologist is one who studies the language, history, and antiquities of Assyria.

1 *Achaemenidae* Persian kings that ruled from about 550 to 331 B.C.

19 *Avernus* Ancient name for a crater near Cumae, Italy, west of Naples.

22 *wildered* Lost, bewildered.

24 *bell . . . book* Apparently a bell to call his newfound students together, and the book could be Tolman's *A Guide to Old Persian Inscriptions* (1893) or *The Behistan Inscription of King Darius Translation and Critical Notes to the Persian Text* (1908). The line could not possibly refer to the Roman Catholic ritual of excommunication involving bell, book, and candle.

28 *Ruler on the Seat* Cf. 2 Corinthians 5:10: "we must all appear before the judgment seat of Christ; that every one may receive the things done in the body, according to that he hath done, whether it be good or bad."

Autumn Love

Published only in *NR*, 20 February 1929, 10.

Tagline The poem consists of three Italian octaves that progress in the manner of the quatrains of many English sonnets—but here towards a single Italian sestet.

2 *cake* Solidification (*OED*, sense 4b).

29 *fowler's gun* A fowler is one who hunts wild birds.

The Feasting of Maionides and Stephen Daedalus

Published only in *NR*, 14 April 1929, 342.

Title Maionides (1135–1204) was a noted Jewish Aristotelian during the Middle Ages. A rationalist and anti-mystic philosopher, he wrote *The Guide for the Perplexed.* He was not a Greek, as the poem suggests. Stephen Dedalus is the hero of James Joyce's *A Portrait of the Artist as a Young Man* (1916).

JCR attached the following footnote to the title of this poem:

> Who are the four-and-twenty blackbirds celebrated in the old rhyme? [see l. 4 below] The answer is very clear: they are the letters of the Greek alphabet, the cause of all our Western learning, fashioned variously into songs after the skill of the contrivers who impress and manage them. Of all the ancient practitioners of this art, Maionides is considered the grandest, claimed by seven cities after his death, who during his life was homeless and a wanderer. And Stephen Daedalus [*sic*] is said to be the most formidable of the modern in the line of succession. But how shockingly has he taken unto himself the name: Stephanos Daldalos [*sic*], the true Contriver wearing the crown! And what a change has come over the pastry-profession in the meantime! Evidently the blackbirds that used to sing like meadowlarks and nightingales have made up their minds to play crows and sullen rooks, and even realistical birds of worser obscenity.—THE AUTHOR.

Stephen's friends refer to him, and he does himself as well, as "Stephanos Dedalos," which JCR (see above) misspells (James Joyce, *A Portrait of the Artist as a Young Man* [New York: Viking, 1965], 168). Apparently JCR assumes that Stephen and Joyce are one and the same, and though Stephen thinks of himself as "a priest of eternal imagination, transmuting the daily bread of experience into the radiant body of everliving life" (221), JCR sees the avatar of modernism as failing to carry on the tradition of forging true literature. Standing on the steps of the library, Stephen listens to the birds' "cries," "squeak[s]," their "shrill twofold note," and this "inhuman clamour soothed his ears" (224); JCR suggests that these birds are an objective correlative of Stephen's/Joyce's aesthetic sense.

3 *Four-and-twenty blackbirds* From "Sing a Song of Sixpence," an English nursery rhyme, possibly going back to the sixteenth century. These blackbirds have been variously interpreted over the years—that they represent the number of hours in a day, or monks during Henry VIII's dissolution of the monasteries, or the whole church—but JCR's assigning to them the characters of the Greek alphabet seems original to him.

4 *fowler of Phoenicia* See "Autumn Love," l. 29n. Phoenicia is an ancient region made up mainly of modern-day Lebanon. The Phoenician alphabet is the ancestor of most modern alphabets.

5 *Greek Maionides* See note to *Title* above.

13 *dainty dish . . . king* Cf. "Sing a Song of Sixpence": "When the pie was opened, / The birds began to sing; / Wasn't that a dainty dish, / To set before the king?"

21 *whir* Ironically, the birds that Stephen Dedalus observes are described as "whirring" (*Portrait of an Artist,* 224).

37 *Achilles* The mighty Greek warrior who, because he was wronged by Agamemnon, sulks through most of Homer's *Iliad.*

40 *Troy* The city besieged for ten years by the Greeks, who were intent upon recovering Menelaus's wife, Helen, who had been carried there by Paris.

43 *Maionides* See note for *Title* above.

Daedalus JCR holds that Stephen Dedalus (see *Title* above) fails to live up to his namesake: The mythical Greek representative of all art, especially architecture, Daedalus created waxen wings, allowing him, together with his son Icarus, to escape the labyrinth at Gnosus and soar to great heights. Stephen Dedalus, in creating "jangl[ing] sibilants" and a "mocking art," goes too far from the traditional limitations on art and thus is really more associated with Icarus, who, getting too close to the sun, caused his waxen wings to melt, and he fell into the sea.

46 *sibilants and surds* Sibilants are hissing sounds; "surds" are sounds lacking sense or perception—stupid or irrational.

55 *no bird singing* Cf. John Keats, "La Belle Dame Sans Merci": "And no birds sing!" (ll. 4, 48).

67 *Troy* See l. 39n above.

2. NEW POEMS IN THE SELECTED POEMS VOLUMES

What Ducks Require (*SP* 45)

First published in *NR,* 27 April 1927, 273.

8 *Cyclops* Mythical Greek giant with one eye in the middle of his forehead.

10 *aquarelles* Paintings with Chinese ink and transparent water colors, usually representing flowers or small landscapes.

13 *estate* Landed property (ironic, since the term implies one of considerable extent).

16 *Lar* In Roman myth, the "tutelary deity of a house, hence 'the home'" (*OED,* sense 1).
invalided Rendered invalid.

19 *quadrate wing* A rectangular one.

20 *fowler* See "Autumn Love," l. 29n.

25 *prodigious* Marvellous (*OED,* sense 3).

29 *Capricornus* One of the constellations and represents a creature that is a blend of fish and goat.

Prelude to an Evening (*SP*45)

First published in *AR* 3 (April–October, 1934), 262–63, and then in *NV* 10 (August 1934), 9–10.

19–20 *peignoir . . . sunny room* Cf. Wallace Stevens, "Sunday Morning": "Complacencies of the peignoir, and late / Coffee and oranges in a sunny chair."

20 *poising* Being held in equilibrium.

22 *metronome* JCR turns the noun for the instrument used in music for marking time into a verb.

26 *buckberries* Huckleberries (wild blueberries), common in the American South.

30 *Eumenides* The Greek goddesses of vengeance.

Of Margaret (*SP*45)

First published in *SatR,* 29 September 1934, 137.

6 *gelid* Cold as ice.

12 *substant* Substantial.

Painted Head (*SP*45)

First published in *NR*, 26 December 1934, 185.

2 *capital* Pun: a human head and the uppermost part of an architectural column.

3 *Platonic* Suggesting reason and "pure idea" (Buffington 124).

4 *depending* Hanging.

12 *stem* Offshoot from a family tree.

19 *capital* First rate.

23 *egg* Suggesting "egghead" (Buffington 125).

33 *blue birds* The eyes.
Sea; *sea-shell flats* The teeth (Buffington).

34 *caves* The mouth or ears (Buffington).

35 *hyacinthine hair* Cf. Edgar Allan Poe, "To Helen": "On desperate seas long wont to roam, / Thy hyacinth hair."

36 *olive garden* The mind.

Address to the Scholars of New England (*SP*45)

First published in the *KR* 1 (Autumn 1939), 406–8. This was JCR's first poem in five years and written to be read at the meeting of the Harvard chapter of the Phi Beta Kappa Society on 23 June 1939.

1 *Sarah Pierrepont . . . rage* The wife of eighteenth-century Puritan divine Jonathan Edwards (1703–1758), a graduate of Yale, Sarah Pierrepont Edwards (1710–1758) was known for her enthusiastic conversion narrative, which is alluded to in ll. 5–6 below.

3 *the Bear* Ursa Major, a constellation visible all year in the Northern Hemisphere.

12 *Pure Idea* A reference to Plato's theory of pure ideas; see "Survey of Literature" (*TGB*), l. 1n.

15 *levees* Assemblies.

21 *entail* A settlement of the inheritance of property.

22 *merchant . . . thumb* One who leaves his thumb on the scale to cheat his customers.

31 *megrims* "Whims" or possibly "low spirits" (*OED*, sense 2, 3).

41 *Plato . . . Plotinus* The Greek philosopher Plotinus (204–270 A.D.) was in the Platonic tradition; the way to happiness was given emphasis in his philosophy. See "Survey of Literature," l. 1n.

46 *witch . . . water* A reference to dunking practiced by seventeenth-century Puritans: if the accused woman sank, she was deemed innocent; if she floated, she was a witch.

47 *blasphemer . . . stocks* Those who outraged strict Puritan religious views were, like murderers, put in a wooden stock, which secured the legs in place, so that the populace could ridicule the offender.

48 *woman branded . . . sin* A reference to Hester Prynne, who in Hawthorne's *The Scarlet Letter* (1850) wore an "A" for her adultery.

50 *British tea . . . water* A reference to the Boston Tea Party in 1771.

55 *giddying . . . clouds* The "Puritans were out of their natural element in the 'transcendent clouds'"; the "giddying" stems from the Old English *gydig,* which means "god-possessed," "in a state of divine frenzy" (Buffington 127).

Old Man Pondered (*SP63*)

First published in *SatR,* 15 June 1929, 1107, "Old Man Pondered" was apparently a last-minute addition to *SP63*, for it does not appear in the page proofs. This poem was revised as "Four Threesomes; or Three Foursomes," *SR* 81:3 (Summer 1973), 387–88, and as "The Eye Can Tell," *SoR* 19:4 (Autumn 1983), 836–37.

3. ALTERNATE VERSIONS OF POEMS

Sonnet of a Sure Heart

Published in *EP* (in Morley's "The Bowling Green") on 18 February 1920, 8, a precursor of a sixteen-line version published in *F* 1 (June 1922), 54, which was also part of the original "Chills and Fevers" manuscript that JCR sent to Morley on 31 December 1922 (the title was "Heart Too Sure"); and of the twelve-line version published in *CF* under the title "Spring Posy." Morley selected this sonnet for his *The Bowling Green: An Anthology of Verse* (New York: Doubleday, Page, 1924), 125.

Winter Remembered (1922)

This Shakespearian sonnet, published in *SR* 30:1 (January 1922), 1, was expanded into a twenty-line poem in *CF* and remained so thereafter.

The Handmaidens

Published only in *F* 1:1 ([April] 1922), 26–32, as by Roger Prim, this poem is a significant expansion of "The Power of God" (*PAG*), a 24-line poem, to one of 134 lines. Another expanded version of "The Power of God" was included as part of the manuscript of "Chills and Fevers" that JCR sent to Christopher Morley on 31 December 1922 (see introduction to *CF*). The most obvious difference between this and the *F* version is that the "Chills and Fevers" version is arranged in couplet-stanzas and is divided into five numbered sections of different lengths. This manuscript version also has 20 fewer lines (those not included in "Chills and Fevers" are 9–10, 45–48, 55–58, 62–63, 79–80, 85–86, and 111–14) as JCR had sought to pare down a very long poem. He did, however, add one couplet in the unpublished manuscript, one drawing from the Song of Solomon (7:7) describing Eve's breasts: "Her stature like to a palm with clusters of grape, / Whereof a cunning workman had wrought the shape" (between ll. 100 and 101). In addition, JCR rewrote five lines and throughout made changes in diction and punctuation. Variants from the "Chills and Fevers" manuscript will not be recorded in the notes because that manuscript was never connected with any publication, and it is not a distinct version.

3 *the Force* A reference to an element of the American Expeditionary Forces (AEF) during World War I.

7 *limbered* To limber is "to fasten together the two parts of a gun-carriage, as a preparation for moving away" (*OED*).

Fontevrault The monastery of Fontevrault, founded in 1099, is about two and a half miles south of the Loire, near Saumur (see l. 9n).

9 *Saumur* A commune in the Maine-et-Loire Department in western France.

12 *sabots* Wooden shoes.

53 *bone . . . bone* Cf. Genesis 2:23: "This is now bone of my bones, and flesh of my flesh; she shall be called Woman."

55 *It is writ . . . toil* Cf. Genesis 3:23.

62 *gird* Jest or gibe (*OED*, sense 4).
villain Casting opprobrium (*OED*, sense 3b—obsolete).

75 *impounding* Seizing.

88 *sweat . . . face* Cf. Genesis 3:19.

89 *seraphim* See "Our Two Worthies" (*TGB*), l. 42n.

93 *vaunted* Praised vaingloriously.

94 *Delilah* The Philistine who betrayed Samson (Judges 16: 4–22).
Sheba Queen of Sheba, whose visit to Solomon is recorded in 1 Kings 10:1–13.

95–97 *Madam Helen . . . battle* See "The School" (*PAG*), ll. 3–4n.

99–100 *fair . . . armies* Cf. Song of Solomon 6:10: "Who is she that looketh forth as the morning, fair as the moon, clear as the sun, and terrible as an army with banners."

101 *breasts . . . twin-born* Cf. Song of Solomon 7:3: "Thy two breasts are like two young roes that are twins."
Heshbon Cf. Song of Solomon 7:4: "thine eyes like the fishpools in Heshbon." (Heshbon was an ancient town east of the Jordan River.)

102 *teeth . . . shorn* Cf. Song of Solomon 4:2: "Thy teeth are like a flock of sheep that are even shorn."
Hermon Mount Hermon in Lebanon, simply called "Hermon" in Song of Solomon, 4:8.

103 *Rose of Sharon* Cf. Song of Solomon 2:1: "I am the rose of Sharon, and the lily of the valleys." (The plain of Sharon is between the mountains of central Palestine.)

105–9 *they sinned . . . must sweat* Cf. Genesis 3:17–19, 23.

111 *lily . . . toil not* Cf. Matthew 6:28: "And why take ye thought of raiment? Consider the lilies of the field, how they grow: they toil not, neither do they spin."

115 *daughters of Eve* Cf. Genesis 3:20.

117 *wen* Wart (*OED*, obsolete).

123 *encircuit* See "The Power of God" (*PAG*), l. 19n.

127 *ancient of days* A name of God, the term appears in Daniel 7:9, 13–14; and in the hymn "Immortal, Invisible, God Only Wise": "Most blessed, most precious, the Ancient of Days, / Almighty, victorious, Thy great name we praise." Also, William Blake produced a watercolor etching *The Ancient of Days* (1794).

Blue Girls (1924)

Published in *F* 3:3 (June 1924), 82.

2 *seminary* See "Blue Girls" (*TGB*), l. 2n.

Implacable Tower (1925)

Published in *APM*, an earlier version of a poem by the same title in *TGB*. The octave is, after the first four words, entirely different, the sestet the same.

2 *churl* Serf (*OED*, sense 3—obsolete).

5 *buds* Undeveloped breasts.

7 *stiff-necked* See "Night Voices" (*CF*), l. 14n.

The Vanity of the Bright Young Men (*SP*63)

A thorough rewriting of "Tom, Tom, the Piper's Son" (*CF*).

14 *Druid trees* The Druids, ancient Celtic priests, performed secret rites at midnight in oak groves.

23 *dammed* See "Tom, Tom, the Piper's Son," l. 27n.

25 *changeling* See "Tom, Tom, the Piper's Son," l. 29n.

34 *litten* See "Tom, Tom, the Piper's Son," l. 38n.

Master's in the Garden Again (*SP*63)

First published in *KR* 24 (Summer 1962), 439–40, as "Conrad in Twilight."

Title The title alludes to Hardy's "The Master of the Leaves" (1917).

The dedication to the poet Hardy (1840–1928) relates perhaps to the edgy husband-wife relationship in the poem and perhaps to Hardy's enjoyment of relaxing in his garden.

2 *conjugate* Joined together in wedlock.

3 *Conrad* See note to *Title* of "Conrad Sits in Twilight" (*CF*).

15 *miasma* See "Conrad Sits in Twilight" (*CF*), l. 7n.

25 *byre* See "Conrad Sits in Twilight" (*CF*), l. 21n.

29 *Its* The capitalization suggests that the Power is a deity. The speaker employs "It" to suggest that the Power over men and gardens does not possess the moral sensitivity of human beings, an idea also held by Hardy.

34 *tell-tale . . . heart* Obviously glancing at Edgar Allan Poe's short story "The Tell-Tale Heart" (1843).

41 *mumming* Sounding indistinctly (*OED*, obsolete), a term contemptuously bringing to mind religious utterance.

Prelude to an Evening

A rewriting of the *SP*45–*SP*63 (earlier version in the same volume).

30 *buckberries* See "Prelude to an Evening" (*SP*45), l. 26n.

34 *Furies* Same as Eumenides, see "Prelude to an Evening" (*SP*45), l. 30n.

April Treason (*SP*69)

This is an alternate version of the poem first published in *CF*. See note for "April Treason," *Source*, in *CF*.

25 *Venus* See "On the Road to Wockensutter," l. 14n.

Nocturne (*SP*69)

This is an alternate version of the poem first published in *CF*.

Title See "Nocturne" (*CF*) note on title.

3 *Goat-footed* See "Nocturne" (*CF*), l. 2n.

36 *bacchanal* See "Nocturne" (*CF*), l. 18n

Two Gentlemen Scholars (*SP69*)

A total rewriting of "Overtures" (*PAG*).

6 *ribbon of silver* Flowing water (JCR's commentary in *SP69*, 117).

18 *screed* Harangue.

20 *bleed . . . look* Perhaps he looked daggers, that is, in such a way as to wound (see *OED*, 3b).

24 *John Donne* English metaphysical poet (1572–1631).

36 *riddling* Enigmatic in expression (*OED*).

42 *siren* That which charms.

Agitato ma non troppo (*SP69*)

An alternate version of the poem first published in *CF.*

6 *bittern* See "*Agitato ma non troppo*" (*CF*), l. 3n.

8–9 *Dante's fury . . . bury* Beatrice married another man; see "*Agitato ma non troppo*" (*CF*), ll. 5–6n.

11 *Shelley's . . . tremolo* See "*Agitato ma non troppo*" (*CF*), l. 8n.

15 *terrible bier* Perhaps that of one of his children.

The Vanity of the Bright Boys (*SP69*)

A rewriting of "The Vanity of the Bright Young Men" (*SP63*), which was a rewriting of "Tom, Tom, the Piper's Son" (*CF*).

14 *Druid* See "The Vanity of the Bright Young Men," l. 14n.

21 *dammed* See "Tom, Tom, the Piper's Son," l. 27n.

29 *vegetary* Vegetative (*OED*, obsolete).

42 *wantoned* Trifled (*OED*, sense 1e).

45 *purpled* Colored purple, which indicates the dress of a king.

48 *kingdom come* Cf. Matthew 6:10" "Thy kingdom come. Thy will be done."

Birthday of an Aging Seer (*SP*69)

This rewriting of "Semi-Centennial" (*TGB*) portrays an actual man, who though nameless is given a birth date, in place of the generic old man in thc original poem.

Title See note on title for "Semi-Centennial" (*TGB*).

6 *grave* See "Semi-Centennial," l. 6n.

35 *theogony* See "Semi-Centennial," l. 35n.

Unpublished Poems

Typescripts for the unpublished poems are in the Ransom Papers, Special Collections and University Archives, Heard Library, Vanderbilt University, and the Christopher Morley Collection, Harry Ransom Center, University of Texas at Austin.

Hallowe'en Poem

This poem, with JCR's name typed at the manuscript bottom right, is in the same folder with several poems written by his daughter, Helen Ransom Forman, in the Ransom Collection at Vanderbilt.

Guarded Protest

Withdrawn from the original manuscript of "Chills and Fevers" (1922), which manuscript is at HRC.

10 *Empery* A territory of an absolute and powerful ruler (*OED*).

Quarrel

Withdrawn from the original manuscript of "Chills and Fevers" (1922, HRC).

Mr. Hopper

Withdrawn from the original manuscript of "Chills and Fevers" (1922, HRC).

4 *asymptote* That which approaches but never meets.

9 *started* Broke loose (*OED*, sense 8).

12 *Atlas* The Titan who held up the celestial spheres, in Greek myth.

26 *Deliver . . . Lord!* The refrain in "The Litany of General Supplication": "Good Lord, deliver us" (Book of Common Prayer).

Address to the Importunate Deacons

Withdrawn from the original manuscript of "Chills and Fevers" (1922, HRC).

Emendations

The following emendations have been made to the copy-texts:

Two Gentlemen in Bonds

Blue Girls

l. 13. The VMS colon, which properly sets up the illustrative story, is restored.

l. 16. The wordy "and yet" in the first edition is emended to "yet" according to VMS, MS*SP*45, *SP*45, *PE, SP*63, and *SP*69.

Vain Protestations

The intended space between octave and sestet is restored. That space appeared in the copy of the poem that JCR read at a meeting of the Fugitives, in the poem as it appears in *APM,* and in his own copy of the first edition, where he made a marginal note recreating the break. Further, all the other poems in the series of sonnets "Two Gentlemen in Bonds," save "Wrong" (see below), observe the break.

Wrong

The intended space between octave and sestet is restored, for the same reasons applying to "Vain Protestations."

Semi-Centennial

l. 22. The copy-text contains the word "word" when the other texts (*F* and *SP*69a)—and the context almost demands it—give the reading as "world." Furthermore, the marked-up first edition at Vanderbilt shows that JCR recognized "word" as an error.

Appendix A
Tables of Contents for Volumes of *Selected Poems*

Selected Poems (1945)

Winter Remembered
Miriam Tazewell
Dead Boy
Spectral Lovers
Necrological
Bells for John Whiteside's Daughter
The Tall Girl
Good Ships
Emily Hardcastle, Spinster
Parting at Dawn
Vaunting Oak
Spiel of the Three Mountebanks
Here Lies a Lady
Tom, Tom, the Piper's Son
Conrad in Twilight
Armageddon
Judith of Bethulia
Blue Girls
Philomela
Old Man Playing with Children
Captain Carpenter
Old Mansion
Piazza Piece
Eclogue
Her Eyes
Parting, Without a Sequel
Janet Waking
Lady Lost
Two in August
Somewhere Is Such a Kingdom
Antique Harvesters

Our Two Worthies
Puncture
Dog
Man Without Sense of Direction
Survey of Literature
The Equilibrists
What Ducks Require
Prelude to an Evening
Of Margaret
Painted Head
Address to the Scholars of New England

Selected Poems (1963)

Winter Remembered
Miriam Tazewell
Dead Boy
Spectral Lovers
Agitato ma non troppo
Necrological
Bells for John Whiteside's Daughter
The Tall Girl
First Travels of Max
Good Ships
Emily Hardcastle, Spinster
Parting at Dawn
Vaunting Oak
In Process of a Noble Alliance
Spiel of the Three Mountebanks
Here Lies a Lady
The Vanity of the Bright Young Men
Conrad in Twilight
Armageddon
Prometheus in Straits
Judith of Bethulia
Blue Girls
Philomela
Old Man Playing with Children
Captain Carpenter
Old Mansion

Selected Poems (1969)

The Innocent Doves

Janet Waking
Eclogue
Vaunting Oak
Two in August
Emily Hardcastle, Spinster
Moments of Minnie
Somewhere Is Such a Kingdom
Parting at Dawn
Good Ships
Romance of a Youngest Daughter
Vision by Sweetwater
April Treason
Judith of Bethulia
Her Eyes
Parting, Without a Sequel
Hilda

The Manliness of Men

Winter Remembered
Dead Boy
First Travels of Max
Necrological
Captain Carpenter
Spiel of Three Mountebanks
Nocturne
Dog
Blackberry Winter
Armageddon
Old Man Playing with Children
Prometheus in Straits
Our Two Worthies
Philomela
Crocodile
Survey of Literature
Old Mansion (after Henry James)
On the Road to Wockensutter (a Western)
Morning
Jack's Letter
Persistent Explorer

Puncture
Man without Sense of Direction
Antique Harvesters
The Equilibrists
To the Scholars of Harvard
What Ducks Require
Painted Head

TWO GENTLEMEN IN BONDS
(*in twelve sonnets*)

Pink and Pale
Thinking, Drinking
Epithalamion of a Peach
Bad News
L'état C'est Moi
Misanthrope
Kingdom Come
In Bed Not Dead
Primer for Statesmen
Fait Accompli
Rain
Injured Sire

SIXTEEN POEMS IN EIGHT PAIRINGS
(with original and final versions studied comparatively)

Preface
I A Overtures
B Two Gentlemen Scholars (a pastoral)

II A Conrad Sits in Twilight
B Master's in the Garden Again

III A *Agitato ma non troppo*
B *Agitato ma non troppo*

IV A Tom, Tom, the Piper's Son
B The Vanity of the Bright Boys

V A Semi-Centennial
B Birthday of an Aging Seer

VI A Here Lies a Lady
B Here Lies a Lady

VII A Of Margaret
B Of Margaret

VIII A Prelude to an Evening
B Prelude to an Evening

Appendix B
Ransom's Prefaces

This appendix contains Ransom's introduction to Poems About God *and his prefaces for the* Selected Poems *volumes.* CF *and* TGB *did not have prefaces.*

Poems About God

INTRODUCTION

Most of these poems about God were complete a year ago, that is at about the time when the great upheaval going on in God's world engulfed our country too. Since then I have added a little only, and my experience has led me so wide that I can actually look back upon those antebellum accomplishments with the eye of the impartial spectator, or at most with a fatherly tenderness, no more. In this reviewing act I find myself thinking sometimes that the case about God may not be quite so desperate as the young poet chooses to believe. But it is not for that reason that I shall ever think of suppressing a single one of his poems. For I am deeply engaged by the downright evident honesty of the young man, though I may wonder at the source of his excitement; esteeming honesty more highly than those amiable Southern accents into which he seems determined not to lapse, and indeed more highly than anything else in the world. So that it is altogether as his apologist that I undertake this introduction.

"God moves in a mysterious way, His wonders to perform," says the poet in an effort to render our hearts properly humble before him. And we remember the story of how a certain Samaritan woman was rebuked once for thinking that God was to be worshiped only in that mountain where her fathers had always worshiped him; the point of the story being that he can be found just as readily on one mountain as another.

The first three or four poems that I ever wrote (that was two years ago) were done in three or four different moods and with no systematic design. I was therefore duly surprised to notice that each of them made considerable use of the term God. I studied the matter a little, and came to the conclusion that this was the most poetic of all terms possible; was a term always being called into requisition during the great moments of the soul, now in tones of love, and now indignantly; and was the very last word that a man might say when standing in the presence of that ultimate mystery to which all our great experiences reduce.

Wishing to make my poems as poetic as possible, I simply likened myself to a diligent apprentice and went to work to treat rather systematically a number of the occasions on which this term was in use with common American men. And since these occasions fairly crowded into mind even at the most casual inventory, I also likened myself to a sovereign and a chooser; and I very quickly ruled that I should consider only those situations as suitable in which I could imagine myself pronouncing the name God sincerely and spontaneously, never by that way of routine which is death to the aesthetic and religious emotions.

I anticipate the objection that the name of God is frequently taken here in ways that are not the ways of the fathers. I reply in advance, There are many mountains; and probably every one of them is worthy of being charted on the true Chart of God's world.

France
May 13, 1918

Selected Poems 1945

PREFACE

Most of these poems come from the two volumes, *Chills and Fever* and *Two Gentlemen in Bonds*; and I have not included any from my earliest volume, *Poems About God.* But there are five poems, the last in this text, which have had only a periodical publication previously. For their use I wish to make acknowledgments to the *New Republic,* the *Saturday Review of Literature,* the *American Review,* and the *Kenyon Review.*

There are two items of information which I think I should offer. It would be difficult for me to recover exactly the order in which these poems were composed, but I believe the present arrangement is substantially in that order. And some of the earlier poems I have felt impelled to trim and revise a little.

April 10, 1945

Selected Poems 1963

PREFACE

In the page proof of the preface for this edition, JCR carried out significant revisions. I shall insert in brackets the original reading following the revision, as well as other editorial interpolations.

This edition of *Selected Poems* contains all that were in the original edition. Some of them have been gone over critically and revised a little; but perhaps [I hope] the new phrases will not perceptibly be out of tone with the body of them that is left untouched. One poem's title has been changed; from "Tom, Tom, the Piper's Son" to "The Vanity of the Bright Young Men" [*the following five words, preceded by a semi-colon, were deleted:* it is more pointedly descriptive]. But in addition to the original poems I have entered, at the places where they seem to belong chronologically, a few [five] others taken from my old single volumes. I shall not name them here, because the test of their belonging in the selection is whether the reader will want to stop and raise the question in his own right when he happens to come upon them. The total volume of my verse is not very large, and the *Selected Poems* will have to be modest proportionately [cannot expect to be other than proportionate in volume. I should not like to seem to cull unworthy poems.] [*Then the following sentence was added in the margin but withdrawn before the 1963 volume was published:* The items number just over fifty].

But the greatest pleasure in preparing this edition came from the last two items of the text. "Master's in the Garden Again" is a completely new version of the old and rather ignominious "Conrad in Twilight," elaborating it as the situation demanded in a style which did not try to resemble that of the original, except partly in the second of the three movements. This is the first verse I have written in more than twenty years, and it was very hard trying to "get my hand in" [*next fourteen words crossed out*: again. Perhaps it is my illusion that I succeeded, but it has been exhilarating.] [*Replaced by the following nine words*: again. I am not sure how well I succeeded].[1]

The last item is "Prelude to an Evening: Revised and Explicated." The original eight stanzas remain pretty much what they were, but five [four] new stanzas have been added which change the ending completely. The prose commentary follows the poem [*the following eight*

1. In the actual edition, JCR changed the last statement to "I do not know how well I succeeded."

words, following a comma, were deleted before the final publication: and I need not dwell on it here]. Both this item [poem] and the preceding one have been published in the *Kenyon Review.*

Gambier, Ohio

Selected Poems 1969

There is no preface for the volume, but JCR precedes the essays of eight pairings of poems with a "Preface," which follows. This edition does not include JCR's commentary on the individual pairings

Here follows, completing the text of this final edition of *Selected Poems,* a set of pairings or couplings of poems which are closely related. The first poem of each pairing is designated A, and reports a vision or a meditation which will just manage as a prompter to the B poem, its superior. Let *A* stand for Average, for the sort of poem which is good enough to look for publication. And let *B* stand for Better; I must not say for Best. My purpose is didactic, and even euphuistic: to see how a deficient poem may be whipped into something more satisfactory—if only it has sufficient "makings." As the proverb goes, the poet not only must be "born" with the heritage of an individual talent, but also must be "made" by his own best labor of will and imagination.

I sometimes find myself wishing that the idiom for the two stages of the poem might be "born and bred"; a usage that seems to call for the more admirable actions and sentiments of mankind, therefore steeped in morals and manners. But always on second thought it occurs to me that we require also a poetry of many humors, of satire, and even of naked evil. That kind of poetry would be permissive, and instructive as to one of the built-in halves of our personalities. And I do not recall many ages whose poets at large have dwelt more insistently upon evil than have those of our own generation. They display on purpose the dark and animal side of our divided selves; but probably, with or without knowing it, they mean to remind themselves and the rest of us of the parity of the two sides. This is the principle of old Heraclitus himself, now renewed with great rigor; and I for one have not resisted it. I must have observed several times in print that the man who limits himself, aspiring to pure goodness or saintliness, seems to us very far from possessing that entire vitality which Providence has meant for him. He has not elected the whole joy of life.

The date and publisher of each *A* poem will be recorded as we come to it. But it needs to be stated positively that the date of all the *B* poems is Now; they are final versions that have been arrived at in this year of 1968. Furthermore, I have revised, and promoted to the text of *Selected Poems,* a dozen or so poems which existed in my three single volumes: in *Poems About God,* Henry Holt, 1919; in *Chills and Fever,* Alfred A. Knopf, 1924; and in *Two Gentlemen in Bonds,* Alfred A. Knopf, 1927.

Appendix C
Poems Read at Fugitive Meetings

This appendix contains a selection of unpublished versions of Ransom's poems read and discussed at meetings of the Fugitives. The poems are significantly different from any of their published forms. If the titles of the published versions differ from the manuscript copies, the published titles will be given in parentheses.

Spectral Lovers

Deep in the haunted thickets of an April mist
They wandered, across my melancholy mirth;
Immaculate as two angels fallen to earth;
Lovers they knew they were, but still unclasped, unkissed.
And why should two lovers be frozen asunder in fear?
But yet they were, they were.

Quick in the shredding of an April blossom
Her thrilling fingers touched him; and her hair;
Of her pedestrian postures she made a fugitive snare;
But shily the red heart must beat in the pale bosom;
Her face as of cunningly tinctured ivory
Was hard with an agony.

Too shrewdly pressed the batteries of an April night.
These being the passionate essences of the field,
Should the penetrable walls of delicate spirit yield
And open her treasure to the first adventurous knight?
"This is the mad moon, and must I surrender all?
If he but speak, I shall."

And gesturing largely to the very moon of Easter,
Mincing his steps and swishing the jubilant grass
That had died and come from death since Michaelmas,

He was an utter troubadour and poetaster;
But soberer tunes were pounding at his heart
Unfitted for his art.

"Am I reeling with the sap of April like a drunkard?
Blessed is he that taketh this radiant city.
Yet it is so stainless and cold, besieging is pity;
This is that rocky fortress not to be conquered,
Lest its white peace in the black flame turn to tinder
And an unutterable cinder."

Thus they passed once in April, in the mist.
No other season is there, when one walks and discovers
Two clad in the shapes of angels, being spectral lovers,
Trailing much glory of moon-gold and amethyst,
Who touch their quick fingers fluttering like a bird
Whose songs shall never be heard.

Philomela

Procne, Philomela, and Itylus,
Liquid procession of names, whose lickerous tale
Is recited in the classic numbers of the nightingale:
Ah, but our numbers are less felicitous,
It goes not liquidly with us!

Perched on a Roman ilex, and duly apostrophized,
The nightingale descanted unto Ovid;
Even the Teutons have heard her, the swilled and gravid;
At Versailles, it may be, the bird was gallicized,
But she was never baptized.

To England came Philomela with her pain,
Fleeing the hawk her husband; like a faithful ghost
She issues when he sits heavy on his roost,
And utters her woe in the original refrain,
The untranslatable strain.

Not to our shores she came! This other Thrace
Is environ barbarous for the royal Attic,
How could her delicate dirge run democratic,
Sung in a cloudless boundless public place
To a hyperkinetic race?

I pernoctated with the Oxford students once,
And in the quadrangles, in the cloisters, on the Cher
Precociously knocked on the antique doors ajar,
Fatuously touched the hem of the Hierophants,
Sick of my dissonance.

I went out to Bagley Wood; I climbed the hill
Until the moon had slanted off on a twinkling,
I heard the sepulchral owl and a few bells tinkling,
The villainous day was gone after serving me ill—
Diuturnity was still.

Up from the darkest wood where Philomela sat
Her fairy numbers issued: what then ailed me?
My ears were called capacious but they failed me,
Her classics quavered thinly, woefully flat!
I rose, and venomously spat.

Philomela, Philomela, lover of song,
I have despaired of thee and am unworthy,
My scene is prose, these people and I are earthy;
Unto more beautiful, persistently more young
Thy fabulous realms belong.

Minnie's Way

(Moments of Minnie)

Minnie was a more difficult problem in curves
Than my laborious geometry deserves,
And piqued me with her wholly irregular style.
Yet it oppressed me when an evil while
Had thrilled so lazy and beautiful a creature,
Scaring, misshaping her most sumptuous feature—

The mouth-corners were pulled down, and the outleaning
Of her strange lips drew back their gallant meaning.
Pain is hideous: it pinched the vaulted line
Till I feared to see what was no fault of mine.
I was ashamed, though knowing it was not my
Reproach—I was a neutral—as if I,
By only being of a stronger order,
Conspired with the infernal skies to accord her
More doom than a girl should bear. And I did not even
Know what her sin was, nor to whom given.

I trembled when I heard that which could not
Be foreseen, nor afterwards forgot:
Oh, oh, oh! Not a word, not a name,
And no tears flowed, but wry and dry it came,
Till I trembled—and I fled—I had to go
From this too, too infectious woe.

Then I washed my mind with its old memories.
For it was better to reconstitute the trees
And the bridegroom scarlet bird of April crying
To his brown one embowered, and the flying
Mirth that bubbled off this woman's mouth
From secret wells abundant as the South,
Which spilled their joy too thickly for shaped speech:
Ah, ah, ah! she sighed deeply, and each
Sighing was a new Ah! until I heard
Better than had it been some lettered word.

Husband Betrayed

Why did he christen her his Pigeon
If not for seeing how she flew and fluttered
And in what strange sweet monotone she twittered?
Nothing was said of her religion.

There was wood-wildness in her—say a dove,
For doves are pigeons not domesticated

And whoso snares them is forthwith frustrated,
Expecting quick return of love.

At all events she had a snowy bosom
And trod so mincingly that you would say
She only wanted wings to fly away,
Easy and light and lissom.

She pecked her food with ravished cries,
She sunned her bosom by the wall in the morning,
Preening prettily in the sun and turning
In her bird-wise.

But fancy then his dudgeon,
When he that should have married him a woman
To sit and drudge and serve him as was common
Discovered he had wived (had wived!) a pigeon.

The Miller's Daughter

I have seen, O, the miller's daughter
And on her neck a coral necklace lies
And yellow glint like corn is in her eyes
Which are a blue stillwater.

The strange miller hath strange daughter
For he is pink and painfully doth walk
And life demandeth of them little talk
Beside the small stillwater.

At candlelight I hear she goes
And on a bed of snow like snow she lies
Yet warmer much and lids her sleepy eyes.
Long lies the tall white tower which uprose.

At daylight some vague bird
Tinkles his little bell and she comes down
Coiling her hair as queens would coil a crown.
Yet queens are most absurd,

And so am I, poor bookish hind,
Who come by fabulous roads around the hill
To bring the famous daughter of the mill
No combs to sell, no corn to grind,

But too much pudding in my head
Of learned characters and scraps of love
Which O that she might peck at (dainty dove!)
And words vain to be said.

What then to do but stare—
A learned eye of our most Christian nation
And foremost philosophical generation—
At primary monochromatic hair,

Incontrovertible Oes of eyes,
And the white moons I tremble to behold
As tales in our vast libraries untold
And all her parts likewise.

She dwells beside a water
And counts the bins and ties the sacks pardee
And smiles both night and day and seems to me
A most rare miller's daughter.

Blue Girls

If I were younger, traveling the bright sward
Under the towers of your seminary,
I should get a look, and a thought, or even a word;
But you find me old, of a countenance contrary,
Clearly too wise and weary.

Why do you bind white fillets about your tresses
And stare so haughtily on the wayfaring?
Why do you whirl so lovingly your blue dresses,
Like bluebirds in the snow that preen a wing,
And make a noise of spring?

Practice your beauty, blue girls, if you will;
The lean preceptress of your history
Showed you the manifold of good and ill,
But all you saw was the crook of a nobleman's knee
And Queens of great decree.

Do you think there are thrones enough, one to each Queen?
Some thrones are chairs, some three-legged milking-stools,
Or you even sit the floor where throne should have been;
And worse than little laws of little schools
Are other grave misrules.

Practice your beauty, young girls, nevertheless;
For once the mistress, the lean puckered one,
Printed the sward as she tripped in a purple dress
And was a beautiful princess mounting her throne;
And where has her kingdom gone?

Parting—Without a Sequel

She has finished and sealed the letter
At last, which he so richly has deserved,
With characters venomous and hatefully curved,
And nothing could be better.

But even as she gave it
Saying to the blue-capped conveyancer of doom,
"Into his hands," she hoped the leering groom
Might somewhere lose and leave it.

And she wrung her hands,
The proud young lady; she was close to tears,
Unfruited after all her younger years;
And now she stands

Under the vaunting oak
Who kept his peace in the wind and sun, and glistened
Stoical in the rain; to whom she listened
If he spoke.

So mild and strong a tree
That her own father's spirit when he was dead
Had entered into it, and inhabited
So near her doorway: he and she.

The agitation of the rain
Rasped his sere leaves, and he talked low and gentle
Reproaching his wan daughter by her lintel;
Ceasing, the beginning again.

Away went the messenger's bicycle,
His serpent's track coiled up the hill forever,
And all the time she stood there hot as fever
And cold as any icicle.

Lady Lost

This morning again and again
The mournful ladybird by our birdbath
Stood eying her sharp image grave as death;
This afternoon she knocked on our windowpane
To be let in from the rain.

And when I caught her eye
She looked aside, but at the clap of thunder
When the whole city seemed to blaze like tinder
Looked in on us again most miserably,
Indeed as if she would cry.

So I will go out into the park and say,
"Who has lost a delicate brown-eyed lady
In the West End section? Or has anybody
Injured some fine woman in some dark way
Last night or yesterday?

"Let the owner come and take possession,
No questions will be asked. But stroke her tenderly
With loving words, and she will evidently
Return to her full soft-haired soft-breasted fashion
And her right home and her right passion."

Sociological
(Dog)

Cock-a-doodle-doo the brass-lined rooster says,
Brekki-ki-kax reiterates the Greek frog—
These fantasies do not terrify me as
The bow-wow-wow of dog.

I had a little doggie who used to sit and beg,
A pretty little creature with tears in his eyes,
Anomalous hand extended on a leg—
Housebroken was my Hundchen, and so wise.

Booms the voice of a big dog like a bell.
But Fido sits, Madam Incy, on your lap
And bored beyond his tongue's poor skill to tell
Conjugates nicely his pink verb, To yap.

However—up the lane trot-trots the bull
Yearning for his kine—Queen June envied them
Their lovely eyes—thinking how beautiful,
In his heart love, no treason nor mayhem.

But on arriving at the gap in the fence,
Behold! again the ubiquitous hairy dog—
Like a numerous army shaking the battlements
With shouting, though it is only his monologue—
With a lion's courage and a bee's diligence,
Though he is only one dog.

Shrill is the fury of the proud red bull,
His knees quiver, and the honeysuckle vine
Distils sweet anguish as his voice, terrible,
Cries, "What do you want with my twenty lady kine?"

Ah, doubtless nothing; yet his fang is out and keen
And will not even permit the marriage rites
Enacted in the dark if they are obscene.
Heart of a dog! censorious of delights.

Suspires in deprecation one vast Moo
From the twenty innocent ladies of the mead;
Their lord must fight, this is too much ado!
The sun sets and the gloom is gory indeed.

The hooves of the red bull slither the claybank
And cut the green tendrils of the vine; his poll
Splinters the young trees to the living shank
And cannot find whom he would toss and roll.

Across the red sky comes master, Hodge by name,
Unright, biped, tall-browed, and self-assured;
In his hand a cudgel, in his cold eye a flame:
"Have I beat my dog so sore, and he is not cured?"

With stick and stone he harries the tawny brute
That pipped his bull of gentle pedigree
Till leonine smarts with pain and disrepute
And bovine weeps in the bosom of his family.

Old Hodge stays not his hand, but whips to kennel
The renegade; then imprecation rolls
From his tongue; but in the box grown round with fennel
The red eyes shine with chemistry of coals.

Jack's Letter

Do not consider that Jack and Rose apart
Can thrive much, for they cannot lie together
Nor under the same roof nor in the same weather;
These are the moons of absence grieving the heart.

But Jack, sore-hearted, puts his wits to use;
He must convey to Rose his pent-up love
And then receive acknowledgment thereof;
A letter is his passionate excuse.

But cold and dry he finds the paper sheet
And atrabilious and sour is ink;

He'd set his matter forth, but stops to think
His passion must in transit lose its heat;

So plants on four sides of the folio
Himself in bulbs of cunning charactry,
But Rose must guess the cipher! seeing she
Must water him with tears in he would grow.

The glade is not so green now, Jack says there;
The fish have all swum down the dwindled stream;
The birds have scattered and become a dream;
Eheu, Eheu! he latinizes despair.

Here then lies Jack beneath a penny seal.
The dainty lady of the superscription
If she have very delicate perception
With eyes may see and with sharp fingers feel.

And if I knew the gods upon the hill
I'd ask the kindest: Wet your lip and bless
The little ones that die of separateness,
Absent and impotent and unspoken still.

The poet is gone, and the event will tell.
If only she should lay it to her bosom,
Soon might her parcel thicken to a blossom
Which would be soft to hold and sweet to smell.

Index of Poem Titles